Lecture Notes in Computer Science 4498

Commenced Publication in 1973
Founding and Former Series Editors:
Gerhard Goos, Juris Hartmanis, and Jan van Leeuwen

T0223132

Nabil Abdennadher   Fabrice Kordon (Eds.)

Reliable Software Technologies – Ada-Europe 2007

12th Ada-Europe International Conference
on Reliable Software Technologies
Geneva, Switzerland, June 25-29, 2007
Proceedings

 Springer

Volume Editors

Nabil Abdennadher
University of Applied Sciences Western Switzerland, HES.SO
École d'ingénieurs de Genève
Rue de la Prairie 4, 1202 Geneva, Switzerland
E-mail: Nabil.Abdennadher@hesge.ch

Fabrice Kordon
Université Pierre et Marie Curie
Laboratoire d'Informatique de Paris 6
104 Avenue du Président Kennedy, 75016 Paris, France
E-mail: Fabrice.Kordon@lip6.fr

Library of Congress Control Number: 2007929319

CR Subject Classification (1998): D.2, D.1.2-5, D.3, C.2.4, C.3, K.6

LNCS Sublibrary: SL 2 – Programming and Software Engineering

ISSN   0302-9743
ISBN-10   3-540-73229-2 Springer Berlin Heidelberg New York
ISBN-13   978-3-540-73229-7 Springer Berlin Heidelberg New York

Springer is a part of Springer Science+Business Media

springer.com

© Springer-Verlag Berlin Heidelberg 2007

Typesetting: Camera-ready by author, data conversion by Scientific Publishing Services, Chennai, India
Printed on acid-free paper   SPIN: 12080861   06/3180   5 4 3 2 1 0

Preface

Reliable Software Technologies is an annual series of international conferences devoted to the promotion and advancement of all aspects of reliable software technologies. The objective of this series of conferences, initiated and sponsored by Ada-Europe, the European federation of national Ada societies, is to provide a forum to promote the development of reliable softwares both as an industrial technique and an academic discipline.

Previous editions of the Reliable Software Technologies conference were held in: Porto (Portugal) in 2006, York (UK) in 2005, Palma de Mallorca (Spain) in 2004, Toulouse (France) in 2003, Vienna (Austria) in 2002, Leuven (Belgium) in 2001, Potsdam (Germany) in 2000, Santander (Spain) in 1999, Uppsala (Sweden) in 1998, London (UK) in 1997 and Montreux (Switzerland) in 1996.

The 12th International Conference on Reliable Software Technologies took place in Geneva, Switzerland, June 25-29, 2007, under the continued sponsoring of Ada-Europe, in cooperation with ACM SIGAda. It was organized by members of the University of Applied Sciences, Western Switzerland (Engineering School of Geneva), in collaboration with colleagues from various places in Europe. The 13th conference, in 2008, will take place in Venice, Italy.

Continuing the success achieved in previous years, the conference included a three-day technical program, where the papers contained in these proceedings were presented. The technical program was bracketed by two tutorial days where attendants had the opportunity to catch up on a variety of topics related to the fields covered by the conference, at both introductory and advanced levels. The technical program also included an industrial track, with contributions illustrating challenges faced and solutions devised by industry from both sides of the Atlantic, as well as from the rest of the world (we note several contributions from South-East Asia). Furthermore, the conference was accompanied by an exhibition where vendors presented their products for supporting the development of reliable software.

The conference featured four distinguished speakers, who delivered state-of-the-art information on topics of great importance, both for the present and the future of software engineering:

- Challenges for Reliable Software Design in Automotive Electronic Control Units *by Klaus D. Mueller-Glaser (University of Karlsruhe, Germany)*
- Synchronous Techniques for Embedded Systems *by Gerard Berry (Esterel Technologies, France)*
- Perspectives on Next-Generation Software Engineering *by Ali Mili (New Jersey Institute of Technology, USA)*
- Observation Rooms for Program Execution Monitoring *by Liviu Iftode, (Rutgers University, USA)*

We would like to express our sincere gratitude to these distinguished speakers for sharing their insights with the conference participants.

A large number of regular papers were submitted, from as many as 15 different countries. The Program Committee worked hard to review them, and the selection process proved to be difficult, since many papers had received excellent reviews. The Program Committee eventually selected 18 papers for the conference and these proceedings.

The industrial track of the conference also received valuable contributions from industry, and the Industrial Committee selected nine of them for presentation in Geneva. The final result was a truly international program with contributions from Australia, Austria, China, France, Germany, Italy, Republic of Korea, Spain, Tunisia, and the UK, covering a broad range of topics: real-time systems, static analysis, verification, applications, reliability, industrial experience, compilers and distributed systems.

The conference also included an interesting selection of tutorials, featuring international experts who presented introductory and advanced material in the domain of the conference:

- An Overview of Model-Driven Engineering, *William Bail*
- CbyC: A UML2 Profile Enforcing the Ravsenscar Computational Model, *Tullio Vardanega*
- Verification and Validation for Reliable Software Systems, *William Bail*
- Object-Oriented Programming in Ada 2005, *Matthew Heaney*
- Security by Construction, *Rod Chapman*
- Synchronous Design of Embedded Systems: the Esterel/Scade Approach, *Gerard Berry*
- Building Interoperable Applications with PolyORB, *Thomas Quinot and Jérôme Hugues*
- Situational Method Engineering: Towards a Specific Method for Each System Development Project, *Jolita Ralyté*

We wish to extend our gratitude to these experts for the work they put into preparing and presenting this material during the conference.

The 12th Reliable Software Technologies (Ada-Europe 2007) conference was made possible through the generous support and diligent work of many individuals and organizations. A number of institutional and industrial sponsors also made important contributions and participated in the industrial exhibition. Their names and logos appear on the Ada-Europe 2007 Web site. We gratefully acknowledge their support. A subcommittee comprising Nabil Abdennadher, Dirk Craeynest, Fabrice Kordon, Dominik Madon, Ahlan Marriott, Tullio Vardanega and Luigi Zaffalon met in Geneva to elaborate the final program selection. Various Program Committee members were assigned to shepherd some of the papers. We are grateful to all those who contributed to the technical program of the conference.

We would like to thank the members of the Organizing Committee for their valuable effort in taking care of all the details needed for a smooth run of the conference. Dominik Madon did a superb job in organizing an attractive tutorial program. Luigi Zaffalon took on the difficult task of preparing the industrial track. We would also like to thank Dirk Craeynest and Ahlan Marriott, who worked very hard to make the conference prominently visible, and to all the members of the Ada-Europe board for helping with the intricate details of the organization. Special thanks go to Régis Boesch and Albena Basset, who took care of all details of the local organization.

Finally, we also thank the authors of the contributions submitted to the conference, and to all the participants who helped in achieving the goal of the conference: to provide a forum for researchers and practitioners for the exchange of information and ideas about reliable software technologies. We hope they all enjoyed the program as well as the social events of the 12th International Conference on Reliable Software Technologies.

June 2007

Nabil Abdennadher
Fabrice Kordon

Organization

Conference Chair

Nabil Abdennadher, University of Applied Sciences, Geneva, Switzerland

Program Co-chairs

Nabil Abdennadher, University of Applied Sciences, Geneva, Switzerland
Fabrice Kordon, Université Pierre & Marie Curie, Paris, France

Industrial Committee Chair

Luigi Zaffalon, University of Applied Sciences, Geneva, Switzerland

Tutorial Chair

Dominik Madon, University of Applied Sciences, Geneva, Switzerland

Exhibition Chair

Neville Rowden, Siemens Switzerland

Publicity Co-chairs

Ahlan Marriott, White-elephant, Switzerland
Dirk Craeynest, Aubay Belgium and K.U.Leuven, Belgium

Local Chair

Régis Boesch, University of Applied Sciences, Geneva, Switzerland

Ada-Europe Conference Liaison

Fabrice Kordon, Université Pierre et Marie Curie, Paris, France

Program Committee

Abdennadher Nabil, University of Applied Sciences, Geneva, Switzerland
Alonso Alejandro, Universidad Politécnica de Madrid, Spain
Asplund Lars, Mälardalens Högskola, Sweden
Barnes Janet, Praxis High Integrity Systems, UK

Blieberger Johann, Technische Universität Wien, Austria
Boasson Maartin, University of Amsterdam, The Netherlands
Burgstaller Bernd, University of Sydney, Australia
Craeynest Dirk, Aubay Belgium and K.U.Leuven, Belgium
Crespo Alfons, Universidad Politécnica de Valencia, Spain
Devillers Raymond, Université Libre de Bruxelles, Belgium
González Harbour Michael, Universidad de Cantabria, Spain
Gutiérrez José Javier, Universidad de Cantabria, Spain
Hadded Serge, Université Paris-Dauphine, France
Hately Andrew, Eurocontrol CRDS, Hungary
Hommel Günter, Technische Universität Berlin, Germany
Keller Hubert, Institut für Angewandte Informatik, Germany
Kermarrec Yvon, ENST Bretagne, France
Kienzle Jörg, McGill University, Canada
Kordon Fabrice, Université Pierre et Marie Curie, France
Llamosi Albert, Universitat de les Illes Balears, Spain
Lundqvist Kristina, MIT, USA
Mazzanti Franco, ISTI-CNR Pisa, Italy
McCormick John, University of Northern Iowa, USA
Michell Stephen, Maurya Software, Canada
Miranda Javier, Universidad Las Palmas de Gran Canaria, Spain
Moldt Daniel, University of Hamburg, Germany
Pautet Laurent, Telecom Paris, France
Petrucci Laure, LIPN, Université Paris 13, France
Pinho Luís Miguel, Polytechnic Institute of Porto, Portugal
Plödereder Erhard, Universität Stuttgart, Germany
de la Puente Juan A., Universidad Politécnica de Madrid, Spain
Real Jorge, Universidad Politécnica de Valencia, Spain
Romanovsky Alexander, University of Newcastle upon Tyne, UK
Rosen Jean-Pierre, Adalog, France
Ruiz José, AdaCore, France
Schonberg Edmond, New York University and AdaCore, USA
Seinturier Lionel, INRIA Lille, France
Shing Man-Tak, Naval Postgraduate School, USA
Tokar Joyce, Pyrrhus Software, USA
Vardanega Tullio, Università di Padova, Italy
Wellings Andy, University of York, UK
Winkler Jürgen, Friedrich-Schiller-Universität, Germany
Zaffalon Luigi, University of Applied Sciences, Geneva, Switzerland

Sponsoring Institutions

Ada-Europe
AdaCore
Aonix

Ellidiss Sowftare
Green Hills Software Inc.
Praxis

PostFinance
Sun Microsystems
Siemens
Telelogic

Fédération des Entreprises Romandes
Swiss Informatics Society
The Quality Software Foundation

Table of Contents

Real-Time Utilities for Ada 2005*

Andy Wellings and Alan Burns

Department of Computer Science, University of York, UK
{andy,burns}@cs.york.ac.uk

Abstract. Modern large real-time systems are becoming more complex. Whilst
Ada 2005 provides a comprehensive set of programming mechanisms that allow
these systems to be implemented, the abstractions are low level. This paper argues
that there is a need for a standardised library of real-time utilities that address
common real-time problems. The paper presents some initial considerations on
what could be in such a library and how it could be structured.

1   Introduction

Ada has comprehensive support for priority-based real-time systems. The approach has
been to provide a set of low-level mechanisms that enable the programmer to construct
systems solving common real-time problems. Whilst eminently flexible, this approach
requires the programmer to re-implement common paradigms in each new system. In
the past, these structures have been quite straightforward, perhaps just involving simply
periodic or sporadic tasks communicating via protected data. However, modern large
real-time systems are much more complex and include hard, soft and non real-time
components. The resulting paradigms are similarly more involved, and require activities
like deadline miss detection, CPU budget overrun detection, the sharing of CPU budgets
between aperiodic threads etc. Ada 2005 has responded admirably, expanding its set of
low-level mechanisms. However, the common problems are now much more complex,
and it is no longer appropriate to require the programmer to reconstruct the algorithms
in each new system. Instead, what is required is a library of reusable real-time utilities;
indeed, ideally such a library should become a de facto secondary standard – perhaps in
the same way that Java has developed a set of concurrency utilities over the years that
have now been incorporated into the Java 1.5 distribution.

The goal of this paper is to initiate a discussion in the Ada community to both confirm
the need for a library of common real-time utilities and to propose (as a starting point)
a framework for their construction.

2   Real-Time Utilities – Framework Overview

In the field of real-time programming, real-time tasks are often classified as being periodic, sporadic or aperiodic. Simple real-time periodic tasks are easy to program but

---

* This work has been undertaken within the context of the EU ARTIST2 project.

N. Abdennahder, F. Kordon (Eds.): Ada-Europe 2007, LNCS 4498, pp. 1–14, 2007.

once more complicated ones are needed (such as those that detect deadline misses, execution time (budget) overruns, minimum inter-arrival violations etc), the paradigms become more complex. Hence, there is a need to package up some of these and provide them as real-time tasking utilities.

A programmer wanting to use a real-time tasking abstraction will want to indicate (for example):

- whether the abstraction is periodic, sporadic or aperiodic (each task is "released" in response to a release event, which is usually time triggered for periodic tasks and event triggered for sporadic and aperiodic tasks);
- whether to terminate the current release of the task in the event of a deadline miss or to simply inform the program that this event has occurred (in which case, the programmer can choose to react or ignore the event);
- whether to terminate the current release of the task in the event of an execution time overrun or to simply inform the program that this event has occurred (in which case, the program can choose to react or ignore the event);
- whether a task is associated with an execution-time server that can limit the amount of CPU-time it receives.
- whether a task can operate in one or more modes, and if so, the nature of the mode change.

This paper illustrates how real-time task abstractions, supporting some of these variations, can be developed in Ada 2005. The approach that has been taken is to divide the support for the tasks into four components.

1. The functionality of the task – this is encapsulated by the `Real_Time_Task_-State` package. Its goal is to define a structure for the application code of the tasks. It is here that code is provided: to execute on each release of the task, to execute when deadline misses occur and when execution time overruns occurs. In this paper, it is assumed that the task only wishes to operate in a single mode.
2. The mechanisms needed to control the release of the real-time tasks and to detect the deadline misses and execution time overruns – this is encapsulated in the `Release_Mechanisms` package. Each mechanism is implemented using a combinations of protected objects and the new Ada 2005 timer and execution time control features.
3. The various idioms of how the task should respond to deadline misses and execution time overruns – this is encapsulated in the `Real_Time_Task` package. It is here that the actual Ada tasks are provided.
4. The mechanisms needed to encapsulate subsystems and ensure that they are only given a fixed amount of the CPU resource (often called temporal firewalling) – this is the responsibility of the `Execution_Servers` package. This paper considers using these mechanisms to support aperiodic task execution only.

Figure 1 illustrates the top level packages that make up the abstractions. The details are discussed in the following sections.

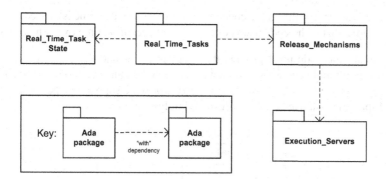

Fig. 1. Top-Level Packages

3   Framework Design

This section describes the details of the design of the framework introduced in Section 2. It assumes fixed priority scheduling and that the deadlines of all periodic tasks are less than or equal to their associated periods.

3.1   Real-Time Task State

First, it is necessary to provide a structure within which the programmer can express the code that the real-time task wishes to execute, along with its associated state variables. This is achieved, in the usual Ada object-oriented fashion, by defining the state within a tagged type, and providing operations to execute on the state. The following package shows the state and operations that all real-time tasks need.

```
-- with and use clauses omitted
package Real_Time_Task_State is
  type Task_State is abstract tagged record
    Relative_Deadline : Time_Span := Time_Span_Last;
    Execution_Time : Time_Span := Time_Span_Last;
    Pri : Priority := Default_Priority;
  end record;
  procedure Initialize(S: in out Task_State) is abstract;
  procedure Code(S: in out Task_State) is abstract;
  procedure Deadline_Miss(S: in out Task_State) is null;
  procedure Overrun(S: in out Task_State) is null;
  type Any_Task_State is access all Task_State'Class;
end Real_Time_Task_State;
```

Every real-time task has a deadline, an execution time and a priority. Here, these fields are made public, but they could have just as well been made private and procedures to 'get' and 'set' them provided. No additional assumptions have been made about the values of these attributes. The operations to be performed on a task's state are given by four procedures:

- Initialize: this is used to initialize the state when the real-time task is created;
- Code: – this is the code that is executed on each release of the task;

- `Deadline_Miss`: this is the code that is executed if a deadline is missed.
- `Overrun`: this is the code that is executed if an execution time overrun occurs.

Note, all real-time code must provide the `Initialize` and the `Code` procedures. There are default null actions on a missed deadline and on an execution time overrun.

Child packages of `Real_Time_Task_State` provide support for periodic, aperiodic and sporadic task execution (as illustrated in Figure 2).

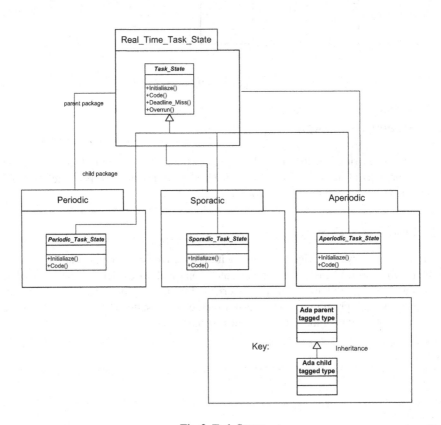

Fig. 2. Task States

A periodic task's state includes that of a real-time task with the addition of its period of execution. In other words, it has regular time-triggered releases.

```
package Real_Time_Task_State.Periodic is
   type Periodic_Task_State is abstract new Task_State with record
      Period : Time_Span;
   end record;
   procedure Initialize(S: in out Periodic_Task_State) is abstract;
   procedure Code(S: in out Periodic_Task_State)is abstract;
   type Any_Periodic_Task_State is access all Periodic_Task_State'Class;
end Real_Time_Task_State.Periodic;
```

There is more than one model of a sporadic task; here, it is assumed that the task must have an enforced minimum inter-arrival time between releases (another approach would be to enforce a maximum arrival frequency). Hence, the state includes this value.

```
package Real_Time_Task_State.Sporadic is
  type Sporadic_Task_State is abstract new Task_State with record
    MIT : Time_Span;
  end record;
  procedure Initialize(S: in out Sporadic_Task_State) is abstract;
  procedure Code(S: in out Sporadic_Task_State) is abstract;
  type Any_Sporadic_Task_State is access all Sporadic_Task_State'Class;
end Real_Time_Task_State.Sporadic;
```

The state for aperiodic tasks has no new fields over the normal Task_State, but for uniformity, a new type can be created.

Application real-time tasks choose the appropriate real-time state to extend, and add their own state variables. For example, the following shows the application code to be used with the declaration of a periodic real-time task that is not interested in any missed deadlines or execution-time overruns.

```
type My_State is new Periodic_Task_State with record
  -- state variables
end record;

procedure Initialize(S: in out My_State);
procedure Code(S: in out My_State);

Example_State: aliased My_State := (Pri=> System.Default_Priority + 1);
```

3.2   Real-Time Task Release Mechanisms

Real-time tasks can be released by the passage of time or via a software or hardware event. The following package (Release_Mechanisms) provides the common interfaces for all mechanisms (illustrated in Figure 3).

The root of the interface hierarchy (Release_Mechanism) simply supports the facility for a real-time task to wait for notification of its next release to occur (be that a time triggered or an event triggered release). The Release_Mechanism_With_-Deadline_Miss interface is provided for the case where the real-time task wishes to be informed when it has missed a deadline. Similarly, the Release_Mechanism_-With_Overrun interface is provided for the case where the real-time task wishes to be informed when it has overrun it execution time. Finally, Release_Mechanism_-With_Deadline_Miss_And_Overrun allows both detection of deadline misses and execution time overruns. The Ada code is shown below for some of the above.

```
package Release_Mechanisms is
  type Release_Mechanism is synchronized interface;
  procedure Wait_For_Next_Release(R : in out Release_Mechanism) is abstract;
  type Any_Release_Mechanism is access all Release_Mechanism'Class;

  type Release_Mechanism_With_Deadline_Miss is
      synchronized interface and Release_Mechanism;
  procedure Wait_For_Next_Release(R : in out
      Release_Mechanism_With_Deadline_Miss) is abstract;
  procedure Inform_Of_A_Deadline_Miss(R : in out
      Release_Mechanism_With_Deadline_Miss) is abstract;
```

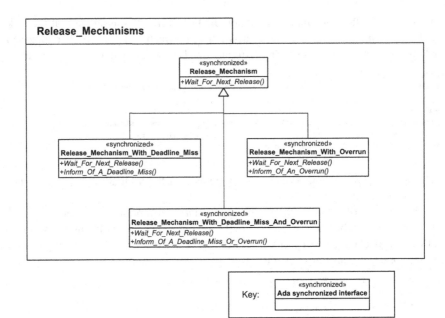

Fig. 3. Release Mechanism Interfaces

```
type Any_Release_Mechanism_With_Deadline_Miss is access all
      Release_Mechanism_With_Deadline_Miss'Class;
  ...
end Release_Mechanisms;
```

Child packages provide the actual release mechanisms – as illustrated in Figure 4 for periodic real-time tasks.

For example, the following shows the structure of a protected type that implements a periodic release mechanisms. The period of the task is obtained from the task's state, which is passed in as an access discriminant. The application code simply calls the Wait_For_Next_Release entry.

```
-- with and use clauses omitted
package Release_Mechanisms.Periodic is
  protected type Periodic_Release(S: Any_Periodic_Task_State) is
          new Release_Mechanism with
    entry Wait_For_Next_Release;
    pragma Priority(System.Interrupt_Priority'Last);
  private ...
  end Periodic_Release;
end Release_Mechanisms.Periodic;
```

Another protected type can support deadline miss detection:

```
-- with and use clauses omitted
package Release_Mechanisms.Periodic_And_Deadline_Miss_Detection is
  protected type Periodic_Release_With_Deadline_Miss(
      S: Any_Periodic_Task_State; Termination : Boolean) is
          new Release_Mechanism_With_Deadline_Miss with
    entry Wait_For_Next_Release;
```

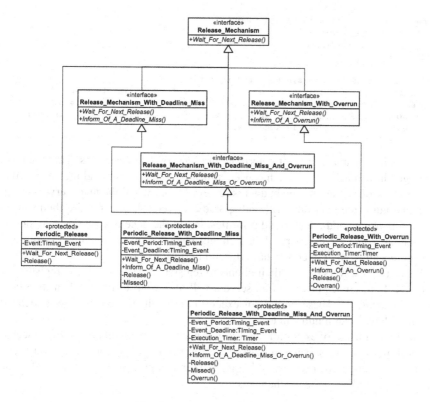

Fig. 4. Release Mechanism Classes

```
    entry Inform_Of_A_Deadline_Miss;
    pragma Priority(System.Interrupt_Priority'Last);
  private ...
    end Periodic_Release_With_Deadline_Miss;
end Release_Mechanisms.Periodic_And_Deadline_Miss_Detection;
```

Here, a boolean indicates whether the application requires notification or termination of a deadline miss. If termination is required, the Inform_Of_A_Deadline_Miss entry can be used by the framework in a select-then-abort statement.

The implementation of these and the other release mechanism packages are discussed in Section 4.

3.3 Aperiodic Release Mechanisms and Execution servers

The final type of release mechanism is that for handling aperiodic releases. Typically, the CPU time allocated to aperiodic tasks must be constrained as they potentially can have unbounded resource requirements. The Ada 2005 group budget facility can be used to implement the various approaches.

Before the release mechanism can be programmed, it is necessary to consider how it interacts with the execution severs. This paper will only consider periodic execution servers. The following package specification defines the common interface.

```
type Server_Parameters is tagged record
  Period : Time_Span;
  Budget : Time_Span;
end record;

type Execution_Server is synchronized interface;
procedure Register(ES: in out Execution_Server; T : Task_Id) is abstract;
procedure Start_Session(ES: in out Execution_Server; T : Task_Id) is null;
procedure Complete_Session(ES: in out Execution_Server; T : Task_Id) is null;
type Any_Execution_Server is access all Execution_Server'Class;
end Execution_Servers;
```

All servers have parameters that determine the servers' characteristics. They include: the budget, how much CPU time has been allocated to the server, and the period (this relates to how often the server's budget is replenished). Two of the main servers found in the literature (the deferrable [2] and sporadic servers[5]) also require their clients to have foreground and background priorities, but in the general case this may not be the situation. Some servers suspend their clients when their execution time expires, and other servers allow their clients to have different priorities.

All execution servers require their clients to register. Here, any task can register any other task. Some types of execution servers will also want to know when the client tasks are executable. These periods of execution are called *sessions*. The associated procedures have default null values.

To facilitate the use of execution servers, it is necessary to modify the release mechanism to allow the actual server to be passed as a discriminant. The approach is illustrated by considering aperiodic releases (although, the same approach could be applied to the periodic or sporadic release mechanisms).

```
package Release_Mechanisms.Aperiodic is
 protected type Aperiodic_Release(S: Any_Aperiodic_Task_State;
      ES: Any_Execution_Server) is new Release_Mechanism with
   entry Wait_For_Next_Release;
   procedure Release;
   pragma Priority(System.Interrupt_Priority'Last);
 private ...
  end Aperiodic_Release;
end Release_Mechanisms.Aperiodic;
```

3.4   Real-Time Tasks

The Real_Time_Tasks package provides the code that integrates the task states with the release mechanisms to provide the required application abstraction. Several task types are shown in the following package specification .

```
-- with and use clauses omitted package
Real_Time_Tasks is
  task type Simple_Real_Time_Task(S : Any_Task_State;
      R : Any_Release_Mechanism; Init_Prio : Priority) is
    pragma Priority(Init_Prio);
  end Simple_Real_Time_Task;

  task type Real_Time_Task_With_Deadline_Termination(S : Any_Task_State;
      R : Any_Release_Mechanism_With_Deadline_Miss; Init_Prio : Priority) is
    pragma Priority(Init_Prio);
  end Real_Time_Task_With_Deadline_Termination;
```

```
task type Real_Time_Task_With_Overrun_Termination ...;
   task type Real_Time_Task_With_Deadline_And_Overrun_Termination ...;
end Real_Time_Tasks;
```

Simple_Real_Time_Task – This can be used for the cases where there is no required termination of the current release in the advent of a missed deadline or execution time overrun.

Real_Time_Task_With_Deadline_Termination – This can be used for the cases where the current release of the task must be immediately terminated on the occurrence of a deadline miss.

Real_Time_Task_With_Overrun_Termination – This can be used for the cases where the current release of the task must be immediately terminated if the execution time is exceeded.

Real_Time_Task_With_Deadline_And_Overrun_Termination – This can be used for the cases where the current release of the task must be immediately terminated on the occurrence of a deadline miss or an execution time overrun.

Note that the priority at which the task activates can be given as a discriminant (this can be changed in the application initialization code for the execution phase of the task).

Note also that if the Simple_Real_Time_Task is used with one of the release mechanisms that support deadline miss or execution-time overrun detection, it should set the Termination discriminant to false. This will allow the task to be notified using a direct call to the Deadline_Miss and Overrun operations via the Task_State.

The body of this package shows the various structures. Note the use of the 'select-then-abort' statement to achieve the termination semantics.

```
package body Real_Time_Tasks is

   task body Simple_Real_Time_Task is
   begin
     S.Initialize;
     loop
       R.Wait_For_Next_Release;
       S.code;
     end loop;
   end Simple_Real_Time_Task;

   task body Real_Time_Task_With_Deadline_Termination is
   begin
     S.Initialize;
     loop
       R.Wait_For_Next_Release;
       select
         R.Inform_Of_A_Deadline_Miss;
         S.Deadline_Miss;
       then abort
         S.code;
       end select;
     end loop;
   end Real_Time_Task_With_Deadline_Termination;

   -- similar structures for the other task types
end Real_Time_Tasks;
```

3.5   A Simple Example

Consider a simple example of two identical periodic tasks that wish to detect deadline misses: one requires termination semantics, the other just wishes to be notified. First, the application code is defined:

```
type My_State is new Periodic_Task_State with record I : Integer; end record;

procedure Initialize(S: in out My_State);
procedure Code(S: in out My_State);
procedure Deadline_Miss(S: in out My_State);

Example_State1: aliased My_State;
Example_State2: aliased My_State;

Releaser1 : aliased  Periodic_Release_With_Deadline_Miss(
          Example_State1'Access, Termination => True);
Releaser2 : aliased Periodic_Release_With_Deadline_Miss(
          Example_State2'Access, Termination => False);
```

In the above, two instances of the state are created, one for each real-time task. There are two protected objects for the release mechanisms : `Release1` supports the termination model, and `Release2` supports the notification model

Now, the real-time tasks can be declared:

```
T1 : Real_Time_Task_With_Deadline_Termination(
          Example_State1'Access, Releaser1'Access, Default_Priority);
T2 : Simple_Real_Time_Task (
          Example_State2'Access, Releaser2'Access, Default_Priority);
```

Here, `T1` uses the real-time task type that supports the termination semantics, and `T2` uses the simple real-time task type.

For completeness, the code of the tasks are given (they are identical, in this example and simply manipulate an integer state variable).

```
procedure Initialize(S: in out My_State) is
begin
  S.I := 2;
  S.Pri := Default_Priority + 2;
  S.Relative_Deadline := To_Time_Span(0.1);
  -- set up execution time if needed
end Initialize;

procedure Code(S: in out My_State) is
begin S.I := S.I * 2; end Code;

procedure Deadline_Miss(S: in out My_State) is
begin  S.I := 2; end Deadline_Miss;
```

The body initializes the state, sets the priority and the deadline; it then squares the state value on each periodic release. On a deadline miss, the value is reset to 2.

4   Release Mechanisms in Detail

In Section 3.2 a framework for constructing various mechanisms for releasing tasks was given. Here, the detailed implementation of one of them is shown in order to both test the framework and to show the expressive power of the Ada 2005 real-time support mechanisms

4.1 Periodic Release Mechanisms

The `Periodic` child package of `Release_Mechanism` implements time triggered releases. First, the full package specification is given:

```
-- with and use clauses omitted
package Release_Mechanisms.Periodic is
  protected type Periodic_Release(S: Any_Periodic_Task_State) is
         new Release_Mechanism with
    entry Wait_For_Next_Release;
    pragma Priority(System.Interrupt_Priority'Last);
  private
    procedure Release(TE : in out Timing_Event);
    Event : Timing_Event;
    Next : Time;
    New_Release : Boolean := True;
    First: Boolean := True;
  end Periodic_Release;
end Release_Mechanisms.Periodic;
```

In the above package, a protected type is defined that implements the synchronized `Release_Mechanism` interface. The type takes as a discriminant an access value to any periodic task state. It defines two protected actions. The first implement the required abstract operation of the `Release_Mechanism` interface (the `Wait_For_Next_Release` entry). The other (`Release`) provides the operation that will be called to provide the releases at the appropriate times. Note, this has been made private as it should not be called by the real-time tasks. Also note that as this mechanism provides no support for deadline miss or execution time overrun detection, the `Relative_Deadline` and `Execution_Time` state attributes are not used.

The periodic release mechanism uses Ada's new timing events facility to generate the calls to the `Release` procedure. Hence, the private part of the protected type defines the `Event` object as part of the state (and the ceiling priority is set to `Interrupt_Priority'Last`). The other variables are used to control the actual release of the real-time threads, as shown in the body below.

```
with Epoch_Support; use Epoch_Support;
package body Release_Mechanisms.Periodic is
  protected body Periodic_Release is
    entry Wait_For_Next_Release when New_Release is
    begin
      if First then
        First := False;
        Epoch_Support.Epoch.Get_Start_Time(Next);
        Next := Next + S.Period;
        Event.Set_Handler(Next, Release'Access);
        New_Release := False;
        requeue Periodic_Release.Wait_For_Next_Release;
      else New_Release := False;
      end if;
    end Wait_For_Next_Release;

    procedure Release(TE : in out Timing_Event) is
    begin
      New_Release := True;
      Next := Next + S.Period;
      TE.Set_Handler(Next, Release'Access);
    end Release;
```

```
end Periodic_Release;
end Release_Mechanisms.Periodic;
```

The release mechanisms for all periodic activities assume that the first release should be relative to some common program start time. This is maintained by an `Epoch_Support` package that allows this time to be acquired.

The first time the `Wait_For_Next_Release` entry is called, it sets up the timing event to expire at one period from the epoch, and then requeues the calling task. When the timer expires, the system automatically calls the `Release` procedure, which sets up the next timing event and opens the barrier on the entry.

To support deadline miss detection requires a different release mechanism, which is provided by the following package:

```
-- with and use clauses omitted
package Release_Mechanisms.Periodic_And_Deadline_Miss_Detection is
   protected type
    Periodic_Release_With_Deadline_Miss(
        S: Any_Periodic_Task_State; Termination : Boolean) is
            new Release_Mechanism_With_Deadline_Miss with
      entry Wait_For_Next_Release;
      entry Inform_Of_A_Deadline_Miss;
      pragma Priority(System.Interrupt_Priority'Last);
   private
      procedure Release(TE : in out Timing_Event);
      procedure Missed(TE : in out Timing_Event);
      Event_Period : Timing_Event;
      Event_Deadline : Timing_Event;
      Next : Time;
      New_Release : Boolean := True;
      First: Boolean := True;
      Missed_Deadline : Boolean := False;
      Completed : Boolean := True;
    end Periodic_Release_With_Deadline_Miss;
end Release_Mechanisms.Periodic_And_Deadline_Miss_Detection;
```

The main differences between this and the previous package is that an additional timing event is required to track the deadline of the real-time task. Furthermore, it is necessary to know if the task has completed its last release. In the body, the timer to detect the deadline miss is set when the release event occurs. The next release event is also set at this time. When the task completes, it calls the `Wait_For_Next_Release` entry, which cancels the deadline timer and requeues the task to wait for its next release event to occur.

For convenience, the above mechanisms support both notification and termination semantics on a deadline miss. The required semantics is set via the discriminant. An additional entry and an additional procedure is provided to support the deadline timing event. Note, the `Inform_Of_A_Deadline_Miss` entry is provided for the termination case – the intention is for it be called within a 'select-then-abort' statement (as was done in section 3.4).

To support execution time overrun detection again requires a different release mechanism – the implementation of this would use the new Ada 2005 facilities for managing CPU-time.

4.2 Sporadic Release Mechanisms

The sporadic release mechanisms mirror that of the periodic ones. One of the main issues is the handling of minimum inter-arrival time (MIT) violations. Here, the approach adopted is not to allow the release event to occur until the MIT has passed. To implement this requires a timing event. The specification of the simple sporadic release mechanism is given below.

```
package Release_Mechanisms.Sporadic is
  protected type Sporadic_Release(S: Any_Sporadic_Task_State)
            is new Release_Mechanism with
    entry Wait_For_Next_Release;
    procedure Release;
    pragma Priority(System.Priority'Last);
  private
    procedure Release_Allowed(TE : in out Timing_Event);
    Event_MIT : Timing_Event;
    Last : Time;
    New_Release : Natural := 0;
    Minimum_Separation: Boolean := True;
  end Sporadic_Release;
end Release_Mechanisms.Sporadic;
```

Note that the `Release` procedure is now public as it will be called by the application. In the body of the package, only when the `Release` procedure has been called and the MIT has passed, is the barrier on the `Wait_For_Next_Release` entry opened.

The code for the body of this package and the other sporadic release mechanisms are omitted due to space limitations.

5 Related Work

Work on real-time programming models for fixed priority systems can be divided into two categories: those that use research-based languages (usually based on C – for example see [3]) or real-time operating systems (such as the Shark kernel [1]), and those that attempts to bring the result of research into international standards. Ada, of course, falls into the latter category. Of this class, the main technologies that it can be compared to is the Real-Time POSIX extensions [4] and the Real-Time Specification for Java [6].

Real-Time POSIX, like Ada, attempts to provide low-level real-time mechanisms. It supports CPU-Time clocks that can be integrated into its other timing abstractions (e.g., timers that can take any clock type, and signals that can be generated when timers expire). However, it chooses to support a particular execution-time server: the sporadic server. There is no other notion of thread group budgets, and consequently constructing other servers is not possible.

The Real-Time Specification for Java provides higher level models than Ada or POSIX. It directly supports periodic, aperiodic and sporadic programming abstractions. It also supports the notion of a processing group. Threads can be associated with a group and the group can be given a budget and a replenishment period. Moreover, unlike the sporadic and deferrable servers, the threads can have different priorities, and they are suspended when the budget is exhausted. By constraining the priorities, a deferrable server can be implemented but the more complicated sporadic sever is not possible. Ada in contrast can implement both server technologies.

6   Conclusions and Final Comments

The Ada designers have learned well the lesson of trying to support too higher level abstractions for real-time programming, that was evident in Ada 83. That version was heavily criticised. Ada 95 responded to those criticisms and is an efficient language for high-reliable long-lived real-time applications. Ada 2005 has continued the recovery, and the language now provides a comprehensive set of mechanisms that can support the development of modern large real-time systems.

However, the complexity of modern real-time systems means that there is now the need to provide high-level real-time programming abstractions in the form of standardised library utilities. The goal of this paper has been to start the debate on how the Ada community should respond to this challenge. The initial focus has been on the construction of a framework that allows the provision of real-time tasking utilities. The framework has been implemented using the evolving Ada 2005 compiler from AdaCore along with a local simulation facilities for the Ada 2005 new real-time mechanisms.

The experience of using the new Ada 2005 facilities has been a positive one. The mechanisms appear to be well integrated with each other and, with one exception, appear to be complete. That exception is not being able to requeue using a synchronized interface. This did cause some problems when trying to implement execution servers (in particular, a sporadic server). However, workarounds were possible.

Acknowledgements

The authors wish to thank member of ISO committee ARG and attendees of the IRTAW series for their input to the issues discussed in this paper. We also would like to thank AdaCore for allowing access to early releases of their Ada 2005 compiler, which was used to test the algorithms presented in this paper.

References

1. Gai, P., Abeni, L., Giorgi, M., Buttazzo, G.: A new kernel approach for modular real-time systems development. In: Proceedings of the 13th IEEE Euromicro Conference on Real-Time Systems, pp. 199–207 (2001)
2. Lehoczky, J.P., Sha, L., Strosnider, J.K.: Enhanced aperiodic responsiveness in a hard real-time environment. In: Proceedings 8th IEEE Real-Time Systems Symposium, pp. 261–270 (1987)
3. Palopoli, L., Buttazzo, G., Ancilotti, P.: A C language extension for programming real-time applications. In: Proceedings of the 6th IEEE International Conference on Real-Time Computing Systems and Applications, pp. 102–110 (1999)
4. Aldea Rivas, M., Gonzalez Harbour, M.: Evaluation of new POSIX real-time operating systems services for small embedded platforms. In: Proceedings of the 15th IEEE Euromicro Conference on Real-Time Systems, pp. 161–168 (2003)
5. Sprunt, B., Lehoczky, J., Sha, L.: Exploiting unused periodic time for aperiodic service using the extended priority exchange algorithm. In: Proceedings 9th IEEE Real-Time Systems Symposium, pp. 251–258 (1988)
6. Wellings, A.J.: Concurrent and Real-Time Programming in Java. Wiley, Chichester (2005)

Handling Temporal Faults in Ada 2005*

José A. Pulido, Santiago Urueña, Juan Zamorano, and Juan A. de la Puente

Universidad Politécnica de Madrid (UPM), E28040 Madrid, Spain
{pulido,suruena,jzamorano,jpuente}@dit.upm.es

Abstract. Hard real-time systems have stringent deadline requirements, which can be guaranteed at system design time by restricting the computational model so that a careful analysis of execution-time budgets and response-time values can be performed. However, design-time guarantees are not enough in many high-integrity systems, in which some degree of run-time fault-tolerance has to be implemented as well. This paper deals with run-time mechanisms for temporal fault detection and recovery, based on some of the new features available in Ada 2005. Fault detection mechanisms are based on execution-time clocks and timers, and timing events. Fault recovery schemes are application-dependent, but some basic patterns are proposed that can be used to develop such kinds of mechanisms.

1 Introduction

The distinctive characteristic of hard real-time systems is to have strict temporal requirements, usually in the form of hard deadlines relative to the activation time of tasks [1]. Most such systems have also high integrity requirements, and thus must be shown to be fully predictable in operation and have all the properties required from them. This is usually achieved by applying static analysis to the software before it is deployed for operation, in addition to the more common approach of performing dynamic tests on the application code. Response-time analysis (RTA) methods [2,3] are particularly useful for analysing the temporal behaviour of hard real-time systems.

Static analysis methods are not always compatible with the full expressiveness of computer languages. In the case of Ada, an ISO report [4] provides guidelines for restricting the language in order to apply different kinds of static analysis techniques. The Ravenscar profile [5,6] (RP) defines a restricted tasking model that can be enforced at compilation time and enables response-time analysis of Ada programs. The profile is part of the new Ada 2005 standard [7, D.13.1]. Available experience supports the claim that the profile is expressive enough for useful hard real-time applications to be developed [8,9] and it provides a solid base for implementing high-integrity real-time systems [10].

* This work has been funded in part by the Spanish Ministry of Education, project no. TIC2005-08665-C03-01 (THREAD), and by the IST Programme of the European Commission under project IST-004033 (ASSERT).

N. Abdennahder, F. Kordon (Eds.): Ada-Europe 2007, LNCS 4498, pp. 15–28, 2007.

However, in some applications with stringent dependability requirements static analysis is not enough, and additional run-time mechanisms have to be provided in order to ensure appropriate levels of fault tolerance at execution time. In particular, appropriate mechanisms for detecting and handling violations of the specified temporal behaviour of the system are of major importance for highly critical real-time systems.

While Ada 95 provided only some basic mechanisms for detecting real-time temporal faults, Ada 2005 has been enhanced with a full set of run-time mechanisms aimed at monitoring the temporal behaviour of a system at run time [7, Annex D]. A previous paper by the authors [11] analysed the usefulness of some of the new mechanisms, and made some suggestions about the proposals that had been discussed for Ada 2005 at the time of writing it. This paper completes that preliminary analysis, taking into account the final definition of time monitoring mechanisms in the Ada 2005 standard, and refining and systematizing error detection and handling strategies based on them. Section 2 categorizes the most common kind of temporal faults in hard real-time systems, and describes some techniques for detecting them using the new Ada mechanisms. Section 3 describes some basic strategies for handling temporal faults. The next section (Sect. 4) gives some guidelines for using the proposed techniques, and Section 5 discusses some application and implementation details. Finally, Section 6 summarizes the main conclusions of this work.

2   Detecting Temporal Faults

2.1   Temporal Fault Characterization

The main temporal requirement for real-time tasks is to complete their activity by the specified deadline in each execution cycle. Therefore, the main problem a task can face is *deadline overrun*. While it may be acceptable for soft real-time tasks to occasionally miss a deadline, hard real-time tasks must always fulfill this requirement.

Although rate-monotonic or response-time analysis [3] can be used to guarantee deadlines at system design time, deadline overruns may still happen during operation if some of the static analysis assumptions are violated. Such violations may come from two sources:

– Violations of the task arrival model, in particular *minimum inter-arrival time* (MAT) of sporadic tasks. A sporadic task executing more often than specified results in an increase of the processor load, which may lead to deadline overruns in the misbehaving task or, more often, in lower-priority tasks.
– Violations of the execution-time budget of some tasks. Temporal analysis assumes that the *worst-case execution-time* (WCET) of all code sequences is known. However, the complexity of modern processor architectures may make it difficult or even impossible to accurately estimate WCET values, which in turn may result in one or more tasks consuming more CPU time

than expected. This may result in the faulty task missing its deadline or, more likely, delaying lower-priority tasks and making them miss theirs.

Since deadline overruns come from these kinds of faults, it is desirable to detect or event prevent them, when possible, before any deadline is missed. In this way, errors can be detected in the faulty task, which often is not the same as the task missing its deadline, and there is more time available for corrective actions to be taken.

There may be other temporal anomalies, which are not dangerous as they cannot result in deadline overruns, but can still expose other problems. For example, a task completing its job much earlier than expected (i.e. violating its assumed best-case execution time), may imply that some required functionality is not executed. We are not considering here such rare cases, and will concentrate only on deadline and WCET overruns, and MAT enforcement.

2.2   Timing Mechanisms in Ada 2005

The current revision of the Ada standard provides a choice of time monitoring mechanisms that can be used to detect temporal faults. The Ada.Real_Time package, including a monotonic real-time clock, which was already part of Ada 95, can be used to check real-time related properties, such as minimum inter-arrival times or task deadlines. Real-time timers were not available as such in Ada 95, but delay statements and asynchronous transfer of control (ATC) provided a similar functionality at a higher abstraction level (see e.g. [1]). However, ATC has a complex implementation and is thus excluded from the Ravenscar profile, which makes it difficult to detect deadline overruns in critical systems adhering to the profile. Unfortunately, critical systems are the kind of systems more prone to require temporal fault detection.

This has been solved in Ada 2005 by providing a lower-level mechanism, *timing events*, which can be used with the Ravenscar profile [7, D.15]. Timing events are a light-weight mechanism for specifying an action to be executed at a given time. A timing event can be set to occur at an absolute time or after a real-time interval. A protected procedure handler is executed whenever the event occurs, unless it is cancelled before that time. It should be noticed that only library-level timing events are allowed by the Ravenscar profile.

Ada 2005 also includes mechanisms for measuring and monitoring execution-time, namely *execution-time clocks*, *execution-time timers*, and *group execution-time budgets*. These mechanisms can be used to estimate the execution time of code segments, and also to handle some kinds of aperiodic events, but this paper will concentrate on their use for detecting execution-time related temporal faults. In Ada 2005 each task has an execution-time clock that computes the amount of CPU time it has consumed, including the run-time services invoked by the task. Implementations are also allowed to allocate the time spent in interrupt service routines or global system services (e.g. scheduling) to the currently running task.

Execution-time timers are objects that are associated with a task —and hence with the task execution-time clock— when they are declared. A timer can be armed to expire at an absolute value of that clock or after some execution-time interval. When the timer expires, a protected procedure handler is executed. Setting again the handler cancels any previous temporization that might be in effect. Group execution-time budgets is a similar mechanism, which can be used with a set of tasks instead of a single task. A task can belong to at most one such group. A global budget of execution-time can be allocated to the whole group, and then it decreases as any task in the group consumes execution time. As with timers, a protected procedure handler can be specified to be executed whenever the budget is exhausted (i.e. it reaches zero). The budget can also be replenished at any time.

Execution-time clocks are allowed in the Ravenscar profile, but timers and group budgets are not. However, we believe that these mechanisms can be safely used in high-integrity systems, provided that some restrictions are put in place:

- Timers and groups are declared only at the library level;
- There is at most one execution-time timer per task;
- Ada.Execution_Time.Timers.Min_Handler_Ceiling is equal to the interrupt priority of the hardware-timer which is used to implement the execution-time timers [12]

In the following, we shall assume an extended profile based on Ravenscar augmented with static execution-time timers and group budgets with the above restrictions.

2.3   Fault Detection Patterns

There are two possible approaches when detecting a temporal fault: to detect it *before* or *after* its effects can be propagated. Corrective actions can be performed if the fault is detected before it is propagated (affecting other tasks), but this approach usually introduces more overhead. On the other hand, detecting faults after having been propagated may be useless as there is no time left to do any corrective action.

All the following patterns detect the fault *before* being propagated, except for the minimum inter-arrival time. In this case the pattern directly avoids its effects, and furthermore some additional code is used to detect and report past MAT violations. Of course, a task can detect all the temporal anomalies if the techniques are combined. This is the preferred approach because the patterns do not introduce much overhead as shown in Section 5, but further analysis should be done for tasks with very tight deadlines.

Deadline Overrun.   For hard real-time tasks, where no single deadline can be missed, we propose the schemes in patterns 1 (for periodic tasks) and 2 (for sporadic tasks) to detect deadline overruns using a timing event.

If the task does not finish its job before the absolute deadline, the handler will be invoked directly by the hardware timer interrupt routine, in much the same way as it is done in cyclic executives. Of course, special care must be taken to avoid unbounded non-preemptible actions. Otherwise, if the interrupts of the hardware clock are inhibited during long time intervals, all of the fault-detection techniques described in this paper will fail. As a side note, the ceiling of the handler must be System.Interrupt_Priority 'Last, as specified in the ARM [7, D.15(14/2)].

For periodic tasks it is worth noting that the handler is set *before* going to sleep, and not afterwards, in order to minimize activation jitter. In this case there is no need to make a call to Cancel_Handler because the timing event is rearmed within the call to Set_Handler which is made at the end of the cycle (see pattern 1).

The code for sporadic tasks has some differences. As shown in pattern 2, the call to Set_Handler is placed *after* the task is released, as the absolute deadline is not known until this time. For this reason the timing event must be cancelled at the end of the execution cycle.

The activation time is recorded inside the Release_Event protected object — before opening the Wait barrier in the Signal procedure— instead of setting it in the body of the sporadic task (after the Wait entry returns). In this way, the interference that the sporadic task suffers from higher priority tasks does not disrupt the measurement of the activation, and therefore the absolute deadline is computed with the best precision.

It should be noticed that a deadline overrun cannot happen before arming the timing event —even when the interference is very long— if the response time analysis is correct, and every task with a higher or equal priority uses the fault-detection and isolation techniques described in this section. To simply arm the timing event inside the protected object does not work, due to race conditions. This method would also add some extra blocking time.

Finally, in some cases the timing event must also be cancelled just after completing its job in a periodic task, but this is only needed if additional code (e.g. data logging) is executed at the end of the cycle. Since this kind of code is usually non-critical, the expiration of a timing event within it should not be identified as a deadline overrun.

Minimal Inter-Arrival Time Enforcement. A pattern for preventing a sporadic task from being activated more often than specified by its minimal inter-arrival time is shown as pattern 3. Once the task has completed its job, it suspends itself until the minimum inter-arrival time (counted from the activation time) has elapsed.

This technique is derived from a well known code template [6, §5.7], with two main differences: First, as in pattern 2, the activation time is recorded inside the protected object, so that the next activation is delayed just the required MAT. The second difference is that this pattern also incorporates additional code inside the protected object to detect the MAT violation (see pattern 4). If the barrier is still open when the procedure Signal is invoked, it means the last event was not processed. Then a counter with the current number of missing events is incremented, and the interarrival time is recorded. Therefore, the Wait

Pattern 1. Deadline overrun detection for periodic tasks

```
Overrun  :  Ada. Real_Time . Timing_Events . Timing_Event ;

task body Periodic_Task is
  Next_Activation  :  Ada . Real_Time . Time := Epoch ;
begin
  loop
    Overrun . Set_Handler ( At_Time => Next_Activation + My_Deadline ,
                            Handler => My_Monitor . Deadline_Handler ' Access );
    delay until Next_Activation ;
    Do_Actual_Work ;
    Next_Activation := Next_Activation + My_Period ;
  end loop ;
end Periodic_Task ;
```

Pattern 2. Deadline overrun detection for sporadic tasks

```
Overrun  :  Ada . Real_Time . Timing_Events . Timing_Event ;

task body Sporadic_Task is
  New_Data          :  Data ;
  Activation_Time   :  Time ;
  Deadline_Missed   :  Boolean ;
begin
  loop
    Release_Event . Wait ( New_Data ,  Activation_Time );
    Overrun . Set_Handler ( At_Time => Activation_Time + My_Deadline ,
                            Handler => My_Monitor . Deadline_Handler ' Access );
    Do_Actual_Work ( New_Data );
    Overrun . Cancel_Handler ( Deadline_Missed );
    -- Log if detected a deadline overrun
  end loop ;
end Sporadic_Task ;
```

Pattern 3. Minimal inter-arrival time enforcement

```
task body Sporadic_Task is
  Activation_Time    :  Time ;        New_Data          :  Data ;
  Interarrival_Time  :  Time_Span ;   Next_Activation   :  Time ;
  Num_Missing_Events :  Natural ;
begin
  loop
    Monitoring_Event . Wait ( New_Data ,            Activation_Time ,
                              Interarrival_Time ,   Num_Missing_Events );
    Do_Actual_Work ( New_Data );
    -- Log the number of missing events and the inter-arrival time
    Next_Activation := Activation_Time + My_Min_Interarrival_Time ;
    delay until Next_Activation ;
  end loop ;
end Sporadic_Task ;
```

entry returns the activation time of the *last invocation* of the Signal procedure, as well as the minimum inter-arrival time and number of missing events since the previous Wait call. The sporadic task can later use this information to report the problem or take an appropriate action.

WCET Overrun. In the same way as timing events can be used to detect missed deadlines, execution-time timers can be used to detect WCET overruns, as shown in pattern 5. This technique is not very intrusive, as it only adds a call to set the timer on each activation. The CPU timer is set just before going to sleep, at the end of the execution cycle, and not after the delay until, in order to minimize the activation jitter. It should also be noticed that there is no need to call Cancel_Handler, as the timer is reset again at the beginning of the loop if there is no WCET overrun. Actually this is the preferred approach because the whole execution cycle should be accounted for, including even the CPU time needed to set the execution-time timer. The pattern for sporadic tasks is similar to this one.

If the task consumes more CPU time than expected, (e.g. due to a programming bug leading to an infinite loop), the timer will expire and corrective actions can be performed, as explained in the next section. Otherwise, the faulty task could interfere with the correct execution of other tasks, making them miss their deadlines. However, if the CPU timer expires when the task is inside a protected operation some of the possible corrective actions (e.g. task abortion or priority lowering) will not be effective until the task leaves the protected object. This is not a problem in Ravenscar because task abortion and dynamic priorities are not allowed, but this can be an issue in full Ada. Therefore, protected operations must be carefully coded, as is always the case, because WCET overruns within them cannot always be immediately corrected. In the worst case, an infinite loop in a protected operation will lead to the whole system being stuck.

The handler will be invoked directly by the hardware timer interrupt routine, as for a timing event. This is the reason for the requirement that the constant Ada.Execution_ Time.Timers.Min_Handler_Ceiling is equal to the hardware-timer interrupt priority.

3   Fault Handling Strategies

Once a temporal anomaly has been detected by means of any of the methods described in Sect. 2, it must be properly handled in order to minimize its impact on the system. While fault handling is a system issue which can be implemented in different ways depending on the application characteristics and the possible consequences of each kind of fault, three basic strategies can be defined: log temporal errors, give the faulty task a second chance, and force a system mode change.

3.1   Error Logging

The first strategy, and the less intrusive one, is just keeping an error log, e.g. for statistical purposes. Obviously, this kind of *soft* strategy, which cannot even be classified as a corrective action, is only valid for systems with a very low level of criticality because, in high-integrity systems, a temporal misbehaviour even from a low criticality task is a potential hazard for the rest of the system and thus this approach is not admissible.

Pattern 4. Release event with inter-arrival time monitoring for sporadic tasks

```
protected Monitoring_Event is
  procedure Signal (New_Data : in Data);
  entry Wait (New_Data             : out Data;
              Activation_Time       : out Time;
              Interarrival_Time     : out Time_Span;
              Missing_Events        : out Natural);
private
  pragma Priority (My_Ceiling);
  Current_Data                  : Data;
  Signalled                     : Boolean := False;
  Arrival_Time                  : Time     := Time_First;
  Current_Interarrival_Time     : Time_Span;
  Num_Missing_Events            : Natural;
end Monitoring_Event;

protected body Monitoring_Event is
  procedure Signal (New_Data : in Data) is
      This_Arrival      : constant Time      := Ada.Real_Time.Clock;
      This_Interarrival : constant Time_Span := This_Arrival − Arrival_Time;
  begin
    if Signalled then
       Num_Missing_Events := Num_Missing_Events + 1;
       if This_Interarrival < Current_Interarrival_Time then
          Current_Interarrival_Time := This_Interarrival;
       end if;
    else
       Signalled                  := True;
       Num_Missing_Events         := 0;
       Current_Interarrival_Time  := This_Interarrival;
    end if;
    Current_Data := New_Data;
    Arrival_Time := This_Arrival;
  end Signal;

  entry Wait (New_Data             : out Data;
              Activation_Time       : out Time;
              Interarrival_Time     : out Time_Span;
              Missing_Events        : out Natural) when Signalled is
  begin
    New_Data            := Current_Data;
    Activation_Time     := Arrival_Time;
    Missing_Events      := Num_Missing_Events;
    Interarrival_Time   := Current_Interarrival_Time;
    Signalled           := False;
  end Wait;
end Monitoring_Event;
```

Pattern 5. WCET overrun detection

```
My_Identity : aliased constant Task_Id := Periodic_Task'Identity;
WCET_Timer  : Ada.Execution_Time.Timers.Timer(My_Identity'Access);

task body Periodic_Task is
  Next_Activation : Ada.Real_Time.Time := Epoch;
begin
  loop
    WCET_Timer.Set_Handler(In_Time=>My_WCET_Budget,
                           Handler=>My_Monitor.Overrun_Handler'Access);
    delay until Next_Activation;
    Do_Actual_Work;
    Next_Activation := Next_Activation + My_Period;
  end loop;
end Periodic_Task;
```

Another possible usage of this strategy is the testing phase, where temporal data, including possible overruns, can be collected in order to get insight into the system behavior.

3.2   Second Chance Algorithm

The second strategy that we propose is to use a *second chance algorithm*. It is a bit more intrusive than the previous one, as it slightly modifies the schedule. The basic idea is to compute the *slack time* of the faulty task, i.e. the amount by which its execution time can be enlarged while still keeping the system schedulable [13]. Slack time can be computed as part of static analysis, as a simple derivation from worst-case response time computation. Then the available slack time can be used to give the faulty task an extra budget in order to let it complete its job.

The justification for using this technique comes from the fact that there are basically two possible causes for an overrun:

– There is a misbehavior (e.g. an infinite loop) which makes the task unable to properly finish its job.
– The WCET value that has been used for static temporal analysis has been miscalculated.

The first kind of failure is really serious because it is likely to prevent the task from ever completing its job, even though its budget is increased. This approach is clearly not suitable for such kind of failure. On the other hand, overruns due to WCET underestimation are the effect of a possibly transitory overload. In this case, giving the task some extra budget may solve a possibly occasional problem without the overhead of more drastic methods such as those discussed in the next section. In other words, provided that there is enough spare processor utilization, it is possible to give a try to the faulty task and check whether it is just a transitory situation that will not happen again, and let the system continue its normal schedule afterwards.

3.3   Mode Change

A last strategy is still possible and essential. When a task is not able to finish its job within the estimated budget, not even after being given additional time with the *second chance algorithm*, it may seriously jeopardize the system integrity. Therefore, corrective actions must be taken in order to prevent undesirable effects.

Acceptable approaches are:

– Go to a safe state and stop the system *(fail-safe)*.
– Change to a safe mode and continue execution with a degraded functionality *(fail-soft)*.

Both are classical examples of fault recovery actions. There is also the possibility of ensuring full fault tolerance, i.e. continuing execution with full system functionality, but this approach requires a high level of hardware and software redundancy, and we shall not consider it in the following.

A fail-safe behaviour can be implemented in Ada by terminating the faulty task and setting a global termination handler, which is allowed by the Ravenscar profile [7, D.13.1]. The termination handler must include everything which is required to ensure a safe stop. On the other hand, switching to a safe mode requires that the faulty task is disabled or "quarantined" in some way so that it no longer interferes with the rest of the system. This purpose can be achieved by lowering the faulty task priority, so that it can only execute when there are no other ready tasks, using only spare CPU time. Alternatively, the faulty task can be aborted, as it can be supposed that it is not able to do its work any more. However, both approaches are a source of temporal indeterminism, and consequently their temporal behaviour may be difficult to analyse. In fact, both dynamic priority changes and task abortion are forbidden by the Ravenscar profile for this reason.

Moreover, any functional dependence or synchronization with the damaged task must be taken into account because it can induce undesirable collateral effects. For instance, a task may be suspended *ad infinitum* waiting on a barrier that the faulty task should open, or it may return wrong values due to parameters that are never updated by the task. Therefore, just removing a task from the system is only acceptable if there are no other tasks depending on it. Care should also be taken that the task functionality is not vital for the system, so that the rest of the tasks can continue executing without compromising the system integrity. On the other hand, when the functionality of the faulty task is essential for the system, it must be replaced in some way so that the system can continue working, even though its functionality is reduced. This can be accomplished by a mode change.

A mode change involves a deep alteration of the system configuration. As such, the static environment implied by the Ravenscar profile may be altered and temporal analysis may be made difficult or impossible. However, it is possible to implement mode changes in a Ravenscar-compatible way as long as some constraints are in place [14]. Another source of complexity has to do with the number of different modes that have to be planned in order to face all the potential failures of the system. Given that a typical real system can have several dozens of tasks, it is clearly not feasible to envisage a different mode for covering every potential failure of every task. A more achievable solution is to provide a small number of *degraded modes* [15], and switch the system to one of them whenever an important task fails. Typically only basic services are provided in degraded modes. If no degraded mode can be used, then a fail-safe stop can still be performed, provided it is acceptable for the application.

4   Guidelines for Building Monitored Systems

In order to get the maximum profit from modern computing devices it is becoming more and more common to build partitioned systems. These systems execute a number of applications, possibly with different levels of criticality, on a single computer platform. In order to preserve the integrity of applications from failures occurring in other applications, temporal and spatial isolation mechanisms have to be put in place. Temporal separation can be based on hierarchical scheduling using Ada 2005 priority bands [16], but architectural mechanisms must be supplemented at run-time with monitoring mechanisms for temporal fault detection and handling. The rest of this section provides some guidelines on how to protect the different subsystems of a partitioned system from temporal faults occurring in other subsystems.

The main strategy is to monitor the CPU-time consumption of every individual task. As above discussed, execution-time timers can be used for this purpose, as shown in pattern 5. Group execution-time budgets can also be used in a similar way to account for global overruns affecting a whole subsystem. The next step is to choose a handling strategy among those discussed in Sect. 3. Although the choice is application-dependent, some general guidelines can be given.

The second chance algorithm should be used whenever possible, as it is the best way to face occasional overloads without significantly altering the system configuration. If after a second chance the overload persists, then it can be assumed that there is a serious error and one of the overrun handlers must be used. An annotation in a log may be enough for non-critical tasks with low priority values (possibly monitored by means of group execution-time budgets), as it is the less intrusive technique. If a failure in one of these tasks does not compromise the whole system, it is better to avoid any action outside the Ravenscar profile, leaving more extreme actions for the situations when they are required.

When the overrun occurs in a critical task a mode change is mandatory. In some cases a safe stop is enough, although this may not be acceptable in some kinds of systems. In these cases the last chance to rescue the system consists in changing to a degraded mode, where only the main functionalities can be executed, in order to to minimize as much as possible the effects of a temporal overrun.

5   Implementation and Applications

The Ada 2005 timing mechanisms have been implemented by the authors on GNATforLEON, a compilation system for the LEON2 processor, a radiation-hardened derivative of the SPARCv8 RISC architecture for the space domain. The implementation has been based on a previous experimental implementation on top of the Open Ravenscar kernel [12]. The modified compilation system is being used as the execution platform for the ASSERT project[1]. The fault detection patterns described in this paper have been successfully applied to a comprehensive example of a spacecraft software system including some critical components [17].

---

[1] ASSERT (Automated proof based System and Software Engineering for Real-Time) is an FP6 Integrated Project coordinated by the European Space Agency. The main goal of the project is to improve the system-and-software development process for critical embedded real-time systems, in the Aerospace and Transportation domains.

Table 1 provides information about the overhead included in a context switch due to the new timing mechanisms (execution-time timers, group budgets, and timing events), comparing the values which have been obtained for GNAT Pro for ERC32, GNATforLEON 1.0 (without the new timing mechanisms), and GNAT-forLEON 1.3 (including the new timing mechanisms). The values shown in this section have been measured using a pilot application, and therefore should be considered as average values, not as worst-case metrics.

Table 1. Context switch in GNATforLEON

Operation	GNAT Pro ERC32	GNAT LEON 1.0	GNAT LEON 1.3
Context switch	362	405	606

Values are expressed in terms of instructions as the overall timing impact is highly dependant on hardware elements such as caches or registers. The ideal situation is one cycle for instruction, and taking into account that the simulator used in the test runs at 50 MHz, the ideal performance would be 50 MIPS. However, real experiments show that the real performance is about one third of the ideal one.

Table 2. Overhead of timing mechanisms

Operation	Instructions
Ada.Real_Time.Timing_Events.Set_Handler	240
Ada.Execution_Time.Timers.Set_Handler	271
Timing event handler latency	396
Execution-time handler latency	415
Basic_Event.Signal	685
Release_Event.Signal	787
Monitoring_Event.Signal	833

Table 2 shows some measurements, including the cost of signalling a sporadic task by means of different patterns in GNATforLEON 1.3. Basic_Event is the protected object used to release sporadic tasks [6, §5.6], which only opens the barrier (and stores the new data). This object is not used in any of the fault-detection patterns, but its metrics are shown for comparison purposes. The protected object Release_Event is used in pattern 2, and its procedure Signal also reads the clock before opening the barrier. Finally, the protected object Monitoring_Event (pattern 4) reads the clock, detects a minimum inter-arrival time violation when it occurs, and finally opens the barrier. Of course, a sporadic task combining MAT enforcement and deadline-overrun detection uses only one protected object (Monitoring_Event in pattern 2).

Finally, table 3 shows the memory size needed for the different types used in this paper.

Table 3. Memory size

Type	Size (bytes)
Timing_Event	24
Execution_Time.Timers.Timer	20
Basic_Event	32
Activation_Event	48
Monitoring_Event	56

6   Conclusions and Future Work

An analysis of the timing monitoring mechanisms available in Ada 2005 has been carried out, and some patterns for temporal fault detection based on these mechanisms have been developed. Strategies for handling temporal faults have been discussed, taking into account different levels of criticality and real-time requirements. The patterns have been used in a sample on-board embedded system, using a pilot implementation of Ada 2005 timing mechanisms.

Most of the proposed patterns and strategies use some features excluded by the Ravenscar profile definition. The most important ones are execution-time timers and group budgets. An extended profile allowing a limited use of both mechanisms, while still preserving the static nature of the system, can be a solution to this limitation.

Given the fact that system integrity is greatly enhanced by means of the presented protection mechanisms, and the metrics provided show that the overhead produced on the system is within acceptable values, its use in high-integrity systems is highly recommended.

Planned future work includes code instrumentation for obtaining timing metrics of Ravenscar tasks, and modification of the run-time system to gather statistics about relevant temporal values (e.g. jitter, blocking, response time, computation time).

References

1. Burns, A., Wellings, A.J.: Real-Time Systems and Programming Languages, 3rd edn. Addison-Wesley, Reading (2001)
2. Joseph, M., Pandya, P.: Finding response times in real-time systems. BCS Computer Journal 29, 390–395 (1986)
3. Klein, M.H., Ralya, T., Pollack, B., Obenza, R., González-Harbour, M.: A Practitioner's Handbook for Real-Time Analysis. Guide to Rate Monotonic Analysis for Real-Time Systems. Kluwer Academic Publishers, Boston (1993)
4. ISO/IEC: TR 15942:2000 — Guide for the use of the Ada programming language in high integrity systems (2000)
5. Burns, A., Dobbing, B., Romanski, G.: The Ravenscar tasking profile for high integrity real-time programs. In: Asplund, L. (ed.) Ada-Europe 1998. LNCS, vol. 1411, pp. 263–275. Springer, Heidelberg (1998)

6. ISO/IEC: TR 24718:2005 — Guide for the use of the Ada Ravenscar Profile in high integrity systems. (2005) Based on the University of York Technical Report YCS-2003-348 (2003)
7. Taft, S.T., Duff, R.A., Brukardt, R.L., Ploedereder, E., Leroy, P. (eds.): Ada 2005 Reference Manual. LNCS, vol. 4348. Springer, Heidelberg (2006)
8. Dobbing, B., Romanski, G.: The Ravenscar profile: Experience report. Ada. Letters XIX, 28–32 (1999) Proceedings of the 9th International Real-Time Ada Workshop
9. Vardanega, T.: Reflections on the use of the Ravenscar profile. Ada. Letters XXIII, 93–95 (2003) Proceedings of the 12th International Ada Real-Time Workshop (IRTAW12)
10. Vardanega, T.: Development of on-board embedded real-time systems: An engineering approach. Technical Report ESA STR-260, European Space Agency (1999)
11. de la Puente, J.A., Zamorano, J.: Execution-time clocks and Ravenscar kernels. Ada. Letters XXIII, 82–86 (2003) Proceedings of the 12th International Ada Real-Time Workshop (IRTAW12)
12. Zamorano, J., Alonso, A., Pulido, J.A., de la Puente, J.A.: Implementing execution-time clocks for the Ada Ravenscar profile. In: Llamosí, A., Strohmeier, A. (eds.) Ada-Europe 2004. LNCS, vol. 3063, Springer, Heidelberg (2004)
13. Davis, R.I., Tindell, K.W., Burns, A.: Scheduling slack time in fixed priority preemptive systems. In: IEEE Real-Time Systems Symposium (1993)
14. Alonso, A., de la Puente, J.A.: Implementation of mode changes with the Ravenscar profile. Ada Letters. In: Proceedings of the 11th International Real-Time Ada Workshop, vol. XXI (2001)
15. Lundqvist, K., Srinivasan, J., Gorelov, S.: Non-intrusive system level fault-tolerance. In: Vardanega, T., Wellings, A.J. (eds.) Ada-Europe 2005. LNCS, vol. 3555, pp. 156–166. Springer, Heidelberg (2005)
16. Pulido, J.A., Urueña, S., Zamorano, J., Vardanega, T., de la Puente, J.A.: Hierarchical scheduling with Ada 2005. In: Pinho, L.M., González Harbour, M. (eds.) Ada-Europe 2006. LNCS, vol. 4006, Springer, Heidelberg (2006)
17. Dissaux, P., Moretti, R., Barone, M.R., Puri, S., Cancila, D., Bordin, M., Prochazka, M., Najm, E., Hamid, I.: Experience in modelling a general PP problem. Technical report, ASSERT Consortium, D3.1.3-1 I2R0 (2006)

Implementation of New Ada 2005 Real-Time Services in MaRTE OS and GNAT[*]

Mario Aldea Rivas[1] and José F. Ruiz[2]

[1] Departamento de Electrónica y Computadores, Universidad de Cantabria,
39005-Santander, Spain
aldeam@unican.es
[2] AdaCore, 8 rue de Milan, 75009 Paris, France
ruiz@adacore.com

Abstract. The paper presents the implementation of some of the new Ada 2005 real-time services ("Execution Time Clocks", "Execution Time Timers", "Timing Events" and "Dynamic Priorities for Protected Objects") in the MaRTE OS/ GNAT run-time library for GNU/Linux. For each these new services we discuss different implementation alternatives and evaluate they performance. As a consequence of the results obtained, our view is that the new services can be implemented in an efficient way in a existing run-time system without requiring major changes. To illustrate the usefulness of the new Ada services, the implementation of a complex scheduling policy is described.

Keywords: Ada 2005, Real-Time Systems, Compilers, POSIX.

1 Introduction

Some of the most exciting Ada 2005 [1] innovations are those targeting the real-time community, providing capabilities that are neither addressed by other programming languages nor supported by most industrial execution platforms. The most important of these new services are: execution time clocks and timers, group execution time budgets, timing events, dynamic priorities for protected objects, immediate priority changes, and the new scheduling and task dispatching mechanisms. This audacious step forward reinforces Ada leadership for real-time programming, but needs to be endorsed by run-time systems that provides those new services.

MaRTE OS [2][3] is a real-time operating system that can also be configured as a POSIX-thread library for GNU/Linux. MaRTE OS provides some specific real-time features, as "timed handlers" or "application-defined scheduling interface", together with most of the advanced features defined in the real-time extension to POSIX [4] (among others the CPU-time clocks and timers).

---

[*] This work has been funded by AdaCore, the *Comisión Interministerial de Ciencia y Tecnología* of the Spanish Government under grant TIN2005-08665-C03-02 (THREAD project) and by the *Commission of the European Communities* under contract IST-004527 (ARTIST2 Network of Excellence).

N. Abdennahder, F. Kordon (Eds.): Ada-Europe 2007, LNCS 4498, pp. 29–40, 2007.

The GNAT run-time library has been adapted to run on top of MaRTE OS in order to use the advanced real-time support provided by this operating system. These features are required to implement the new Ada 2005 real-time services. In this paper we describe the implementation of four features: timing events, execution time clocks, execution time timers, and dynamic priorities for protected objects.

The first objective of this implementation is to provide a reference platform for GNU/Linux, fully compliant with Ada 2005, available for industrial, research, and teaching environments. Additionally, this platform can be used as a test bed before cross-development, providing a more user-friendly environment for testing and debugging.

MaRTE OS was originally implemented as a real-time kernel for embedded PCs, so this development will culminate in a run-time for embedded real-time Ada 2005 applications on bare x86 computers.

This paper is organized as follows: section 2 presents the MaRTE OS run time. Sections 3, 4, 5, and 6 discuss the implementation and performance of timing events, execution time clocks, execution time timers and dynamic priorities for protected objects, respectively. Section 7 shows an usage example of some of the new Ada 2005 real-time features. Finally, Section 8 summarizes our conclusions and outlines some ideas about the continuation of this work.

2 MaRTE OS Run-Time System

The GNAT run-time system has been carefully designed to isolate target dependencies by means of a layered architecture. There is a target independent layer, called GNU Ada Run-Time Library (GNARL), which provides the interface to the compiler. The part of the run time that depends on the particular machine and operating system is known as GNU Low-Level Library (GNULL), which provides a target independent interface. GNULL is some glue code that translates this generic interface into calls to the underlying multitasking library interface, thus facilitating portability.

MaRTE OS was originally implemented as a real-time kernel for embedded x86 targets, and it has been later adapted to behave as a POSIX-threads library for the GNU/Linux operating system. It is a very practical and flexible platform for real-time development in the industrial, research, and teaching communities. We have adapted GNARL to run on top of MaRTE OS using a specialized GNULL layer that maps Ada tasking constructs to MaRTE concurrency features.

Executing on top of the underlying Linux kernel limits its usability for developing hard real-time applications. However, using a properly configured GNU/Linux system allows for the development of soft real-time systems with time requirements longer than 50 ms [5]. This MaRTE OS run-time system will be adapted in the future to support embedded real-time Ada 2005 on bare x86 computers (including industrial controllers with x86 architecture), where hard real-time requirements can be supported.

The advantages of using GNU/Linux as the target platform are that it is a widespread system, with a large availability of drivers, mature and stable, and a very user-friendly environment for testing and debugging.

3 Timing Events

3.1 Description

Timing events are defined in Ada 2005 as an effective and efficient mechanism to execute user-defined time-triggered procedures without the need to use a task or a delay statement. They are very efficient because the event handler is executed directly in the context of the interrupt handler (it does not need a server task). Timing events have been included in the standard as a new language-defined package (Ada.Real_Time. Timing_Events).

The use of timing events may reduce the number of tasks in a program, and hence reduce the overheads of context switching. It provides an effective solution for programming short time-triggered procedures, and for implementing some specific scheduling algorithms, such as those used for imprecise computation [6]. Imprecise computation increase the utilization and effectiveness of real-time applications by means of structuring tasks into two phases (one mandatory and one optional). Scheduling algorithms that try to maximize the likelihood that optional parts are completed typically require changing asynchronously the priority of a task, which can be implemented elegant and efficiently with timing events.

3.2 Implementation

Three possible implementations of Ada timing events have been considered:

- Run-time system implementation using an auxiliary Ada task.
- Implementation based on POSIX timers.
- Implementation based on a MaRTE OS specific functionality called "timed handlers".

The first option has been chosen in recent versions of GNAT as a simple way to support timing events just for demonstration purposes. It uses an auxiliary Ada task at System.Priority'Last priority and a queue of timing events. This task is activated periodically to execute handlers of queued events whose expiration time has passed.

Another option in a POSIX operating system would be to implement timing events based on timers. POSIX timers can be set to expire at a desired time. When a timer expires, a signal is sent to the process. The implementation should use an auxiliary thread at the maximum priority to catch that signal and execute the timing event handler. Handlers expect the timing event object to be passed as parameter. This information can be passed to the auxiliary thread in the additional information field that is associated with every POSIX signal.

Although both implementation alternatives are feasible and functionally correct, they involve too much complexity for a functionality like timing events, intended for being a fast mechanism to execute simple actions at a particular time.

For that reason we have chosen the third alternative. It is based on "timed handlers", a MaRTE OS specific (non-POSIX) service that allows executing user's code in interrupt context at the desired time. "Timed handlers" support all the functionality included in Ada.Real_Time.Timing_Events, together with some other services such as periodic handlers and temporarily disabling handlers execution.

Therefore implementation of Ada timing events on top of "timed handlers" is straightforward, does not require any auxiliary task and is more efficient than the other alternatives.

As said before, timing events has been included in the Ada 2005 standard as a new package without defining any new language construct. Therefore, it has not been necessary to make any modifications in the compiler nor in the run-time to implement this functionality.

3.3 Evaluation

The alternative in Ada 95 to the timing events would be to use a dedicated high priority task. This is in fact the way timing events have been implemented in the test implementation included in recent versions of GNAT. So, in order to compare the performance of our implementation against the use of an auxiliary task we have compared both alternatives.

Table 1. Timing events performance

Metric	Time (µs) (auxiliary task)	Time (µs) (timed handlers)
From user´s task to handler	67.1	21.5
From handler to user's task	46.4	11.2

Table 1 shows the time required by both implementations to preempt the running task in order to execute a handler and to come back from the handler to the preempted task. The first row shows the time elapsed from the last instruction executed by the user's task until the first instruction of the timing event handler is executed. The second row shows the time elapsed from the handler executing its last instruction until the user's task is able to continue executing.

As it can be seen in the table, our implementation using "timed handlers" is between 3 and 4 times faster than the alternative implementation using an auxiliary task.

4 Execution Time Clocks

4.1 Description

Monitoring execution time is important for many real-time systems, and Ada 2005 provides a standardized interface to obtain CPU consumption of every task in the system. This service has been included in the standard in the new language-defined package Ada.Execution_Time.

This feature can be used to detect at run time an excessive usage of computational resources, which is usually caused by either software errors or errors made in the computation of worst-case execution times.

4.2 Implementation

The POSIX standard has "thread CPU-time clocks" to measure the execution time consumed by threads in the system. Implementation of Ada execution time clocks on top of POSIX CPU-time clocks is straightforward for systems where every Ada task is mapped onto one POSIX thread. This is the case of the GNAT run-time system for MaRTE OS.

Two possible issues in the mapping of Ada execution time clocks on top of POSIX CPU-time clocks are solved thanks to the coincidence in the definition of the "execution time" concept in both standards:

- None of the standards, Ada 2005 and POSIX, define which task is charged the execution time that is consumed by interrupt handlers and run-time services on behalf of the system.
- The Ada 2005 standard states the execution time is set to zero at the creation of the task. Activation of the task is executed by the task itself and, therefore, it must be charged to its execution time clock. In the same way, POSIX says the thread CPU-time clock is set to zero at the creation of the thread. Both concepts fit because the run-time system executes the activation part in the context of the low level thread used to implement the Ada task.

As a consequence, no modifications to the compiler or to the run-time system have been necessary to implement this functionality.

4.3 Evaluation

Execution time accounting introduces a small overhead in context switch times but, as it was shown in [7], this overhead is fully acceptable (enabling this service in MaRTE OS increments the context switch time by less than 5%).

Another interesting metric is the time necessary to read execution time clocks. Table 2 shows a comparison between the times[1] needed to invoke `Ada.Real_Time.Clock` and `Ada.Execution_Time.Clock` for the current task and for another task different from the one that is making the call.

The larger value in the second row is because the execution time consumed by the current task is obtained by adding the accumulated execution time consumed in past activations, plus the difference between the current time and the last activation time of

Table 2. Time to read execution time clocks

Metric	Time (μs)
Invoke Ada.Real_Time.Clock	4.9
Invoke Ada.Execution_Time.Clock for the current task	8.9
Invoke Ada.Execution_Time.Clock for another task	4.5

---

[1] All the measurements given in this paper are average times measured in a computer running Linux. They are given only for comparison purposes between the different alternatives.

the task. Therefore, when `Ada.Execution_Time.Clock` is invoked for the current task, the system is internally invoking `Ada.Real_Time.Clock` to get the current time.

As it can be noticed in the table, reading execution time clocks is not an expensive operation in our implementation.

5 Execution Time Timers

5.1 Description

Ada 2005 defines a timing mechanism which allows creating timers that are triggered when the execution time of a task reaches a given value, providing the means whereby action can be taken when this budget expires. Execution time timers have been included in the standard as a new language-defined package (`Ada.Execution_Time.Timers`).

Schedulability analysis is based on the assumption that the execution time of each task can be accurately estimated. This measurement is always difficult, because, with effects like cache misses, pipelined and superscalar processor architectures, the execution time is highly unpredictable. Run-time monitoring of processor usage permits detecting and responding to wrong estimations in a controlled manner.

CPU clocks and timers are a key requirement for implementing some real-time scheduling policies which need to perform scheduling actions when a certain amount of execution time has been consumed. Examples of this kind of policies are aperiodic servers[2] such as the sporadic server policy defined in the POSIX standard [4] or the constant bandwidth server (CBS) [8]. Another example is the policy used in control applications which implementation is shown in section 7.

5.2 Implementation

Two possible implementations of Ada execution time timers have been considered:

- Implementation based on POSIX CPU-time timers.
- Implementation based on "timed handlers".

The most obvious implementation of Ada execution time timers in a POSIX operating system would be to use CPU-time timers: the POSIX standard defines timers based on "CPU-time clocks", in other words, timers that will send a signal to the process when the value of the CPU-time clock of a particular thread reaches the desired value. Therefore, by using an auxiliary thread in the same way that was described in section 3 for Ada timing events, it would be possible to implement execution time timers on top of POSIX CPU-time timers.

However, sending a signal to activate a thread that will execute the timer handler is a much more complex mechanism than using "timed handlers". For that reason, and taking advantage of the fact that "timed handlers" can also be based on CPU-time

---

[2] The Ada 2005 standard provides a service more suitable than CPU timers to implement servers for a group of tasks: the "Group Execution Time Budgets".

clocks, we have decided to implement Ada execution time timers on top of "timed handlers" instead of POSIX CPU-time timers.

This decision implies another important advantage: it allows us to share to a large extent the same implementation for timing events and execution time timers. In our implementation both types (`Ada.Execution_Time.Timers.Timer` and `Ada.Real_Time.Timing_Events.Timing_Event`) are extensions of the same base type form which they inherit common operations (`Set_Handler`, `Current_Handler` and `Cancel_Handler`).

It has not been necessary to make any modifications to the compiler nor to the run-time to implement this functionality.

5.3 Evaluation

Table 3 compares the performance of the execution time timers and timing events. As it can be noticed, times are very similar in both cases.

Table 3. Execution time timers performance

Metric	Time (μs) (execution time timers)	Time (μs) (timing events)	Metric	Time (μs) (delay until)
From user's task to handler	23.3	21.5	Wake up after delay until	43.3
From handler to user's task	12.2	11.2	Suspension using delay until	25.4

Just to serve as reference, the last column shows the time used by the system to perform a `delay until` operation. The first row in the last column shows the time required by the system to preempt a low priority task because a high priority task has finished its suspension period. The second row shows the opposite situation: the time elapsed from a high priority task invoking the `delay until` operation until a low priority task can execute.

By comparing the times in each row it can be seen that system is roughly twice as fast when invoking and returning from handlers than when activating and suspending tasks.

6 Dynamic Priorities for Protected Objects

6.1 Description

The common practice in real time applications is to assign priorities to tasks and to use `Ceiling_Locking` as the locking policy for protected objects in order to avoid the unbounded priority inversion. When using `Ceiling_Locking`, the priority of the protected object is know as its ceiling priority. For a correct and optimal behaviour, the ceiling priority of a protected object should be equal to the highest value among the priorities of all the tasks that use the resource.

In Ada 95 it was possible to change dynamically the priority of a task (using the standard package `Ada.Dynamic_Priorities`), however it was not possible to dynamically change the ceiling priotity of a protected object. This deficiency was a limitation for some purposes, such as implementing "mode changes" [9] or for utility libraries that include protected objects.

To solve this limitation Ada 2005 has introduced the new attribute `'Priority` for protected objects. The value of this attribute can be read or set inside protected actions. When it is set, the ceiling priority of the protected object is updated just before the end of the protected action.

6.2 Implementation

The GNAT run-time system for POSIX operating systems (as is the case of MaRTE OS) uses mutexes as the mutual exclusion primitive to implement protected objects. The POSIX standard defines the `pthread_mutex_setprioceiling()` operation to change the ceiling priority of an existing mutex, but the standard says this operation must lock the mutex before changing the ceiling. Therefore, calling this operation from inside a protected operation will lead to a deadlock.

POSIX "recursive" mutexes are a solution to this problem: "recursive" mutexes are a type of mutex defined by POSIX standard that allows multiple "lock" operations (the same number of "unlocks" will be necessary to release the mutex). The problem with this type of mutexes is that they are not implemented in many POSIX operating systems, and, in our case, they are not implemented in MaRTE OS.

Although "recursive" mutexes can be a better solution for the long term, in our current implementation we have chosen a simpler, but non-POSIX, solution. We have implemented in MaRTE OS a new operation (`pthread_mutex_setprioceiling_locked()`) that allows changing the ceiling with the mutex already locked.

Implementing this new service has required slight modifications in the run-time system and in the compiler. A new field (`New_Ceiling`) has been defined in the protected object's control block. Setting and getting the `'Priority` attribute of a protected object is transformed by the compiler in setting and getting its `New_Ceiling` field. Before leaving every protected action the value stored in `New_Ceiling` is compared with the current ceiling of the protected object. When they are different the ceiling is updated with the new value and the `pthread_mutex_setprioceiling_locked ()` operation is invoked.

6.3 Evaluation

In order to evaluate the complexity of changing the ceiling of a protected object, we have compared the time to execute an empty protected procedure with the time to execute a protected procedure that just changes the ceiling.

As it can be noticed in table 4, times for both operations are almost equal. The reason is because `pthread_mutex_setprioceiling_locked()` is a very simple operation that only changes the ceiling of the mutex without affecting the active priority of the task

Table 4. Time to change priority ceiling of a protected object

Metric	Time (µs)
Empty protected procedure	11.7
Protected procedure that just changes ceiling	11.8

that is locking the mutex. Such behaviour is allowed in the POSIX standard for `pthread_mutex_setprioceiling()` operation, and it is compatible with the expected behaviour in Ada 2005: the new priority ceiling will be in effect for the next invocation of a protected action.

7 Usage Example

To illustrate the usefulness of some of these new Ada services, in this chapter we present an example in which execution time timers and timing events are used together with "select then abort" statements and dynamic priorities to implement a complex scheduling policy used in control applications. The scheduling problem is very similar to the one that was solved in [10] using Ada 95 primitives.

Figure 1 shows the structure of a control activity. Control activities are divided into four parts: data acquisition, mandatory computation of the control action, solution improvement using an any-time algorithm and output of the control action. In order to minimize jitter, "data acquisition" and "output control action" parts are executed at high priority. A valid output value is calculated during the "mandatory calculation" phase using a time bounded algorithm, later the solution can be improved using an unbounded algorithm that can be aborted when necessary.

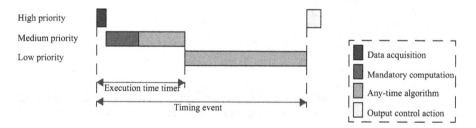

Fig. 1. Structure of a control task

The pseudocode of a control task is shown below. In every activation the task starts executing at high priority to perform the data acquisition and set the execution time timer and the timing event, later it decreases its priority[3] to perform the computation of the control action and starts the any-time algorithm to improve the solution. Once the any-time algorithm is aborted the task, executing at high priority again, outputs control action and waits for next period.

---

[3] In this example we take advantage of priority changes are immediate in Ada 2005.

```
task body Control_Task is
 Task_Id : aliased Ada.Task_Identification.Task_Id :=
    Ada.Task_Identification.Current_Task;
 Output_Control_TE : Ada.Real_Time.Timing_Events.Timing_Event;
 Budget_Timer :
    Ada.Execution_Time.Timers.Timer (Task_Id'Access);
 Activation_time : Ada.Real_Time.Time := Ada.Real_Time.Clock;
begin
loop
--Set execution-time timer
    Ada.Execution_Time.Timers.Set_Handler
       (Budget_Timer,
        Ada.Execution_Time.Clock + Budget,
        PO.Budget_Exhausted_Handler'Access);
--Set timing event
    Ada.Real_Time.Timing_Events.Set_Handler
       (TE,
        Activation_time + Offset_To_Output_Control_Action,
        PO.Output_Control_Action_Handler'Access);
--Data acquisition
    Get_Data;
--Decrease priority and perform mandatory computation
    Ada.Dynamic_Priorities.Set_Priority (Medium_Prio);
    Mandatory_Computation;
--Start any-time control algorithm at medium priority
select
      PO.Time_For_Output_Control_Action_Reached;
then abort
      loop
        Improve_Solution;
      end loop;
end select;
    --At this point task is executing at high priority again
    --Output control action

      Put_Control_Action;
    --Wait for next activation
    Activation_time := Activation_time +
Period;
delay until Activation_time;
end loop;
end Control_Task;
```

The execution time timer and the timing event handlers are in charge of changing task priority. The pseudocode of the protected object where handlers are implemented is:

```
protected body PO is

procedure Budget_Exhausted_Handler
       (Timer : in out
    Ada.Execution_Time.Timers.Timer) is
    begin
    --Budget exhausted => low task priority
    Ada.Dynamic_Priorities.Set_Priority
       (Low_Priority, Control_Task'Identity);
    end Budget_Exhausted_Handler;

  procedure Output_Control_Action_Handler
       (E :in out Ada.Real_Time.Timing_Events.Timing_Event) is
```

```
begin
    Output_Time_Reached := True;
  --Reached time to output control action => raise priority
  Ada.Dynamic_Priorities.Set_Priority
      (High_Priority, Control_Task'Identity);
 end Output_Control_Action_Handler;

entry Time_For_Output_Control_Action_Reached
    when Output_Time_Reached is
    begin
      Output_Time_Reached := False;
  --Clear timer (just in case it has not expired yet)
  Ada.Execution_Time.Timers.Set_Handle
    (Budget_Timer,
     Ada.Execution_Time.CPU_Time_First,
     Handler => null);
  end Time_For_Output_Control_Action_Reached;
end PO;
```

Each job the task sets the execution time timer to bound the time it will execute at medium priority. When the timer expires, its associated handler (`Budget_Exhausted_Handler`) decreases the priority of the task to the background level, so that the task can continue improving the solution while there are not any other active tasks in the system.

Also a timing event is set to expire at the time the control action must be sent to the actuator. Its handler (`Output_Control_Action_Handler`) opens the entry used to abort the any-time algorithm (`Time_For_Output_Control_Action_Reached`) and raises the priority of the task to the higher level.

In [10] four Ada tasks and three protected objects were required to implement every control activity. Taking advantage of some of the new Ada 2005 features (timing events, execution time timers and immediate priority changes) it is possible to simplify implementation using only one task and one protected object for every control activity.

8 Conclusions

We have adapted the GNAT run-time system to use MaRTE OS as the low level Pthreads library. Using services provided by MaRTE OS (as timed handlers and CPU-time clocks and timers) we have implemented four of the new Ada 2005 real-time services: execution time clocks, execution time timers, timing events and dynamic priorities for protected objects.

For each of the new services implemented we have discussed implementation alternatives and evaluated its performance. As a consequence of the results obtained, our view is that the new services can be implemented in an efficient way in a existing run-time system without requiring major changes, as long as the underlaying operating system provides the required services. This is the case of MaRTE OS and of another POSIX operating systems that provide services such as recursive mutexes, CPU-time clocks, timers and CPU-time timers.

Performance measurements show that, in our implementation, times to use the new services are in the same range of values than other Ada constructs. In particular timing events and execution time timers avoid the use of extra tasks and are about twice faster than them.

Finally, to illustrate the usefulness of the new Ada services, we have presented an example in which execution time timers and timing events are used together with "select then abort" statements and dynamic priorities to implement a complex scheduling policy.

We plan to complete the implementation of all the new Ada 2005 real-time services. In a close future, MaRTE OS/GNAT run-time for GNU/Linux will support "Group Execution Time Budgets", the new scheduling policies (EDF, round-robin and non-preemptive) and the "Priority Specific Dispatching".

Once all the new Ada 2005 real-time functionality is implemented for the GNU/Linux platform, we plan to port it to the bare x86 version of MaRTE OS, a platform where hard real-time requirements can be fulfilled.

References

[1] Ada Reference Manual, ISO/IEC 8652:2007(E) Ed. 3.
[2] Rivas, M.A., Harbour, M.G.: MaRTE OS: An Ada Kernel for Real-Time Embedded Applications. In: Strohmeier, A., Craeynest, D. (eds.) Reliable Software Technologies – Ada Europe 2001. LNCS, vol. 2043, Springer, Heidelberg (2001)
[3] MaRTE OS home page: http://marte.unican.es/
[4] IEEE Std 1003.1-2003. Information Technology -Portable Operating System Interface (POSIX). Institute of Electrical and electronic Engineers.
[5] Alonso, A., López, R., de la Puente, J.A., Álvarez, B., Iborra, A.: Using Linux and Ada in the development of distributed computer control systems. In: IFAC Conference on New Technologies for Computer Control, NTCC'01, Hong-Kong (November 2001)
[6] Liu, J.W., Lin, K.J., Shih, W.K., Chuang-Shi, A., Chung, J.Y., Zhao, W.: Algorithms for Scheduling Imprecise Computations, May 1991, vol. 24(5). IEEE Computer Society Press, Los Alamitos (1991)
[7] Rivas, M.A., Harbour, M.G.: Evaluation of New POSIX Real-time Operating Systems Services for Small Embedded Platforms. In: Proceedings of 15th Euromicro Conference on Real-Time Systems (ECRTS'03), pp. 161–168. IEEE Computer Society, Los Alamitos (2003)
[8] Abeni, L., Buttazzo, G.: Integrating Multimedia Applications in Hard Real-Time Systems. In: Proceedings of the IEEE Real-Time Systems Symposium, Madrid, Spain (December 1998)
[9] Real, J., Crespo, A.: Offsets for scheduling mode changes. In: Proceedings of the 13th Euromicro Conference on Real-Time Systems, Delft, The Netherlands, pp. 3–10. IEEE Computer Society Press, Los Alamitos (2001)
[10] Crespo, A., Betoret, P.B., Terrasa, S.: Complex Task Implementation in Ada. In: Strohmeier, A., Craeynest, D. (eds.) Reliable Software Technologies – Ada Europe 2001. LNCS, vol. 2043, pp. 167–178. Springer, Heidelberg (2001)

Enhancing Dependability
of Component-Based Systems

Arnaud Lanoix[1], Denis Hatebur[2], Maritta Heisel[2], and Jeanine Souquières[1]

[1] LORIA – Université Nancy 2, Campus Scientifique BP 239
F-54506 Vandœuvre lès Nancy cedex
{Arnaud.Lanoix,Jeanine.Souquieres}@loria.fr
[2] Universität Duisburg-Essen, Abteilung Informatik und Angewandte
Kognitionswissenschaft, D-47048 Duisburg
{Denis.Hatebur,Maritta.Heisel}@uni-duisburg-essen.de

Abstract. We present an approach for enhancing dependability of component-based software. Functionality related to security, safety and reliability is encapsulated in specific components, allowing the method to be applied to off-the-shelf components. Any set of components can be extended with dependability features by wrapping them with special components, which monitor and filter input and outputs. This approach is supported by a rigorous development methodology based on UML and the B method and is introduced on the level of software architecture.

1 Introduction

Component orientation is a new paradigm for the development of software-based systems. The basic idea is to assemble the software by combination of pre-fabricated parts (called software components), instead of developing it from scratch. This procedure resembles the construction methods applied in other engineering disciplines, such as civil or mechanical engineering. Software components are put together by connecting their interfaces. A *provided* interface of one component can be connected with a *required* interface of another component if the provided interface offers the services needed to implement the required interface. An *adapter* is often necessary to map the provided services to the required ones.

Hence, an appropriate description of the provided and required interfaces of a software component is crucial for component-based development. In earlier papers [12, 18, 22], we have investigated how to formally specify interfaces of software components and how to demonstrate their interoperability, using the formal method B.

In the present paper, we study how dependability features [4], such as safety, security or reliability, can be built into component-based software. The goal is to retain the initial software components as far as possible and only add new software components in a systematic way. This approach works out if the initial software architecture is structured in such a way that the normal behavior

N. Abdennahder, F. Kordon (Eds.): Ada-Europe 2007, LNCS 4498, pp. 41–54, 2007.

is clearly separated from auxiliary functionality that is needed to connect the components implementing the core functionality to their environment.

To make a software-based system more dependable, new components are added, or existing components are replaced by more dependable ones, while the normal behavior remains the same. New or modified interfaces must be taken into account. In order to connect these new interfaces to the given interfaces of components, new adapters must be developed, or existing adapters must be upgraded. These adapters "shield" the components implementing the normal behavior by intercepting and possibly modifying their inputs and outputs.

In Section 2, we describe how we support component-based development using the formal specification language B. We then describe our method to integrate dependability features in Section 3. The method is illustrated by the case study of an access control system, presented in Section 4. The paper closes with the discussion of related work in Section 5 and a summary in Section 6.

2   Using B for Component-Based Development

We first briefly describe the formal language B and then explain how we use B in the context of component-based software. We formally express provided and required interfaces using B models in order to verify their compatibility.

The Formal Method B. B is a formal software development method based on set theory, which supports an incremental development process using refinement [1]. Starting out from a textual description, a development begins with the definition of an abstract model, which can be refined step by step until an implementation is reached. The refinement of models is a key feature for incrementally developing more and more detailed models, preserving correctness in each step.

The method B has been successfully applied in the development of several complex real-life applications, such as the METEOR project [6]. It is one of the few formal methods which has robust and commercially available support tools for the entire development life-cycle, from specification down to code generation [7]. The B method provides structuring primitives that allow one to compose models in various ways. Large systems can be specified in a modular way and in an object-based manner [21, 20]. Proofs of invariance and refinement are part of each development. The proof obligations are generated automatically by support tools such as AtelierB [28] or B4free [13], an academic version of AtelierB. Checking proof obligations with B support tools is an efficient and practical way to detect errors introduced during development.

Specifying Component Architectures. We define component-based systems using different kinds of UML 2.0 diagrams [23]:

— Composite structure diagrams serve to express the overall architecture of the system in terms of components and their required and provided interfaces.
— Class diagrams serve to express interface data models with their different attributes and methods. An interface data model specifies the data that are passed via a given interface.

- The usage protocol of each interface can be modeled by a Protocol State Machine.
- Sequence diagrams serve to express different views of the possible interactions between different components that are connected via some interface.

Component interfaces are then specified as B models, which increases confidence in the developed systems: the correctness of the specifications, as well as correctness of the subsequent refinement process can be checked with tool support. In an integrated development process, the B models can be obtained by applying systematic derivation rules from UML to B [21, 20].

Let us give an example of a software component called TurnstileDriver, presented in Figure 1, with the B model of one of its interfaces TS_P. It represents a software driver that can lock and unlock a turnstile. This component has two interfaces, a provided one TS_P and a required one TS_R. These interfaces express that another component, connected to the TurnstileDriver, can call the lock() and unlock() methods of TS_P, but the TurnstileDriver can reciprocally call a pushed() method from the connected component when the turnstile is pushed.

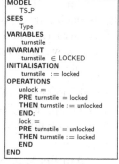

Proving Interoperability of Component Interfaces. In component-based architectures, the components must be connected in an appropriate way. To guarantee interoperability of components, we must consider each connection of a provided and a required interface contained in

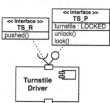

Fig. 1. TurnstileDriver

a software architecture and try to show that the interfaces are compatible. Using the method B, we prove that the provided interface is a correct B refinement of the required interface. This means that the provided interface constitutes an implementation of the required interface, and we can conclude that the two components can be connected as intended. The process of proving interoperability between components is described in [12].

Often, to construct a working component architecture, adapters have to be defined, connecting the required interfaces to the provided ones. An adapter is a piece of glue code that realizes the required interface using the provided interface. On the signature level, it expresses the mapping between required and provided variables. In [22], we have studied an adapter specification and its verification by giving a B refinement of the adaptation that refines the B model of the required interface and includes the provided (previously incompatible) interface.

3   Integrating Dependability Features into a Composite System

We now describe our method to integrate dependability features into a software-based system, whose software part makes use of component technology.

Dependability is the ability to deliver services that can justifiably be trusted. In particular, we consider dependability properties concerning security, safety, and reliability. The latter two are relevant mainly for embedded systems, where some part of the physical world has to be controlled, whereas security is an issue also in pure data-processing systems. The basic idea of our method is to leave the normal behavior of the system untouched, and enhance dependability by

- adding dedicated components needed for realizing dependability features, or replacing used components by more dependable ones;
- constructing and/or upgrading software adapter components that connect the new "dependability components" with the existing (and unchanged) components.

In the following, we first describe the situations where our method can profitably be applied. Then, we describe how different kinds of dependability properties can be added.

3.1 Application Scenario

Our method is intended to support the following scenario. We start out with a component-based system that implements a given normal behavior, for example, controlling access of persons to a building. In the software architecture of the system, one or more components (called *application* components) can be identified that implement the normal behavior. This functionality is clearly separated from the functionality of the other components.

The components should be robust to changes: their normal behavior is to be left unchanged. Their connections to other components in terms of provided and required interfaces are not evolved. This means that enhancing dependability amounts to providing *additional* behavior that has to be executed in case of hazardous conditions, hardware or software failures, or security attacks. The system behavior in the normal case, however, remains the same. Instead of changing the components, we evolve the adapters independently of the components by providing additional functionality and dependability features.

3.2 General Procedure

Adding dependability features to a given system means to adapt the system to new requirements. The new dependability requirements may override existing requirements. For example, a functional requirement for an access control system may be that exactly the persons are admitted to a building who are authorized to be in the building. To find out if a person has permission, a database is queried. A new security requirement might state that if the database is corrupted, nobody is admitted any more, even if they are authorized according to the database. It is realized by updating existing adapters or developing new adapters. The adapters shield the application components by intercepting and possibly modifying their inputs and outputs. In general, we proceed as follows:

1. Express the new dependability requirements.
2. Express how the new requirements are related to the old ones and among each other.
3. For each dependability requirement, state what components are needed for ensuring it. Inspect the given system architecture and decide what new components are necessary, and what components must be replaced or updated.
4. Update the existing adapters and implement new dependability adapters that connect the existing components to the other components.
5. If several dependability adapters are added, it may be suitable to add one or more components that handle the new dependability-relevant events.

We use the B method for specifying component interfaces and implementing adapters. First, we can ensure that the components can indeed be plugged together as intended (see Section 2). Second, the adapter and application specifications expressed in B can be refined until code is reached.

In the following sections, we describe how to add security, safety and reliability features. We do not invent any new mechanisms but show how standard solutions for the given dependability requirements can be added to a component-based system in an incremental way.

3.3   Adding Security Features

Security is mostly concerned with confidentiality, integrity, and availability. More concrete security features concern for example authenticity and non-repudiation. In our method, availability is considered in the context of reliability, see Section 3.5.

When adding security features to a component-based system, the corresponding adapters will often implement the secure (i.e., confidential and integrity-preserving) transmission of data. Typical tasks that have to be performed include:

- checking message authentication codes to ensure integrity
- encrypt or decrypt data to ensure confidentiality
- check credentials to ensure authenticity

Existing security components may be used to realize the required security functionality.

3.4   Adding Safety Features

Safety requirements concern the reaction to hazardous situations in the environment of the system (for example, fire in a building). In these cases, the system must be put into a safe state. The safety adapters must be connected to new external components that make it possible to detect a hazardous situation. Furthermore, they must implement a transition to a safe state, because this cannot be done by the application components. What can be considered to be a safe state cannot be stated in general but depends on the specificities of the given system.

3.5   Adding Reliability Features

A standard technique to achieve reliability is to use fault-tolerance mechanisms, e.g. introducing redundant components, which can be active or passive. An active component can inform its environment when a failure occurs. In contrast, passive components just fail without informing the environment.

To realize fault tolerance with respect to failures of active components, the adapter must be able to shut down the failed component when it is informed of the failure and switch to a redundant one. In case of passive components, the adapter must check if the component works correctly, or if a failure has occurred. It must take the faulty component out of service and handle the fault, e.g. by switching to a redundant component.

4   Case Study

We illustrate our method with the case study of a simple access control system, which controls the access to a building [2]. Persons who are authorized to enter the building are equipped with a smartcard on which a user identification is stored. The access control system queries a database to obtain the information if the person is permitted to enter the building. If access is granted, a turnstile located at the entrance is unblocked, so that the person can enter the building. At the exit of the building, another turnstile is installed. It is always unblocked and only serves to count the number of persons who have left the building.

In a first version, the access control system contains no dependability features. Using our method described in Section 3, we will add two dependability features to the system by integrating appropriate new components, however leaving the basic functionality untouched. The first dependability feature concerns security. Using message authentication codes, it is checked if unauthorized modifications of the database content have occurred. In this case, the person who wants enter to the building is not admitted, and a facility service is notified. The second dependability feature concerns safety. A fire detector is added to the system. In case of fire, nobody is allowed to enter the building until the fire is dealt with, and the facility service is notified.

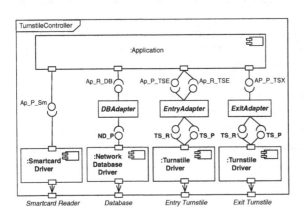

Fig. 2. Software architecture of TurnstileController

4.1   Architecture of the System Without Dependability Features

The access control system communicates with hardware components (a smartcard reader and the turnstiles), as well as software components (the database). The controller software architecture of the access control system is shown in Figure 2, using the syntax of UML composite structure diagrams. Software components are represented as named boxes, and the interfaces between them are represented by "sockets" (required interfaces) and "lollipops" (provided interfaces).

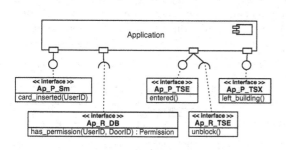

Fig. 3. The different interfaces of the Application

The software architecture of the TurnstileController is a layered one. The highest layer, i.e., the Application component, implements its normal behavior. The lowest layer consists of the software drivers that connect the software to the hardware components. A driver comes with the hardware components and should not be modified. Hence, adapters may be necessary to connect the application component to the software drivers, making up the middle layer of the architecture.

Figure 3 shows the interfaces of the Application component in more detail. For each required and each provided interface, an interface class is specified in UML notation. The interface class shows the operations belonging to the interface, together with their parameters. For example, the interface class Ap_P_Sm describes a provided interface of Application: it expresses that Application implements one method, namely card_inserted(uid), which has a user identifier uid as its parameter. This method may be called by another component connected to the interface Ap_P_Sm.

The access control system uses three kinds of external components, namely a smartcard reader, a network database, and two copies of a turnstile. The corresponding drivers that control these components are named SmartcardDriver, NetworkDatabaseDriver and TurnstileDriver, respectively. Their interfaces are shown in Figure 4.

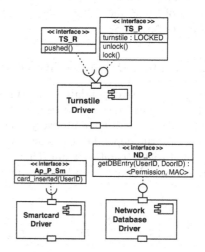

Fig. 4. Components used by the TurnstileController

The DBAdapter. As an example of an adapter, we consider the DBAdapter. Figure 5 gives a scenario of its behavior. The Application calls one of its required methods, has_permission(uid,did), which must be implemented by the DBAdapter. Parameters of the method are a user identification uid and a door identification did. As is shown in Figure 4, the database driver offers an operation getBDEntry(uid,did), which yields a permission and a message authentication code as its result. To implement has_permission(uid,did), the DBAdapter just calls the method getBDEntry(uid,did) and returns only the permission to the application component.

As Figure 3 shows, the required interface Ap_R_DB of the Application has to be implemented, i.e., an implementation of the operation has_permission(uid,did) has to be provided. This is achieved by the DBAdapter, which uses the provided interface ND_P. In Figure 6, we show how the corresponding B models are organized. To verify the correctness of the assembly, we specify a B model of the DBAdapter, which includes the B model of ND_P and refines the B model of Ap_R_DB.

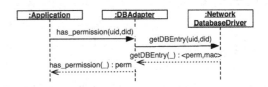

Fig. 5. Sequence diagram for the DBAdapter

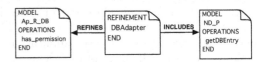

Fig. 6. B architecture for DBAdapter

4.2   Adding Dependability Features to the Access Control System

We now add two dependability features to the system, one for security and one for safety. We introduce a new component called Safety / Security / Service Application that handles security- and safety-related events by notifying the facility service. To realize the dependability features, we must introduce three new components: Secret, FacilityServiceDriver and FireDetectorDriver. Descriptions of their interfaces are given in Figure 7, and the resulting software architecture in Figure 8.

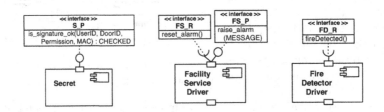

Fig. 7. New components used by the TurnstileController

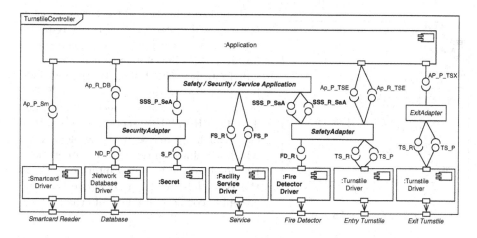

Fig. 8. Software architecture for the dependable TurnstileController

The SecurityAdapter. The security feature concerns the integrity of the database. Its content is now checked using a message authentication code (MAC). A new component Secret is introduced for storing secrets that are needed to check the MAC.

The DBAdapter that connects the Application to the database is changed to use the component Secret. It is renamed to Security-Adapter. A behavioral scenario is presented in Figure 9: the SecurityAdapter still receives a call of the method has_permission(uid, did) from the Application. It still queries the database. But now, the SecurityAdapter ch-

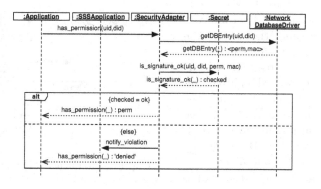

Fig. 9. Sequence diagram for the SecurityAdapter

ecks the message authentication code for each database return. In case of a violation (checked $\neq$ ok), it notifies the Safety / Security / Service Application before it denies access. The Application component remains unchanged.

Here, we see that the new security requirement has a higher priority than the initial functional requirement: if a manipulation of the database is detected, then the access is denied even to persons that normally have permission to enter the building.

```
REFINEMENT
    SecurityAdapter
REFINES
    Ap_R_DB
SEES
    Type
INCLUDES
    ND_P, S_P, SSS_P_SeA
OPERATIONS
    permi ←— has_permission(uid, did) =
    VAR mac, checked IN
        permi, mac ←— getDBEntry(uid, did) ;
        checked ←— is_signature_ok(uid, did, permi, mac) ;
        IF ¬(checked = ok)
        THEN
            ¬ ify_violation ||
            permi := denied
        END
    END
END
```

Fig. 10. SecurityAdapter

The B specification of the SecurityAdapter is given in Figure 10. Again, the required interface Ap_R_DB has to be implemented, however this time not only using the provided interface ND_P, but also the provided interfaces S_P of the Secret, and SSS_P_SeA of the Safety / Security / Service Application. The OPERATIONS section contains the operation has_permission to be implemented, which is defined in terms of the operations provided by the included interfaces. Using the B models, we formally prove that the assembly correctly implements the requirements.

The SafetyAdapter. The safety feature we add to the system concerns the reaction to fire. If a fire occurs, the entry turnstile must remain blocked: nobody is allowed to enter the building until the fire is extinguished (we assume the fire brigade uses another entry). Here, the EntryAdapter has to be changed to receive messages from the fire detector. It is renamed to SafetyAdapter. The SafetyAdapter blocks the entry turnstile in case of a fire and informs the Safety / Security / Service Application.

Figure 11 shows one sequence diagram concerning the SafetyAdapbreak ter, explaining the safety reaction of the adapter when it receives a fire_detected call: the turnstile will be blocked until the fire alert is canceled. Here, we see an example of how signals from the application component are intercepted: the unblock signals of the Application are not passed on to the entry turnstile; hence, it remains blocked.

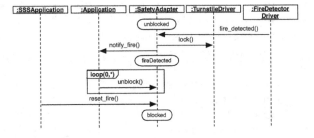

Fig. 11. A sequence diagram for the SafetyAdapter

Figure 12 shows how the SafetyAdapter is specified in B. It implements the interfaces SSS_R_SaA, Ap_R_TSE, FD_R, and TS_R, using the interfaces SSA_P_SaA, Ap_P_TSE, and TS_P. The B model called SafetyAdapter_abs is needed for technical reasons: a B model can only refine a single B model and not several ones.

We do not describe the new application component Safety / Security / Service Application in detail. It serves to pass on a security or safety alarm to the facility service, and it receives a message from the facility service when the alarm is canceled.

```
REFINEMENT
   SafetyAdapter
REFINES
   SafetyAdapter_abs
INCLUDES
   TS_P_U, Ap_P_TSE, SSS_P_SaA
SEES
   Type
VARIABLES
   entry
INVARIANT
   entry ∈ ENTRY_STATES ∧
   ( turnstile  = locked ⇒
        entry ∈ {blocked, fireDetected}) ∧
   ( turnstile  = unlocked ⇒
        entry = unblocked)
INITIALISATION
   entry := blocked
OPERATIONS
   unblock =
   IF
        entry = blocked
   THEN
        unlock ;
        entry := unblocked
   END ;
   pushed =
   IF
        entry = unblocked
   THEN
        entered ;
        lock ;
        entry := blocked
   END ;
   fire_detected =
   IF
        entry ≠ fireDetected
   THEN
        IF ( turnstile  = unlocked) THEN lock END ;
        ¬ ify_fire  ;
        entry := fireDetected
   END ;
   reset_fire =
   IF
        entry = fireDetected
   THEN
        entry := blocked
   END
END
```

Fig. 12. SafetyAdapter

With this case study, we have shown how dependability features can be added to a component-based system in a modular manner. Other dependability features could be added to the access control system in the same way. Examples are an authentication mechanism for the smartcard interface, a redundant arrangement of fire detectors, or checking for memory errors.

5 Related Work

A lot of studies have already been done on component-based approaches. Beugnard et al. [8] propose to define contracts for components, distinguishing four levels of contracts: syntactic, behavioral, synchronization, and quality of service. They do not introduce data models for interfaces, and it cannot easily be checked if two components can be combined. Roshandel and Medvidociv [26] propose to specify four different views of software components, namely the interface, static behavior, dynamic behavior, and interaction protocol views. To ensure dependability, the consistency of the different views is checked. Cheesman and Daniels [11] propose a process to specify component-based software, which starts with an informal requirements description and produces an architecture showing the components to be developed or reused, their interfaces and their dependencies.

Canal et al. [10] use a subset of the polyadic π-calculus to deal with component interoperability at the protocol level. The limitation of this approach is the low-level description of the used language and its minimalistic semantics. Bastide et al. [5] use Petri nets to specify the behavior of CORBA objects, including operation semantics and protocols. The difference to our approach is that we take into account the invariants of the interface specifications. Zaremski and Wing [31] propose an interesting approach to compare two software components. It is determined whether one component can be substituted for another. They use formal specifications to model the behavior of components and the Larch prover to prove the specification matching of components. Others [17, 29] have also proposed to enrich component interface specifications by providing information at signature, semantic and protocol levels. Henzinger and Alfaro [3] propose an approach allowing the verification of interfaces interoperability based on automata and game theories, which is well suited for checking the interface compatibility at the protocol level.

Concerning component adaptation, several proposals have already been made. Some practice-oriented studies analyze different issues when adapting of third-party components [16]. A formal foundation of the notions of interoperability and component adaptation is set up in [30]. Component behavior specifications are given by finite state machines.

Braccalia et al. [9] specify an adapter as a set of correspondences between methods and parameters of the required and provided components. The adapter is formalized as a set of properties expressed in π-calculus. From this specification and from both interfaces, they generate a concrete implementable adapter. Reussner and Schmidt present adapters in the context of concurrent systems. They consider a certain class of protocol interoperability problems and generate adapters for bridging component protocol incompatibilities, using interface described by finite parameterized state machines [27].

In contrast to the above approaches, we prefer to use the B method, because it allows us to not only consider component compatibility at the protocol level, but also at the signature and semantic levels, and because of its tool support.

A general approach to wrappers for common security concerns is described in [15]. Popov et al. [24] show that wrappers are components that monitor and ensure the non-functional properties at interfaces between components. They improve dependability by adding fault tolerance. In [14], the authors propose to structure fault-tolerant component-based systems that use off-the-shelf components, at the architectural level, using constructs similar to the multi-versioning connector [25].

In contrast to the above approaches, our method stresses the methodological aspects of evolving a given component-based system to make it more dependable. In an earlier paper [19], we have addressed to problem of adding features to component-based systems. But there, we did not use the B method, and the newly integrated features did not concern dependability, but the addition of new functionality.

6   Conclusion

The success of the component-construction paradigm in mechanical and electrical engineering has led to calls for its adoption in software development. We have described a method to integrate dependability features into a composite system. We start from an initial software architecture describing the the normal behavior of the system for. Dependability is then enhanced in an incremental way, by modifying adapter components and possibly adding new adapter or new application components.

Using the formal method B and its refinement and assembling mechanisms to model the component interfaces and the adapters, we pay special attention to the question of guaranteeing the interoperability between the different components. The B prover guarantees that the adapter is a correct implementation of the required functionalities in terms of the existing components. With this approach, the verification of the interoperability between the connected components is achieved at the signature, the semantic and the protocol levels. In summary, the advantages of our approach are the following:

• Dependability features can be integrated one by one, as needed.

• The necessary changes to the software architecture are local; the functionality for the normal case is not changed.

• Components and dependability features can be further evolved independently of each other.

• Our method gives guidance on how the addition of dependability features can be performed in a systematic way.

• Using B, it can be checked that the components of the evolved software architecture indeed interoperate as intended.

• The B specifications of the new or evolved software components can be used as the starting point of an implementation. For this purpose, the B refinement mechanism can be used.

In this way, we have proposed a "dependable" process for making component-based systems more dependable.

References

[1] Abrial, J.-R.: The B Book. Cambridge University Press, Cambridge (1996)

[2] Afadl2000. Etude de cas : systéme de contrôle d'accés. In Journés AFADL, Approches formelles dans l'assistance au développement de logiciels. actes LSR/IMAG (2000)

[3] Alfaro, L., Henzinger, T.A.: Interface automata. In: 9 th Annual Aymposium on Foundations of Software Engineering, FSE, pp. 109–120. ACM Press, New York (2001)

[4] Avizienis, A., Laprie, J.-C., Randell, B., Landwehr, C.: Basic concepts and taxonomy of dependable and secure computing. IEEE Trans. on Dependable and Secure Computing 1(1), 11–33 (2004)

[5] Bastide, R., Sy, O., Palanque, P.A.: Formal specification and prototyping of CORBA systems. In: Guerraoui, R. (ed.) ECOOP 1999. LNCS, vol. 1628, pp. 474–494. Springer, Heidelberg (1999)

[6] Behm, P., Benoit, P., Meynadier, J.M.: METEOR: A Successful Application of B in a Large Project. In: Wing, J.M., Woodcock, J.C.P., Davies, J. (eds.) FM 1999. LNCS, vol. 1708, pp. 369–387. Springer, Heidelberg (1999)

[7] Bert, D., Boulmé, S., Potet, M-L., Requet, A., Voisin, L.: Adaptable Translator of B Specifications to Embedded C Programs. In: Araki, K., Gnesi, S., Mandrioli, D. (eds.) FME 2003. LNCS, vol. 2805, pp. 94–113. Springer, Heidelberg (2003)

[8] Beugnard, A., Jézéquel, J.-M., Plouzeau, N., Watkins, D.: Making components contract aware, July 1999, pp. 38–45. IEEE Computer, Los Alamitos (1999)

[9] Bracciali, A., Brogi, A., Canal, C.: A formal approach to component adaptation. Journal of Systems and Software (2005)

[10] Canal, C., Fuentes, L., Pimentel, E., Troya, J-M., Vallecillo, A.: Extending CORBA interfaces with protocols. Comput. J. 44(5), 448–462 (2001)

[11] Cheesman, J., Daniels, J.: UML Components – A Simple Process for Specifying Component-Based Software. Addison-Wesley, Reading (2001)

[12] Chouali, S., Heisel, M., Souquiéres, J.: Proving Component Interoperability with B Refinement. Electronic Notes in Theoretical Computer Science 160, 157–172 (2006)

[13] Clearsy. B4free. (2004), Available at http://www.b4free.com
[14] de Guerra, P.A., Mary, C., Rubira, F., Romanovsky, A., de Lemos R.: A fault-tolerant software architecture for COTS-based software systems (2003)
[15] Fetzer, C., Xiao, Z.: HEALERS: A Toolkit for Enhancing the Robutness and Security of Existing Wrappers. In Proc. International Conference on Dependable Systems and Networks (2003)
[16] Garlan, D., Allen, R., Ockerbloom, J.: Architectural Mismatch: Why Reuse is so Hard. IEEE Software 12(6), 17–26 (1999)
[17] Han, J.: A comprehensive interface definition framework for software components. In: The 1998 Asia Pacific software engineering conference, pp. 110–117. IEEE Computer Society Press, Los Alamitos (1998)
[18] Hatebur, D., Heisel, M., Souquières, J.: A method for component-based software and system development. In: Proceedings of the 32tnd Euromicro Conference on Software Engineering And Advanced Applications, pp. 72–80. IEEE Computer Society Press, Los Alamitos (2006)
[19] Heisel, M., Souquières, J.: Adding features to component-based systems. In: Ryan, M.D., Meyer, J.-J.Ch., Ehrich, H.-D. (eds.) Objects, Agents, and Features. LNCS, vol. 2975, pp. 137–153. Springer, Heidelberg (2004)
[20] Ledang, H., Souquières, J.: Modeling class operations in B: application to UML behavioral diagrams. In: ASE'2001: 16th IEEE International Conference on Automated Software Engineering, IEEE Computer Society Press, Los Alamitos (2001)
[21] Meyer, E., Souquières, J.: A systematic approach to transform OMT diagrams to a B specification. In: Wing, J.M., Woodcock, J.C.P., Davies, J. (eds.) FM 1999. LNCS, vol. 1708, pp. 875–895. Springer, Heidelberg (1999)
[22] Mouakher, I., Lanoix, A., Souquières, J.: Component adaptation: Specification and verification. In: Reussner, R., Weck, W., Szyperski, C. (eds.) 11th International Workshop on Component Oriented Programming (WCOP'06), pp. 23–30 (2006)
[23] Object Management Group (OMG). UML Superstructure Specification, version 2.0 (2005)
[24] Popov, P., Strigini, L., Riddle, S., Romanovsky, A.: Protective Wrapping of OTS components. In: 4th ICSE WWorkshop on Component-Based Software Engineering: Component Certification and System Prediction (2001)
[25] Rakic, M., Medvidovic, N.: Increasing the confidence in off-the-shelf components. In: Symposium on Software Reusability, pp. 11–18 (2001)
[26] Roshandel, R., Medvidovic, N.: Multi-view software component modeling for dependability. In: de Lemos, R., Gacek, C., Romanovsky, A. (eds.) Architecting Dependable Systems II. LNCS, vol. 3069, pp. 286–306. Springer, Heidelberg (2004)
[27] Schmidt, H.W., Reussner, R.H.: Generating adapters fo concurrent component protocol synchronisation. In: Crnkovic, I., Larsson, S., Stafford, J. (eds.) Proceeding of the 5th IFIP International conference on Formal Methods for Open Object-based Distributed Systems (2002)
[28] Steria – Technologies de l'information. Obligations de preuve: Manuel de référence, version 3.0 (1998)
[29] Vallacillo, A., Hernandez, J., Troya, M.: Object interoperability. In: Guerraoui, R. (ed.) ECOOP 1999. LNCS, vol. 1628, pp. 1–21. Springer, Heidelberg (1999)
[30] Yellin, D.D.M., Strom, R.E.: Protocol specifications and component adaptors. ACM Trans. Program. Lang. Syst. 19(2), 292–333 (1997)
[31] Zaremski, A.M., Wing, J.M.: Specification matching of software components. ACM Transactions on Software Engineering and Methodology 6(4), 333–369 (1997)

On Detecting Double Literal Faults in Boolean Expressions*

Man F. Lau[1], Ying Liu[1], Tsong Y. Chen[1], and Yuen T. Yu[2]

[1] Faculty of Information and Communication Technologies,
Swinburne University of Technology
Hawthorn, Victoria, 3122, Australia
{elau,yliu,tchen}@ict.swin.edu.au
[2] Department of Computer Science, City University of Hong Kong
Tat Chee Avenue, Kowloon Tong, Hong Kong
csytyu@cityu.edu.hk

Abstract. Fault-based testing aims at selecting test cases to detect hypothesized faults in a program. When a program contains a fault so that it behaves differently from as is expected, test cases that satisfy the detection condition of the fault will be able to detect it. Detection conditions of single occurrence of hypothesized faults had been studied and used to propose testing strategies and investigate relationships between different types of faults. As software developers may make several mistakes during software development, multiple faults may occur in a program. In this paper, we report our study in detection conditions of double occurrences of faults related to literals in a Boolean expression. This leads to some interesting observations. Some previous studies in double fault discarded equivalent mutants caused by a single fault. However, we observe that such equivalent mutants may give rise to non-equivalent double fault mutants, and hence, cannot be discarded. Moreover, we have developed several supplementary test case selection strategies to detect double faults that cannot be detected by existing test case selection strategies which aim at single-fault detection.

Keywords: Black-box testing, Boolean specification, Fault-based testing, Test case generation.

1 Introduction

Software testing is crucial in ensuring the quality of software. Fault-based testing techniques have been proposed for many years [1]. Test cases generated by fault-based testing techniques can detect hypothesized faults if they indeed appear in the program.

Many industrial software systems in the domain of avionics, air traffic collision avoidance, nuclear power plant control and cruise control have been modelled by specifications using Boolean expressions [2–9]. Representing the specifications in the form of Boolean expressions can help to model check the systems as well as to automatically generate test cases based on the specifications [4, 9]. Moreover, fault-based testing

---

* The work described in this paper was supported in part by a grant from the Australian Research Council, Australia (project id. DP0558597), and in part by a grant from the Research Grants Council of Hong Kong Special Administrative Region, China (project no. CityU 1166/04E).

N. Abdennahder, F. Kordon (Eds.): Ada-Europe 2007, LNCS 4498, pp. 55–68, 2007.

techniques have been studied to generate test cases based on Boolean specifications [9–14]. Even though these studies are mainly related to generating test cases from Boolean specifications, the results can also be applied to the generation of test cases for program-based predicate testing, which usually involves logic expressions [12].

Research studies on detection conditions of hypothesized faults on Boolean expressions [10, 11, 13–15] have been used in two ways. First, the detection conditions are used to develop test case selection strategies aiming at the detection of the hypothesized faults. For example, Chen and Lau [10] proposed three test case selection strategies based on the detection conditions of seven classes of faults. Second, they have been used to develop *fault class hierarchies* [11, 13, 14]. As discussed in Kuhn [11] and Lau and Yu [13], fault class hierarchy can be used to explain empirical results for fault-based testing techniques. A fault class hierarchy establishes the relationships among different classes of faults. Suppose we have two fault classes A and B. If a test case that detects a particular instance of fault in A can always detect another particular instance of fault in B, A is considered to be lower than B in the hierarchy.

Research on fault detection conditions assumes that various types of hypothesized faults may occur in a program. However, when establishing the detection conditions of a particular hypothesized fault, only that fault is assumed to occur in the program.

Many empirical studies on software faults show, however, that in practice multiple faults occur more often in programs [16, 17]. Previous research on multiple faults [18–21] mainly studied the fault coupling effect of double faults, which are a special instance of multiple faults. When two faults combine in such a way that they cannot be detected using test cases that detect these faults in isolation, the two faults are said to be *coupled* together. Both experimental and theoretical research on the coupling effect of double faults have studied the chances of a test set in detecting these double faults, given that it can detect the two individual faults in isolation.

Recently, Lau and Yu [22] explored the use of fault class hierarchy to detect double faults related to terms in Boolean expressions. They found that, given two fault classes A and B, where A is lower than B in the fault class hierarchy, a test case that detects faults in A can also detect the double fault involving faults in A and B. Lau et al. [15] have further studied the detection conditions of double faults related to terms. Five different types of faults are considered. They have found that all double faults formed by these single faults can be detected by test case selection strategies that subsume the BASIC meaningful impact strategy (or, simply the BASIC strategy) proposed in [9].

In this paper, we study the detection conditions of double faults related to literals in Boolean expressions. Unlike the results in double term faults, the analysis of the detection conditions of double literal faults reveals that new fault-based test case selection strategies are required to guarantee their detection. In other words, existing fault-based test case selection strategies aiming at the detection of single fault classes are inadequate for detecting double literal faults. Moreover, based on fault detection conditions, further test case selection strategies can be used to supplement existing fault-based test case selection strategies for double literal fault detection.

The rest of the paper is organized as follows: Section 2 introduces the notation and fault classes studied in this paper. Section 3 discusses the double fault classes and their detection conditions. Section 4 discusses various practical applications related to the study of the detection conditions of double literal fault classes. Section 5 concludes the paper and discusses future work.

2   Preliminary

2.1   Notation

In this paper, 1 and 0 are used to represent 'TRUE' and 'FALSE' respectively. The Boolean operators AND, OR and NOT, are denoted by '$\cdot$', '$+$' and '$^-$', respectively. Usually, '$\cdot$' is omitted whenever it is clear in the context. The set of all truth values ($\{0, 1\}$) is denoted by $\mathbb{B}$.

Let S be a Boolean expression in irredundant disjunctive normal form (IDNF) (that is, disjunctive normal form with no redundant term or literal) and be given by

$$S = p_1 + \cdots + p_m$$

where m is the number of terms and p_i is the i-th term of S. Let $p_i = x_1^i \cdots x_{k_i}^i$ be the i-th term of S where x_j^i is the j-th literal in p_i and k_i is the number of literals in p_i. A literal x is a *missing literal* of a term p_i if both x and $\bar{x}$ do not appear in the term. If S has n variables, the input domain is the n-dimensional Boolean space $\mathbb{B}^n$.

A *true point* of S is a point in $\mathbb{B}^n$ such that S evaluates to 1. We use $TP(S)$ to denote the set of all true points of S. A true point of the i-th term, p_i, of S is a point such that p_i evaluates to 1. We use $TP_i(S)$ to denote the set of all true points of p_i in S. A *unique true point* of p_i in S is a true point of p_i such that terms other than p_i evaluate to 0. The set of all unique true points of p_i is denoted by $UTP_i(S)$. True points that are not unique true points are *overlapping true points*. The set of all overlapping true points of S is denoted by $OTP(S)$. Let $S = ab + ac + cd$. A true point of $p_1 = ab$ in S is 1100 (that is, $a = b = 1$, $c = d = 0$). The set $TP_1(S)$ of all true points of p_1 is $\{1100, 1101,$ $1110, 1111\}$. The point 1100 is a unique true point of p_1 in S. The point 1110 is an overlapping true point of S.

A *false point* of S is a point in $\mathbb{B}^n$ such that S evaluates to 0. We use $FP(S)$ to denote the set of all false points of S. A *near false point* for the j-th literal, x_j^i, of p_i in S is a false point of S such that (1) x_j^i evaluates to 0, and (2) literals in p_i other than x_j^i evaluate to 1. The set of all near false points for x_j^i of p_i in S is denoted by $NFP_{i,j}(S)$. False points that are not near false points are *remaining false points*. The set of all remaining false points of S is denoted by $RFP(S)$. For example, let $S = ab + ac + cd$. A near false point for the first literal a of the first term $p_1 = ab$ is 0100. The set $NFP_{1,\bar{1}}(S)$ of all near false points for the first literal a of the first term ab is $\{0100, 0101, 0110\}$. The point 0000 is a remaining false point of S.

2.2   Fault Class

Lau and Yu [13] have considered and proposed nine common types of single faults that may be committed in Boolean expressions in various research literature [9–11, 14]. Among these fault classes, five of them are related to terms in Boolean expressions, while the remaining four are literal faults. Lau et al. [15] have analysed the detection conditions of double faults involving five single fault classes related to terms. In this paper, we study the detection conditions of double literal faults whose individual faults belong to one the following four single literal faults:

1. *Literal Negation Fault* (LNF): A literal in a particular term in the Boolean expression is negated.

Table 1. Single faults, single-fault expressions and detection conditions ($S = p_1 + \ldots + p_m$)

Fault Class	Faulty Expression	Detection Condition
LNF	$p_1 + \cdots + x_1^i \cdots \bar{x}_j^i \cdots x_{k_i}^i + \cdots + p_m$	any point in $UTP_i(S)$ or any point in $NFP_{i,\bar{j}}(S)$
LOF	$p_1 + \cdots + x_1^i \cdots x_{j-1}^i x_{j+1}^i \cdots x_{k_i}^i + \cdots + p_m$	any point in $NFP_{i,\bar{j}}(S)$
LIF	$p_1 + \cdots + p_i x_l + \cdots + p_m$	any point in $UTP_i(S)$ such that $x_l = 0$
LRF	$p_1 + \cdots + x_1^i \cdots x_{j-1}^i x_{j+1}^i \cdots x_{k_i}^i x_l + \cdots + p_m$	any point in $UTP_i(S)$ such that $x_l = 0$ or any point in $NFP_{i,\bar{j}}(S)$ such that $x_l = 1$

2. *Literal Omission Fault* (LOF): A literal in a particular term in the Boolean expression is omitted.
3. *Literal Insertion Fault* (LIF): A missing literal of a particular term of a Boolean expression is inserted into the term.
4. *Literal Reference Fault* (LRF): A literal in a particular term of a Boolean expression is replaced by a missing literal of the term.

Table 1 lists these four literal fault classes, their corresponding faulty expressions and detection conditions. For example, consider the row of LIF in Table 1 which represents that a LIF is committed during the programming process. Let us use $S = ab + ac + cd$ as an example. If the literal d is inserted into the first term ab in S, the resulting expression I is equivalent to $abd + ac + cd$. This is a *single-fault expression* because it is an expression that (1) differs from the original expression $ab + ac + cd$ by one syntactic change and (2) is not equivalent to the original expression. The corresponding detection condition indicates that any unique true point in $UTP_1(S)$ for which d evaluates to 0 can detect the fault. For example, the test case 1100 (that is, $a = b = 1$ and $c = d = 0$) can detect this LIF because S and I evaluate to different truth values on 1100.

3   Double Fault Classes

Multiple occurrences of any literal fault classes may result in faulty expressions which differ from the original expression by several syntactic changes. For example, $abce + ade$ differs from $abc + de$ by two syntactic changes, namely, the insertions of the literals e and a to the first and second terms, respectively. An expression which differs from the original expression by more than one syntactic change is said to contain multiple faults. In this paper, *double literal fault* is defined as the occurrences of two single literal faults.

When a double literal fault occurs in a Boolean expression, the resulting expression may be equivalent to the original expression or a faulty expression with one syntactic change. For example, if a literal of a particular term in S is negated twice, the resulting expression is equivalent to S. On the other hand, if a literal of a particular term in S is first negated and then omitted from the term, the net result of these two faults is equivalent to a single LOF being committed on the literal. In this paper, we do not study the detection conditions of these expressions because they have been studied in previous research work [10, 13]. Thus, in this paper, a *double-fault expression* is defined as an expression containing two single faults such that it (1) differs from the original expression by two syntactic changes and (2) is equivalent to neither the original expression nor any single-fault expression.

When a double fault is committed in an expression, it is possible that swapping the order of occurrences of the two individual faults will result in two non-equivalent faulty expressions. This kind of double faults is referred to as *double fault with ordering*. However, it is also possible for the two resulting faulty expressions to be equivalent to each other, but not to the original expression. For example, consider the expression $abc + def$. If the literal e is inserted into the first term before the literal c is replaced by another literal d, the resulting faulty expression is equivalent to $abde + def$. On the other hand, if these two faults are committed in the reverse order (that is, the literal c is replaced by the literal d before the literal e is inserted in the first term), the resulting faulty expression is still equivalent to $abde + def$. In other words, the ordering is not important. This kind of double faults is referred to as *double fault without ordering*.

A *mutant* is a program which differs from the original program by small syntactic changes. In this paper, we use *single (double) fault mutant* to mean a mutant with one syntactic change (two syntactic changes). Double fault mutants have been generated in previous studies (such as [21]) in three steps: (1) single fault mutants are generated first by making one syntactic change to the original program, (2) those single fault mutants that are equivalent to the original program are then discarded, and (3) double fault mutants are then generated by making one syntactic change to the remaining non-equivalent single fault mutants. However, during our analysis of double fault without ordering, we have the following interesting observation. Given an original program, it is possible to have a double fault mutant such that the corresponding two single fault mutants (which are separately caused by the two individual single faults) are both equivalent to the original program, as illustrated in Example 1. Hence, when generating double fault mutants, the corresponding equivalent single fault mutants should not be discarded, or else some non-equivalent double fault mutants will be wrongly disposed.

Example 1. Let $S = a + b + cd$. If the literal $\bar{b}$ is inserted in the first term a of S, the resulting expression $a\bar{b} + b + cd$, denoted as I'_1, is equivalent to S. Similarly, if the literal $\bar{a}$ is inserted in the second term b, the resulting expression $a + \bar{a}b + cd$, denoted as I'_2, is equivalent to S. However, when the above two faults are committed on S, the resulting expression $a\bar{b} + \bar{a}b + cd$, denoted by I'', is not equivalent to S because they evaluate to different truth values on 1100.

For double literal faults studied in this paper, Lau and Liu [23] have shown that there are 16 and 10 classes of double literal faults with and without ordering, resulting in 31 and 19 double-fault expressions, respectively. Among these two groups of double-fault expressions, all 31 faulty expressions in the former group have their equivalent counterparts in the latter group, and vice versa. Thus, we only need to study the group of 19 double-fault expressions. Moreover, we will only use the term "*double literal fault*" because there is no need to distinguish between double literal faults with and without ordering. This is different from [15], which shows that the groups of double-fault expressions caused by double term faults with and without ordering are different.

For any two single literal fault classes A and B, we use $A \bowtie B$ to denote the *double literal fault class* formed by A and B. Table 2 lists some double literal fault classes, their corresponding faulty expressions and detection conditions. As shown in Table 2, there are two subcases of LIF $\bowtie$ LIF. Due to space limitation, we only discuss the first subcase of LIF $\bowtie$ LIF where two LIFs are committed on different terms using $S = ab + cd + ef$ as an example. Interested readers may refer to [23] for details of all double literal faults. Suppose the literals a and b are wrongly inserted into the second term cd and the third term ef, respectively. The resulting double-fault expression is $I = ab + acd + bef$. The corresponding detection condition is "any point in $UTP_2(S)$ such that a evaluates to 0 or any point in $UTP_3(S)$ such that b evaluates to 0 or any point in $(TP_2(S) \cap TP_3(S)) \setminus TP_1(S)$ such that $a + b = 0$". The test case 001100 satisfying this condition can detect this fault because $S(001100) = 1 \neq 0 = I(001100)$.

4   Practical Applications

In this section, we discuss the practical applications of the detection conditions of double literal faults. This includes (1) analyzing the fault detection capabilities of existing test case selection strategies for double fault detection, (2) developing new test case selection strategies that supplement the existing fault-based testing strategies to detect double faults, and (3) discussing how to apply these supplementary testing strategies.

4.1   Detection Capabilities of Strategies for Single Fault Detection

There are many test case selection strategies, such as the BASIC, MAX-A, and MAX-B meaningful impact strategies (or simply the BASIC, MAX-A and MAX-B strategies) [9], and the MUMCUT strategy [10], for detecting single faults in Boolean expressions. The MAX-B strategy subsumes the MAX-A strategy, which in turn subsumes the MUMCUT strategy, which in turn subsumes the BASIC strategy.

Lau *et al.* [15] have shown that any test case selection strategy that subsumes the BASIC strategy guarantees to detect all double faults related to terms. It is then natural to ask whether these strategies (the BASIC, MUMCUT, MAX-A and MAX-B strategies) can detect all double literal faults. Unfortunately, the answer is negative, as proved in [24]. We will illustrate this result in Example 2 by using the MAX-B strategy, because it subsumes the other three (BASIC, MAX-A, and MUMCUT) strategies. The MAX-B strategy requires to select (1) all points from $UTP_i(S)$ for every i; (2) all points from $NFP_{i,j}(S)$ for every i and j; (3) $\lceil \log_2(|OTP(S)|) \rceil$ points from $OTP(S)$ where $|OTP(S)|$ denotes the size of $OTP(S)$ (one point is selected if $OTP(S)$ is a singleton set); and (4) $\lceil \log_2(|RFP(S)|) \rceil$ points from $RFP(S)$ where $|RFP(S)|$ denotes the size of $RFP(S)$ (one point is selected if $RFP(S)$ is a singleton set).

Example 2. Let $S = ab + ac + bd$. The set $T = \{1100, 1010, 1011, 0101, 0111, 0100, 0110, 1000, 1001, 0010, 0011, 0001, 1101, 1111, 0000\}$ satisfies the MAX-B strategy. When the literals $\bar{c}$ and $\bar{b}$ are inserted into the first and second terms of S respectively, the resulting double-fault expression is $I = ab\bar{c} + a\bar{b}c + bd$. Since S and I evaluate to different truth values on 1110, they are not equivalent. Note that, T cannot be used to detect this fault because S and I agree on all points in T.

4.2   Proposing New Testing Strategies for Double Fault Detection

Unlike the results of double term faults reported in [15], existing fault-based test case selection strategies for single fault detection discussed previously cannot guarantee to detect all double-fault expressions related to double literal faults. Hence, new test case selection strategies are needed for detecting double literal faults. In developing new strategies based on the derived detection conditions, two approaches can be used.

Table 2. Some double faults, double-fault expressions, detection conditions ($S = p_1 + \ldots + p_m$)

Fault Class[a]	Faulty Expression[b]	Detection Condition[c]
LOF $\bowtie$ LRF	Case 1 ($i_1 < i_2$): $p_1 + \cdots + p_{i_1,\hat{j}_1} + \cdots + p_{i_2,\hat{j}_2}x_{l_2} + \cdots + p_m$ (12)	(C1) any point in $UTP_{i_2}(S)$ such that $p_{i_1,\hat{j}_1} + x_{l_2} = 0$ or (C2) any point in $NFP_{i_1,\hat{j}_1}(S)$ or (C3) any point in $NFP_{i_2,\hat{j}_2}(S)$ such that $x_{l_2} = 1$
	Case 2: $p_1 + \cdots + p_{i_1,\hat{j}_1,\hat{j}_2}x_{l_2} + \cdots + p_m$ (13)	(C1) any point in $UTP_{i_1}(S)$ such that $x_{l_2} = 0$ or (C2) any point in $NFP_{i_1,\hat{j}_1}(S)$ such that $x_{l_2} = 1$ or (C3) any point in $NFP_{i_2,\hat{j}_2}(S)$ such that $x_{l_2} = 1$ or (C4) any point in $FP(S)$ such that $p_{i_1,\hat{j}_1,\hat{j}_2}x_{l_2} = 1$
LIF $\bowtie$ LIF	Case 1 ($i_1 < i_2$): $p_1 + \cdots + p_{i_1}x_{l_1} + \cdots + p_{i_2}x_{l_2} + \cdots + p_m$ (14)	(C1) any point in $UTP_{i_1}(S)$ such that $x_{l_1} = 0$ or (C2) any point in $UTP_{i_2}(S)$ such that $x_{l_2} = 0$ or (C3) any point in $(TP_{i_1}(S) \cap TP_{i_2}(S)) \setminus \left(\bigcup_{\substack{i=1 \\ i \neq i_1,i_2}}^{m} TP_i(S) \right)$ such that $x_{l_1} + x_{l_2} = 0$
	Case 2: $p_1 + \cdots + p_{i_1}x_{l_1}x_{l_2} + \cdots + p_m$ (15)	(C1) any point in $UTP_{i_1}(S)$ such that $x_{l_1}x_{l_2} = 0$
LIF $\bowtie$ LRF	Case 1 ($i_1 < i_2$): $p_1 + \cdots + p_{i_1}x_{l_1} + \cdots + p_{i_2,\hat{j}_2}x_{l_2} + \cdots + p_m$ (16)	(C1) any point in $UTP_{i_1}(S)$ such that $p_{i_2,\hat{j}_2} + x_{l_1} = 0$ or (C2) any point in $UTP_{i_1}(S)$ such that $x_{l_1} + x_{l_2} = 0$ or (C3) any point in $UTP_{i_2}(S)$ such that $x_{l_2} = 0$ or (C4) any point in $NFP_{i_2,\hat{j}_2}(S)$ such that $x_{l_2} = 1$ or (C5) any point in $(TP_{i_1}(S) \cap TP_{i_2}(S)) \setminus \left(\bigcup_{\substack{i=1 \\ i \neq i_1,i_2}}^{m} TP_i(S) \right)$ such that $x_{l_1} + x_{l_2} = 0$.
	Case 2: $p_1 + \cdots + p_{i_1,\hat{j}_2}x_{l_1}x_{l_2} + \cdots + p_m$ (17)	(C1) any point in $UTP_{i_1}(S)$ such that $x_{l_1}x_{l_2} = 0$ or (C2) any point in $NFP_{i_1,\hat{j}_2}(S)$ such that $x_{l_1}x_{l_2} = 1$
LRF $\bowtie$ LRF	Case 1 ($i_1 < i_2$): $p_1 + \cdots + p_{i_1,\hat{j}_1}x_{l_1} + \cdots + p_{i_2,\hat{j}_2}x_{l_2} + \cdots + p_m$ (18)	(C1) any point in $UTP_{i_1}(S)$ such that $p_{i_1,\hat{j}_1} + x_{l_1} = 0$ or (C2) any point in $UTP_{i_1}(S)$ such that $x_{l_1} + x_{l_2} = 0$ or (C3) any point in $UTP_{i_2}(S)$ such that $p_{i_1,\hat{j}_1} + x_{l_1} = 0$ or (C4) any point in $UTP_{i_2}(S)$ such that $x_{l_1} + x_{l_2} = 0$ or (C5) any point in $NFP_{i_1,\hat{j}_1}(S)$ such that $x_{l_1} = 1$ or (C6) any point in $NFP_{i_2,\hat{j}_2}(S)$ such that $x_{l_2} = 1$ or (C7) any point in $(TP_{i_1}(S) \cap TP_{i_2}(S)) \setminus \left(\bigcup_{\substack{i=1 \\ i \neq i_1,i_2}}^{m} TP_i(S) \right)$ such that $x_{l_1} + x_{l_2} = 0$
	Case 2: $p_1 + \cdots + p_{i_1,\hat{j}_1,\hat{j}_2}x_{l_1}x_{l_2} + \cdots + p_m$ (19)	(C1) any point in $UTP_{i_1}(S)$ such that $x_{l_1}x_{l_2} = 0$ or (C2) any point in $NFP_{i_1,\hat{j}_1}(S)$ such that $x_{l_1}x_{l_2} = 1$ or (C3) any point in $NFP_{i_1,\hat{j}_2}(S)$ such that $x_{l_1}x_{l_2} = 1$ or (C4) any point in $FP(S)$ such that $p_{i_1,\hat{j}_1,\hat{j}_2} = 1$ and $x_{l_1}x_{l_2} = 1$

[a] Due to space limitation, only fault classes related to double-fault expressions (12)–(19) are shown here. Please refer to [24] for other double literal faults.

[b] Due to space limitation, only double-fault expressions (12)–(19) are shown here. Please refer to [24] for double-fault expressions (1)–(11).

[c] Since S is in IDNF, the set $UTP_i(S)$ is non-empty for every i and the set $NFP_{i,\hat{j}}(S)$ is non-empty for every i and j. A set that is formed by selecting "any point in $UTP_i(S)$ for every i" and "any point in $NFP_{i,\hat{j}}(S)$ for every i and j" satisfies the detection conditions of double-fault expressions (1)–(11). Please refer to [24] for details.

Table 3. All possible test cases of S where $S = ab + cd + ef$

(a) $UTP_i(S)$ and $NFP_{i,\bar{j}}(S)$

i	1	2	3
$UTP_i(S)$	111010, 111001, 111000, 110110, 110101, 110100, 110010, 110001, 110000	101110, 101101, 101100, 011110, 011101, 011100, 001110, 001101, 001100	101011, 100111, 100011, 011011, 010111, 010011, 001011, 000111, 000011
$NFP_{i,\bar{1}}(S)$	011010, 011001, 011000, 010110, 010101, 010100, 010010, 010001, 010000	100110, 100101, 100100, 010110, 010101, 010100, 000110, 000101, 000100	101001, 100101, 100001, 011001, 010101, 010001, 001001, 000101, 000001
$NFP_{i,\bar{2}}(S)$	101010, 101001, 101000, 100110, 100101, 100100, 100010, 100001, 100000	101010, 101001, 101000, 011010, 011001, 011000, 001010, 001001, 001000	101010, 100110, 100010, 011010, 010110, 010010, 001010, 000110, 000010

(b) $OTP(S)$ and $RFP(S)$

$OTP(S)$	111011, 111111, 111101, 110111, 001111, 011111, 101111, 111110, 111100, 110011
$RFP(S)$	000000

One approach is to develop new test case selection strategies from scratch without referring to any existing fault-based testing strategies. However, the new strategies may not be able to detect all single faults because it is possible to have a test set that detects all double literal faults but not all single literal faults. This is illustrated in Example 3.

Example 3. Let $S = ab + cd + ef$. Table 3 lists the sets $UTP_i(S)$ of all unique true points, the sets $NFP_{i,\bar{j}}(S)$ of all near false points, the set $OTP(S)$ of all overlapping true points and the set $RFP(S)$ of all remaining false points of S. Let T be the set $\{110010, 110101, 001110, 011101, 010111, 101011, 010101, 011010, 100110, 101001, 100101, 101010, 011001, 010110\}$. Test cases in T have been underlined in Table 3 for ease of reference. The test cases in T satisfy all detection conditions of the 19 double-fault expressions in Table 2 (detailed discussions can be found in Appendix A). Hence, T can detect all double literal faults.

Now, T cannot detect the literal insertion fault in the single-fault expression $I_1 = ab\bar{c} + cd + ef$ (where the literal $\bar{c}$ has been inserted into the first term ab of S) because S and I_1 agree on all points in T.

An alternative approach is to supplement existing test case selection strategies for single-fault detection with new strategies so that, when applied together, they will detect all single and double faults under consideration. Moreover, from testing practitioners' perspective, this approach is more practical than the previous one for two reasons.

1. Since time and resources allocated for testing is limited, testing practitioners may opt to select test cases using existing test case selection strategies to first assure that the program is free from single faults. When there is still room for further testing, they may then opt to use supplementary strategies that can help to increase the chance of detecting other fault classes, such as double faults.
2. According to [15], some of the existing test case selection strategies for single fault detection can guarantee to detect certain double faults related to terms in a Boolean

expression. It would be simpler to develop new strategies that focus only on the undetected double faults.

In the rest of this section, we discuss how new strategies can be developed to supplement existing test case selection strategies. Before proposing new strategies, we need to identify which existing test case selection strategies can be used as the basis for detecting all single fault classes. Among the existing strategies discussed earlier, it has been shown that the BASIC strategy cannot guarantee to detect LIF and LRF [10], and the MUMCUT strategy (and hence the MAX-A and MAX-B strategies which subsume the MUMCUT strategy) guarantees to detect all single fault classes in [10, 13] and double faults related to terms [15]. Moreover, empirical studies [9, 25] have shown that the MUMCUT, MAX-A and MAX-B strategies require, on average, 12.0%, 40.6% and 48.2% of the entire input domain, respectively. Thus, the MUMCUT strategy is much more cost-effective than the MAX-A and MAX-B strategies in detecting single faults and double term faults. Furthermore, as reported in [24], the MUMCUT, MAX-A and MAX-B strategies cannot detect 6, 5, and 5 out of the 19 double-fault expressions, respectively. Thus, the MUMCUT strategy is almost as effective as the MAX-A and MAX-B strategies in detecting the double-fault expressions considered in this paper, but at a much smaller sized test sets. Hence, we choose to supplement the MUMCUT strategy for double literal fault detection. Note that although we only discuss the case for MUMCUT strategy, the idea of supplementing other strategies is similar.

Next, we need to identify which double-fault expressions cannot always be detected by the MUMCUT strategy. As reported in [24], the MUMCUT strategy cannot guarantee to detect 6 out of the 19 double-fault expressions, namely, expressions (13), (14), and (16)–(19) in Table 2.

Finally, we develop new test case selection strategies to supplement the MUMCUT strategy aiming at satisfying the detection conditions of these six double-fault expressions. The newly developed test case selection strategies are:

1. *Pairwise Multiple Near False Point (PMNFP)* strategy: To select test cases from every $NFP_{i,j}(S)$ such that, for every pair of missing literals x_{l_1} and x_{l_2} of p_i, all possible combinations of their truth values (that is, 00, 01, 10, and 11) are covered.
2. *Supplementary Multiple False Point (SMFP)* strategy: To select test cases from $FP(S)$ such that, for every term p_i, every two literals $x^i_{j_1}$ and $x^i_{j_2}$ in p_i, and every missing literal x_l of p_i,
   (a) $p_{i,\bar{j}_1,\bar{j}_2}$ evaluates to 1, and
   (b) all possible truth values of x_l are covered.
3. *Supplementary Pairwise Multiple False Point (SPMFP)* strategy: To select test cases from $FP(S)$ such that, for every term p_i, every two literals $x^i_{j_1}$ and $x^i_{j_2}$ in p_i, and every pair of missing literals x_{l_1} and x_{l_2} of p_i,
   (a) $p_{i,\bar{j}_1,\bar{j}_2}$ evaluates to 1, and
   (b) all possible combinations of the truth values of x_{l_1} and x_{l_2} (that is, 00, 01, 10, and 11) are covered.
4. *Pairwise Multiple Unique True Point (PMUTP)* strategy: To select test cases from every $UTP_{i_1}(S)$ such that, for every missing literal x_{l_1} of p_{i_1} and every missing literal x_{l_2} of p_{i_2} for each $i_2 \neq i_1$, all possible combinations of the truth values of x_{l_1} and x_{l_2} (that is, 00, 01, 10, and 11) are covered.

Table 4. Detection conditions aimed by the test case selection strategies

Test Case Selection Strategy	Detection Condition as in Table 2
PMNFP	(C2) of (17); (C2) and (C3) of (19)
SMFP	(C4) of (13)
SPMNFP	(C4) of (19)
PMUTP	(C2) of (16); (C2) and (C4) of (18)
SMUTP	(C1) of (16); (C1) and (C3) of (18)
SMOTP	(C3) of (14); (C5) of (16); (C7) of (18)

5. *Supplementary Multiple Unique True Point (SMUTP)* strategy: To select test cases from every $UTP_{i_1}(S)$ such that, for every missing literal x_l of p_{i_1} and every literal $x_{j_2}^{i_2}$ of p_{i_2} for each $i_2 \neq i_1$,
   (a) all possible truth values of x_l are covered and
   (b) p_{i_2,j_2} evaluates to 0.
6. *Supplementary Multiple Overlapping True Point (SMOTP)* strategy: To select test cases from $(TP_{i_1}(S) \cap TP_{i_2}(S)) \setminus \left(\bigcup_{\substack{i=1 \\ i \neq i_1, i_2}}^{m} TP_i(S) \right)$, for every two different terms p_{i_1} and p_{i_2}, such that, for every missing literal x_{l_1} of p_{i_1} and every missing literal x_{l_2} of p_{i_2}, all possible combinations of the truth values of x_{l_1} and x_{l_2} (that is, 00, 01, 10, and 11) are covered.

Table 4 lists these six new strategies and the corresponding detection conditions at which they are aimed to satisfy. For example, the SMOTP strategy aims at satisfying "any point in $(TP_{i_1}(S) \cap TP_{i_2}(S)) \setminus \left(\bigcup_{\substack{i=1 \\ i \neq i_1, i_2}}^{m} TP_i(S) \right)$ such that $x_{l_1} + x_{l_2} = 0$", which corresponds to (C3), (C5) and (C7) of (14), (16) and (18) in Table 2, respectively.

Due to page limitation, we will illustrate how to select test cases that satisfy the SMOTP strategy using $S = ab + cd + e$ as an example. Interested readers may refer to [24] for other strategies. For $p_1 = ab$ and $p_2 = cd$ of S, the set $(TP_1(S) \cap TP_2(S)) \setminus TP_3(S)$ is {11110}. Hence, by selecting this point, all possible truth value combinations of every missing literal pair from the first and second terms (that is, one missing literal from the first term and the other from the second term) are covered. Similarly, for the first and third terms, the set $(TP_1(S) \cap TP_3(S)) \setminus TP_2(S)$ is {11001, 11011, 11101}. The missing literals of the first term are c, d, and e, whereas those of the third term are a, b, c, and d. In order to cover all possible truth value combinations of every pair of missing literals formed by having one literal from the first term and one literal from the third term, all these three points are selected. Finally, for the second and third terms, the set $(TP_2(S) \cap TP_3(S)) \setminus TP_3(S)$ is {00111, 01111, 10111}. The missing literals of the second term are a, b, and d, whereas those of the third term are a, b, c, and d. In order to cover all possible truth value combinations of every pair of missing literals formed by having one literal from the first second and one literal from the third term, all these three points are selected. As a result, the set of test cases that satisfies the SMOTP strategy is {11110, 11001, 11011, 11101, 00111, 01111, 10111}.

Table 5. Suggested test case selection strategies for each double-fault expression

Expression Id	Test Case Selection Strategies
(1)–(12) and (15)	MUMCUT strategy only
(13)	MUMCUT strategy and then SMFP strategy
(14)	MUMCUT strategy and then SMOTP strategy
(16)	MUMCUT strategy and then PMUTP, SMUTP, and SMOTP strategies
(17)	MUMCUT strategy and then PMNFP strategy
(18)	MUMCUT strategy and then PMUTP, SMUTP, and SMOTP strategies
(19)	MUMCUT strategy and then PMNFP and SPMNFP strategies

4.3   Selective Use of Supplementary Strategies

In the previous section, we proposed six testing strategies to supplement the MUMCUT strategy for the detection of double literal faults. The generation of test cases that satisfy all these six strategies is very time consuming and resource intensive. Hence, from a practical perspective, testing practitioners may want to know which strategies together with the MUMCUT strategy can be used to detect certain double fault expressions. This allows the testing practitioners to focus their testing on particular types of faults when necessary. Table 5 summarizes the testing strategies that can be used to detect particular types of double-fault expressions.

Due to space limitation, we only demonstrate how the SMOTP strategy can be used to supplement the MUMCUT strategy to guarantee the detection of expression (14) in Table 2, which is the result of two literal insertion faults committed on two different terms of a Boolean expression. Interested readers may refer to [24] for other cases and more details. We will illustrate this using the following two examples.

Example 4. Consider the Boolean expression $S = ab + cd$. There are altogether 16 double-fault expressions of type (14). They are $abc + acd$, $abc + \bar{a}cd$, $abc + bcd$, $abc + \bar{b}cd$, $ab\bar{c} + acd$, $ab\bar{c} + \bar{a}cd$, $ab\bar{c} + bcd$, $ab\bar{c} + \bar{b}cd$, $abd + acd$, $abd + \bar{a}cd$, $abd + bcd$, $abd + \bar{b}cd$, $ab\bar{d} + acd$, $ab\bar{d} + \bar{a}cd$, $ab\bar{d} + bcd$, and $ab\bar{d} + \bar{b}cd$. Using the MUMCUT strategy, it is possible to (1) select points from $UTP_1(S) = \{1100, 1101, 1110\}$ such that all possible truth values of every missing literal of $p_1 = ab$ can be covered and (2) select points from $UTP_2(S) = \{0011, 0111, 1011\}$ such that all possible truth values of every missing literal of $p_2 = cd$ can be covered. Every test set generated by the MUMCUT strategy must contain $\{1101, 1110, 0111, 1011\}$ as a subset. Thus, conditions (C1) and (C2) of expression (14) in Table 2 are satisfied. Hence, all the above 16 expressions can be detected by every test set generated by the MUMCUT strategy and there is no need to apply SMOTP strategy.

In Example 4, the MUMCUT strategy is able to select test cases from every $UTP_i(S)$ for every i such that every possible truth values of all missing literals of p_i can be covered. However, it is possible that some of these truth values cannot be covered. In that case, we need the SMOTP strategy to supplement the MUMCUT strategy to guarantee the detection of expression (14) in Table 2, as illustrated in Example 5.

Example 5. Consider the Boolean expression $S = ab + ac + d$. For simplicity, we only illustrate the case of two LIFs committed on the first two terms of S. First of all, there are altogether 16 faulty expressions. They are $abc + acb + d = abc + d$, $abc + ac\bar{b} + d = ac + d$, $abc + acd + d = abc + d$, $abc + ac\bar{d} + d = ac + d$, $ab\bar{c} + acb + d = ab + d$, $ab\bar{c} + ac\bar{b} + d$, $ab\bar{c} + acd + d = ab\bar{c} + d$, $ab\bar{c} + ac\bar{d} + d = ab\bar{c} + ac + d = ab + ac + d$, $abd + acb + d = abc + d$, $abd + ac\bar{b} + d = a\bar{b}c + d$, $abd + acd + d = d$, $abd + ac\bar{d} + d = ac + d$, $ab\bar{d} + acb + d = ab + d$, $ab\bar{d} + ac\bar{b} + d = ab + ac + d$, $ab\bar{d} + acd + d = ab + d$, and $ab\bar{d} + ac\bar{d} + d = ab + ac + d$. Some of these 16 expressions are equivalent to either the original expression (e.g., $ab\bar{d} + ac\bar{d} + d = ab + ac + d$) or a single-fault expression (e.g., $abc + ac\bar{b} + d = ac + d$). Such single-fault expressions can be detected by the MUMCUT strategy [10]. The 5 remaining double-fault expressions are $abc + d$, $ab\bar{c} + ac\bar{b} + d$, $ab\bar{c} + d$, $a\bar{b}c + d$, and d.

Now, $UTP_1(S) = \{1100\}$ and $UTP_2(S) = \{1010\}$. By applying the MUMCUT strategy, these two points will be selected. They can be used to detect double fault expressions $abc + d$ and d.

We then need to use the SMOTP strategy to detect the three remaining double-fault expressions. Since $(TP_1(S) \cap TP_2(S)) \setminus TP_3(S) = \{1110\}$, by applying the SMOTP strategy, we will select 1110 to cover all possible truth value combinations of every pair of missing literals (one missing literal from the first term and the other missing literal from the second term). This test case 1110 can be used to detect the remaining 3 double-fault expressions, namely $ab\bar{c} + ac\bar{b} + d$, $ab\bar{c} + d$, and $a\bar{b}c + d$.

Hence, the MUMCUT strategy together with the SMOTP strategy can guarantee to detect double-fault expression of type (14) in Table 2.

5 Conclusion

This paper presents the detection conditions of double literal faults within a Boolean expression in irredundant disjunctive normal form. We find that there is actually no difference between double literal faults with or without ordering. For the four single literal fault classes, there are altogether 10 classes of double faults resulting in 19 different double-fault expressions. This is different from previous results on double term faults [15], which show that double faults with and without ordering give rise to different groups of double-fault expressions.

Previous study [15] has also shown that any test case selection strategy that subsumes the BASIC strategy (such as the MUMCUT, MAX-A and MAX-B strategies) can guarantee the detection of double term faults. However, in this paper, we show that none of these strategies is adequate for detecting the 19 double-fault expressions studied here. For instance, only 13 out of these 19 expressions can always be detected by the MUMCUT strategy [24]. To guarantee the detection of the remaining six double-fault expressions, we have developed six new test case selection strategies to supplement the MUMCUT strategy.

Empirical study are currently underway to evaluate the cost-effectiveness of these six newly proposed test case selection strategies together with the MUMCUT strategy for detecting all double literal faults in Boolean expressions. Furthermore, double fault classes involving a fault related to term and a literal fault have not been studied yet. Thus, we intend to continue the analysis of detection conditions of these remaining double fault classes. Through our ongoing study of the detection conditions of double faults, we will be able to gain a thorough understanding on the behaviour of multiple faults and how they can be detected.

References

1. Morell, L.J.: A theory of fault-based testing. IEEE Transactions on Software Engineering 16, 844–857 (1990)
2. Atlee, J., Buckley, M.: A logic-model semantics for SCR software requirements. In: Proceedings of 1996 International Symposium on Software Testing and Analysis (ISSTA'96), pp. 280–292 (1996)
3. Atlee, J., Gannon, J.: State-based model checking of event-driven system requirements. IEEE Transactions on Software Engineering 19, 24–40 (1993)
4. Dick, J., Faivre, A.: Automating the generation and sequencing of test cases from model-based specifications. In: Larsen, P.G., Woodcock, J.C.P. (eds.) FME 1993. LNCS, vol. 670, pp. 19–23. Springer, Heidelberg (1993)
5. Hierons, R.M.: Testing from a Z specification. Software Testing, Verification, and Reliability 7, 19–33 (1997)
6. Offutt, J.A., Liu, S., Abdurazik, A., Ammann, P.: Generating test data from state-based specifications. Software Testing, Verification and Reliability 13, 25–53 (2003)
7. Paradkar, A.M., Chung, T.K., Vouk, M.A.: Specification-based testing using cause-effect graphs. Annals of Software Engineering 4, 133–157 (1997)
8. Stocks, P., Carrington, D.: A framework for specification-based testing. IEEE Transactions on Software Engineering 22, 777–793 (1996)
9. Weyuker, E., Goradia, T., Singh, A.: Automatically generating test data from a Boolean specification. IEEE Transactions on Software Engineering 20, 353–363 (1994)
10. Chen, T.Y., Lau, M.F.: Test case selection strategies based on boolean specifications. Software Testing, Verification and Reliability 11, 165–180 (2001)
11. Kuhn, D.R.: Fault classes and error detection capability of specification-based testing. ACM Transactions on Software Engineering and Methodology 8, 411–424 (1999)
12. Tai, K.C.: Theory of fault-based predicate testing for computer programs. IEEE Transactions on Software Engineering 22, 552–563 (1996)
13. Lau, M.F., Yu, Y.T.: An extended fault class hierarchy for specification-based testing. ACM Transactions on Software Engineering and Methodology 14, 247–276 (2005)
14. Tsuchiya, T., Kikuno, T.: On fault classes and error detection capability of specification-based testing. ACM Transactions on Software Engineering and Methodology 11, 58–62 (2002)
15. Lau, M.F., Liu, Y., Yu, Y.T.: On the detection conditions of double faults related to terms in boolean expressions. In: Proceedings of the Thirtieth Annual International Computer Software and Applications Conference, pp. 403–410 (2006)
16. Marick, B.: Two experiments in software testing. Technical Report Technical Report UIUCDCS-R-90-1644, University of Illinois at Urbana-Champaign (1990)
17. Wallace, D., Kuhn, D.: Failure modes in medical device software: i an analysis of 15 years of recall data. International Journal of Reliability, Quality, and Safety Engineering, vol. 8 (2001)
18. How Tai Wah, K.S.: Fault coupling in finite bijective functions. Software Testing, Verification and Reliability 5, 3–47 (1995)
19. How Tai Wah, K.S.: A theoretical study of fault coupling. Software Testing, Verification and Reliability 10, 3–45 (2000)
20. Offutt, A.J.: The coupling effect: fact or fiction. In: Proceedings of the Third Workshop on Software Testing, Verification, and Analysis, pp. 131–140 (1989)
21. Offutt, A.J.: Investigations of the software testing coupling effect. ACM Transactions on Software Engineering and Methodology 1, 5–20 (1992)
22. Lau, M.F., Yu, Y.T.: On the relationship between single and double faults in logical expression. In: Supplementary Proceedings of the 15th International Symposium on Software Reliability Engineering (ISSRE 2004), pp. 41–42 (2004)
23. Lau, M.F., Liu, Y.: The investigation of double faults related to literals. Technical Report SUTICT-TR2006.03, Swinburne University of Technology (2006)

24. Lau, M.F., Liu, Y.: On detecting double faults related to literals. Technical Report SUTICT-TR2006.04, Swinburne University of Technology (2006)
25. Yu, Y.T., Lau, M.F., Chen, T.Y.: Automatic generation of test cases from Boolean specifications using the MUMCUT strategy. Journal of Systems and Software 79, 820–840 (2006)

A   Supplementary Proof in Example 3

We claim in Example 3 that the set T satisfies all detection conditions of the 19 double-fault expressions in Table 2. In the following, we present its proof.

Claim: Using the same notations as in Example 3, the set T satisfies all detection conditions of the 19 double-fault expressions in Table 2.

Proof. (A) For double-fault expressions (1) – (12): Since S is in irredundant disjunctive normal form, all the sets $UTP_i(S)$ and $NFP_{i,j}(S)$ are non-empty for every i and j. Now, the set T contains at least one element in $UTP_i(S)$ for every i and at least one element in $NFP_{i,j}(S)$ for every i and j. Thus, T satisfies the detection conditions of these 12 double-fault expressions. Hence, T detects all these expressions.

(B) For double-fault expressions (13), (16) and (18): Conditions (C3), (C4) and (C6) of double-fault expressions (13), (16) and (18), respectively, as shown in Table 2, are exactly the same: "any point in $NFP_{i_2,\bar{j}_2}(S)$ such that $x_{l_2} = 1$". This condition actually relates to the literal reference fault of replacing $x_{\bar{j}_2}^{i_2}$ of p_{i_2} by x_{l_2}, where x_{l_2} is a missing literal of p_{i_2}. Those test cases in T that are selected from $NFP_{i,\bar{j}}(S)$, for every i and j, collectively satisfy the condition: "the points from $NFP_{i,\bar{j}}(S)$ make every missing literal x_l of p_i evaluate to 1 for every i and j". Hence, T can detect double-fault expressions (13), (16) and (18).

(C) For double-fault expression (14): The detection condition is "(C1) any point in $UTP_{i_1}(S)$ such that $x_{l_1} = 0$ or (C2) any point in $UTP_{i_2}(S)$ such that $x_{l_2} = 0$ or (C3) any point in $(TP_{i_1}(S) \cap TP_{i_2}(S)) \setminus \left(\bigcup_{\substack{i=1 \\ i \neq i_1, i_2}}^{m} TP_i(S) \right)$ such that $x_{l_1} + x_{l_2} = 0$". Those test cases in T that are selected from $UTP_i(S)$, for every i, collectively satisfy the condition: "the points from $UTP_i(S)$ make every missing literal x_l of p_i evaluate to 0 for every i, except for the missing literal $\bar{c}$ of the first term ab and the missing literal $\bar{a}$ of the second term cd in S". Therefore, these test cases from $UTP_i(S)$ can detect all instances of double-fault expressions (14), except possibly $I = ab\bar{c} + \bar{a}cd + ef$. However, I can be detected by test case 111100 in T which is originally selected from $OTP(S)$. Hence, T can detect all double-fault expressions (14).

(D) For double-fault expressions (15), (17) and (19): One of the conditions in the detection conditions of these double-fault expressions is: "any point in $UTP_{i_1}(S)$ such that $x_{l_1} x_{l_2} = 0$". It corresponds to the detection condition of double-fault expression (15) and (C1) of double-fault expressions (17) and (19). This condition actually relates to double literal faults in which x_{l_1} or x_{l_2} is wrong inserted or referenced in p_{i_1} of S, where x_{l_1} and x_{l_2} are two missing literals of p_{i_1}. Those test cases in T that are selected from $UTP_i(S)$, for every i, collectively satisfy the condition: "the points from $UTP_i(S)$ will make $x_{l_1} x_{l_2}$ evaluate 0 where x_{l_1} and x_{l_2} are missing literals of p_i, for every i". Hence, T can detect double-fault expressions (15), (17) and (19).

Static Detection of Livelocks in Ada Multitasking Programs

Johann Blieberger[1], Bernd Burgstaller[2], and Robert Mittermayr[1,3]

[1] Institute for Computer-Aided Automation, TU Vienna, Austria
[2] School of Information Technologies, The University of Sydney, Australia*
[3] Mediornet GmbH, Vienna, Austria

Abstract. In this paper we present algorithms to statically detect livelocks in Ada multitasking programs. Although the algorithms' worst-case execution time is exponential, they can be expected to run in polynomial time. Since the problem is strongly connected to finding infinite loops, which is undecidable in general, our algorithms compute only an approximation to the real solution of the problem. As a consequence our algorithms may compute false positives.

1 Introduction

Concurrent programming is a complex task. One reason is that scheduling exponentially increases the possible program states. Thus a dynamic execution order of the statements executed in parallel is introduced. In general this leads to different behavior between different runs of a program, even on the same input. Because of the nondeterministic behavior, faults are difficult to detect. Static program analysis, which has been used since the beginning of software, can be a valuable aid for the detection of such faults.

One of the problems with concurrent programming are *livelocks*, sometimes also called *infinite internal chatter*. In the context of process calculi, e.g. CSP [15], the term *divergence* is frequently used to denote infinite internal actions. Livelocks are sometimes also referred to as *spinning*. From "outside", a deadlocked and a livelocked system look like no progress is made. In the case of a deadlock this is true, but in the case of a livelock computation still goes on.

The literature contains different definitions for livelock; [14] classifies livelock by three categories: starvation (e.g. [26]), infinite execution (e.g. [33]), and breach of safety properties (e.g. [27]). Our approach addresses programs in the second category. In [32], a livelock is defined as

"...a situation in which two or more processes continuously change their state in response to changes in the other process(es) without doing any useful work."

This and other definitions indicate that in contrast to deadlocks, livelocked systems still do some (although not useful) work.

---

* This work has been partially supported by the ARC Discovery Project Grant "Compilation Techniques for Embedded Systems" under Contract DP 0560190.

N. Abdennahder, F. Kordon (Eds.): Ada-Europe 2007, LNCS 4498, pp. 69–83, 2007.

The above definition of livelock is dynamic in its nature. To devise a static analysis method, we need static program properties that imply a (potential) livelock at run-time.

To distinguish "useful" computations from "purposeless" computations which might be going on during a livelock, we require "useful" computations to have an externally observable effect. Externally observable effect can manifest itself in a multitude of ways in the source code of a program: it can be as simple as writing output to a terminal, or more involved as with memory-mapped I/O or messages sent on a communication channel. In this paper, we model the external observer by task τ_{ext}, which can be envisioned as an additional task that is external to the tasks of the system under consideration. We assume that communication statements to this external observer task are marked by a suitable `pragma` in the source code of the program.

Intuitively, a set T of tasks is livelocking, if each task $\tau \in T$ contains an infinite loop within which it communicates with another task from T, and no communication with the external task τ_{ext} takes place. (NB: this precludes indirect communication with τ_{ext} via further tasks $\tau' \notin T$ as well.)

Definition 1. *A task τ is said to communicate with task $\overline{\tau}$, if*
1. *τ calls an entry of $\overline{\tau}$, or*
2. *τ contains an accept statement which is called by $\overline{\tau}$, or*
3. *τ writes a protected object or a shared variable, which is read by $\overline{\tau}$ (or vice versa), or*
4. *τ and $\overline{\tau}$ perform memory mapped I/O on the same memory cells.*

To detect livelocks, we have to find all infinite loops in a set of tasks and determine those tasks with which they communicate. In this paper we restrict ourselves to communication patterns (1) and (2). An analysis including the other patterns as well is possible, but requires more technicalities such as a relation modeling tasks which execute concurrently (cf. [3]). We construct the *control flow graphs (CFGs)* of tasks and determine *extended regular expressions (EREs)* that contain loop properties (i.e., finite vs. infinite, executed at least zero times vs. executed at least once). Morphisms on EREs allow us to determine the communication behavior of tasks. Because finding infinite loops is *undecidable* in general, our approach has to find a conservative approximation of the problem. As a consequence our approach delivers *false positives*, but we present strategies to reduce the number of false positives.

The remainder of the paper is organized as follows. In Section 2 we give definitions and preliminary results. In Section 3 we describe our approach algorithmically. In Section 4 we survey related work, before we conclude the paper and describe future work in Section 5.

2   Definitions and Preliminaries

Definition 2. *A control flow graph (CFG) $G\langle N, E, r, x \rangle$ is a directed graph with node set N, edge set $E \subseteq N \times N$, and a root node r such that there exists a path from r to every other node in N. Node x denotes the exit node of G.*

CFGs are used to represent programs. In this case nodes represent basic blocks and edges represent the control flow between nodes. Note that CFGs for Ada programs can be generated as for any other program written in different languages. For example, select statements which are not present in other languages can be handled like case statements.

Definition 3. *An* extended regular expression (ERE) *is a regular expression* (RE) *(see e.g. [34]) with additional iteration schemes. In more detail, an ERE has operators* $\cup$, $\cdot$ *and the iteration schemes* $\oplus$, $\circledast$, $+$, *and* $*$; *the empty word is denoted by* ε. *The iteration schemes are defined by the following table.*

$\oplus$	finite loop with at least one iteration
$\circledast$	finite loop with at least zero iterations
$+$	infinite loop with at least one iteration
$*$	infinite loop with at least zero iterations

Examples of $\oplus$- and $\circledast$-loops are for-loops,

```
for i in a..b loop ... end loop;
```

where b$\geq$a in case of a $\oplus$-loop. A simple example of a $+$-loop is

```
loop ... end loop;
```

A simple example of a $*$-loop is

```
while cond loop ... end loop;
```

where the value of cond does not change inside the loop. Note that if cond evaluates to false, the loop body is not executed.

Definition 4. *Let* χ *be a standard RE or an ERE. If for each* $n \in \mathbb{N}$, $n \geq 1$ *there exists a path* $\pi_n(r,x)$ *such that* $\pi_n(r,x)$ *contains* χ n *times, then we say that the CFG G contains an* infinite χ^+-path. *In addition, if there exists a path* $\pi_0(r,x)$ *such that* $\pi_0(r,x)$ *does not contain* χ, *then we say that G contains an* infinite χ^*-path.

Our next step is to define rewrite rules on EREs that determine whether a given task τ communicates with task τ' (cf. Definition 1). We consider extended regular expressions over the alphabet $\{\rho\}$, where ρ denotes a communication statement. An example for such an ERE is given by $(\rho \cup \rho \cdot (\varepsilon \cup \rho^*)) \cdot \rho^{\oplus}$. The rewrite rules are constructed in a way such that the information that ρ is contained in a $+$-loop is conserved.

If we use the conventions $\rho^0 = \varepsilon$ and $\rho^1 = \rho$, we can define the rewrite rules "in terms of the exponents". For example $((\rho^1)^\wedge +)^\wedge \circledast = \rho^+ {}^\wedge \circledast = (\rho^+)^{\circledast} = \rho^*$ corresponds to $(1^\wedge +)^\wedge \circledast = +^\wedge \circledast = *$.

Let $\triangle = \{0, 1, \oplus, \circledast, +, *\}$ be the set of exponents. The rules are given in Tables 1(a), 1(b), and 1(c). Left operands can be found on the left of the tables, right operands on the top. For example $* \cdot 1 = +$ and $1 \cdot * = +$.

The "$\wedge$"-table is set up as follows: We consider nested loops such that the behavior of the inner loop (the left operand) is described by $x \in \triangle$ and that

$\wedge$	0	1	$\oplus$	$\circledast$	+	*
0	0	0	0	0	0	0
1	0	1	$\oplus$	$\circledast$	+	*
$\oplus$	0	$\oplus$	$\oplus$	$\circledast$	+	*
$\circledast$	0	$\circledast$	$\circledast$	$\circledast$	*	*
+	0	+	+	*	+	*
*	0	*	*	*	*	*

(a) Operator "$\wedge$"

$\cdot$	0	1	$\oplus$	$\circledast$	+	*
0	0	1	$\oplus$	$\circledast$	+	*
1	1	$\oplus$	$\oplus$	$\oplus$	+	+
$\oplus$	$\oplus$	$\oplus$	$\oplus$	$\oplus$	+	+
$\circledast$	$\circledast$	$\oplus$	$\oplus$	$\circledast$	+	*
+	+	+	+	+	+	+
*	*	+	+	*	+	*

(b) Operator "$\cdot$"

$\cup$	0	1	$\oplus$	$\circledast$	+	*
0	0	0	0	0	0	0
1	0	1	$\oplus$	$\circledast$	+	*
$\oplus$	0	$\oplus$	$\oplus$	$\circledast$	+	*
$\circledast$	0	$\circledast$	$\circledast$	$\circledast$	*	*
+	0	+	+	*	+	*
*	0	*	*	*	*	*

(c) Operator "$\cup$"

Γ	
0	*false*
1	*false*
$\oplus$	*false*
$\circledast$	*false*
+	*true*
*	*false*

(d) Function Γ

Fig. 1. Operators and Function Γ

of the outer loop (the right operand) is described by $y \in \triangle$. In order to find a description of $(\rho^x)^y$ we have to determine the behavior of the nested loops.

For example consider $(\rho^\circledast)^+$. In this case the inner loop can be executed zero times which means that even when the outer loop is executed more than once, the overall behavior can only be either $\rho^\circledast$ or ρ^*. On the other hand, if the inner loop is executed at least once, and since the outer loop allows for an arbitrary number of iterations, the overall number of iterations cannot be bounded. Thus we get $(\rho^\circledast)^+ = \rho^*$ or given in terms of the exponents $\circledast ^\wedge + = *$.

By similar observations the contents of the "$\wedge$"-table can be completed. Surprisingly, the "$\wedge$"-operator commutes.

For the "$\cdot$"-table we consider concatenation of loops. For example $\rho \cdot \rho^*$ gives ρ^+ or for short $1 \cdot * = +$. For simplicity we assume $1 \cdot 1 = \oplus$. Note that also the "$\cdot$"-operator does commute.

For the "$\cup$"-table we have to consider the effects of if, case, and select statements. For example $\rho \cup \rho^\oplus$ means that on both branches there exists at least one ρ. Hence $1 \cup \oplus = \oplus$. On the other hand, $\rho \cup \rho^\circledast$ contains a path without a ρ on the right side. Thus $1 \cup \circledast = \circledast$. By symmetry, the "$\cup$"-operator has to commute.

Assume that an extended regular expression is represented by an expression tree. Then the rules given in Tables 1(a), 1(b), and 1(c) can be applied to the operators in the tree from bottom up. Thus after a finite number of rewrites we arrive at an expression of the form ρ^x, where $x \in \triangle$. Obviously, the number of rewrites is equal to the number of operators in the extended regular expression.

Definition 5. *Let* $\mathbb{B} = \{false, true\}$ *be the set of boolean truth values. Then we define a function* $\Gamma : \triangle \to \mathbb{B}$ *by enumeration in Table 1(d).*

If function Γ is applied to the simplified result of an ERE, it delivers *true* if and only if the underlying CFG contains an infinite ρ^+-path. If this is not the case, Γ returns *false*.

In [35] Tarjan presents a fast algorithm to determine a regular expression for a given CFG. These regular expressions describe all paths in the CFG from the start node to the exit node compactly. Tarjan's or any other algorithm suitable for this problem can easily be adapted to extended regular expressions.

COMPUTE $\mathcal{C}(\tau)$
```
1   C(τ) := {}
2   for all a ∈ R(τ) do
3       Compute α[ρ | E'_τ(a)]
4       Apply rules to get ρˣ, x ∈ Δ
5       Let C_a(τ) be the set of tasks with which τ communicates via a.
6       if Γ(x) = true then
7           C(τ) := C(τ) ∪ C_a(τ)
8       endif
9   endfor
```

Fig. 2. Algorithm to Compute $\mathcal{C}(\tau)$

Theorem 1. *Let $G\langle N, E, r, x\rangle$ be a CFG. By $\alpha[\rho|E']$ we denote the extended regular expression which we get from α by replacing each occurrence of $e \in E' \subseteq E$ with ρ and by replacing each occurrence of all the other $e' \in E \setminus E'$ with ε.*

As noted above, by successively applying the rules given in Tables 1(a), 1(b), and 1(c) to $\alpha[\rho|E']$ we finally get a result $\sigma = \sigma(\alpha, E') = \rho^x, x \in \Delta$. Now,

$$\Gamma(x) = \begin{cases} true, & \text{if } G \text{ contains an infinite } \rho^+\text{-path,} \\ false, & \text{otherwise.} \quad \square \end{cases}$$

3   Algorithm

Let $R(\tau)$ be the union of all entry calls performed by task τ and of all accept statements being part of τ. If $\tau = \tau_{\text{ext}}$, then $R(\tau) = R(\tau_{\text{ext}})$ contains all communication statements to this external observer task that, as stated above are marked by a suitable **pragma** in the source code of the program.

Each statement $a \in R(\tau)$ can appear in several places in the source code, and thus it can appear in several nodes of the corresponding CFG. Let $N_\tau(a)$ be the set of nodes of the CFG where a appears, or more formally: Let $a \in R(\tau)$ and $N_\tau(a)$ be the set of nodes of the CFG $G\langle V, E, r\rangle$ of τ where a appears in the basic block mapped to $N_\tau(a)$.

Let $E'_\tau(a) = \{(u \to v) \in E \mid v \in N_\tau(a)\}$ be the set of all edges targeting the nodes $N_\tau(a)$.

Let $\mathcal{C}(\tau)$ denote the set of tasks with which task τ communicates. Set $\mathcal{C}(\tau)$ is computed by the algorithm given in Figure 2.

The algorithm proceeds as follows:

1. For each task (type) τ and for each communicating statement a, it computes EREs.
2. The result of simplifying the ERE determines whether τ communicates to some task via a.

```
                               7    task body Server is    17    task body Client is
                               8    begin                  18    begin
1    procedure Main is         9      loop                 19      loop
2      task Server is          10       select             20        Server.E;
3        entry E;              11         accept E;        21      end loop;
4      end Server;             12       or                 22    end Client;
5      task Client is          13         terminate;       23    begin
6      end Client;             14       end select;        24      Server.E;
                               15     end loop;            25    end Main;
                               16   end Server;
```

Fig. 3. A Simple Livelocking Example

3. In $\mathcal{C}(\tau)$ the tasks with which τ communicates are aggregated.
4. Upon completion, $\mathcal{C}(\tau)$ contains all tasks with which τ communicates.

Concerning interprocedural analysis we assume that inlining is performed. This works well as long as there are no recursive subroutines. For recursive subroutines we apply the following solution: If there exist paths (from the start to the exit node of the CFG of the recursive subroutine) not containing a recursive call which can be described by some ERE β and which simplifies to $\rho^x, x \neq 0$ by applying our rules from above then we replace all recursive calls with ρ^x. Otherwise we replace all recursive calls with ε. Obviously, this construction is correct.

It is possible that a task calls an entry of the same task type (e.g. consider an array of tasks where each task communicates with its neighbors). Such "recursive" entry calls are handled correctly by our algorithm in that $\mathcal{C}(\tau)$ simply contains τ itself.

Definition 6. *We define the* communication graph $CG\langle T, E_{\mathcal{C}}\rangle$ *where T is the set of all task types including the environment task, i.e., the main program and the external observer task τ_{ext} in the analyzed program and*

$$E_{\mathcal{C}} = \{(\tau_1 \to \tau_2) \mid \tau_2 \in \mathcal{C}(\tau_1)\}.$$

Theorem 2. *If the communication graph $CG\langle T, E_{\mathcal{C}}$ of a program is not weakly connected (cf. [29]), then the program contains a livelock.*

Proof. By construction of $CG\langle T, E_{\mathcal{C}}\rangle$, the algorithm to compute $\mathcal{C}(\tau)$ (see Figure 3), and Theorem 1.

3.1 Example

Figure 3 shows the Ada source code of a simple livelocking task set. The CFGs of tasks Server and Client are shown in Figures 4(a) and 4(b). The CFG of the environment task (Main) is very simple and is not depicted.

The accept statement in Server is situated on edge $(1 \to 2)$. Node 3 is the terminate statement. Hence we obtain the ERE $\alpha[\![\rho | \{(1 \to 2)\}]\!] = (\rho \cdot \varepsilon)^+ \cdot \varepsilon$ for Server. Applying the simplification rules we get $\alpha[\![\rho | \{(1 \to 2)\}]\!] = \rho^+$. Hence $\mathcal{C}(\text{Server}) = \{\text{Client}\}$.

The entry call in `Client` is performed on edge $(4 \to 5)$. Thus we obtain the ERE $\alpha[\![\rho|\{(4 \to 5)\}]\!] = (\rho \cdot \varepsilon)^+$. Applying the simplification rules we get $\alpha[\![\rho|\{(1 \to 2)\}]\!] = \rho^+$. Hence $\mathcal{C}(\texttt{Client}) = \{\texttt{Server}\}$.

For `Main` we get ERE ρ and $\mathcal{C}(\texttt{Main}) = \{\}$.

The communication graph CG is depicted in Figure 4(c). Note that one single entry call in `Main` does not generate an arc in CG from `Main` to `Server`. Since thus CG is not weakly connected, the example contains a livelock by Theorem 2.

3.2 Notes on Time and Space Behavior

Generating CFGs for programs is straight-forward and can be done in linear time. Determining (extended) regular expressions for a given CFG can be done in almost linear time (cf. [35]). In addition there exist linear algorithms to determine whether a graph is weakly connected (see e.g. [11]).

Detecting the correct iteration scheme of loops requires heuristics for non-trivial cases like loops with exit statements. However, we assume that such heuristics can be implemented efficiently.

Applying the rules given in Tables 1(a), 1(b), and 1(c) needs time and space linear in the number of operators in α, which is denoted by $\|\alpha\|$ in the following.

Different algorithms used to solve the path problem produce different values for $\|\alpha\|$. In the worst-case $\|\alpha\| = O(a^n)$ for some $a > 1$, where n denotes the number of nodes of the underlying CFG.

We have observed that Tarjan's algorithm [35] applied to the SPEC2000 benchmark suite produces regular expressions both of polynomial and of exponential sizes. However, we are unable to spot a pattern in the CFGs that would make it possible to predict whether Tarjan's RE size is polynomial or exponential.

In contrast, an algorithm [30] based on decomposition properties of reducible CFGs delivered only polynomial sizes for the SPEC2000 benchmark suite. This algorithm is known to produce exponential RE sizes only if the number of backedges (i.e., loops) is large compared to the overall number of edges in the CFG. Since this is rarely the case in practical applications, this algorithm seems to be a good candidate for producing the extended regular expressions for the purposes of this paper.

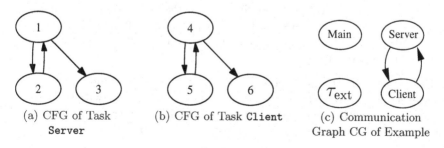

(a) CFG of Task **Server**   (b) CFG of Task **Client**   (c) Communication Graph CG of Example

Fig. 4. Graphs for Example

```
1    procedure Main is
2      X : Boolean;
3      task body T is
4      begin
5        Write_Ln();
6      end;
7    begin
8      if X then
9        l: loop
10           Write_Ln();  -- Path p
11         end loop;
12     end if;
13   end Main;
```

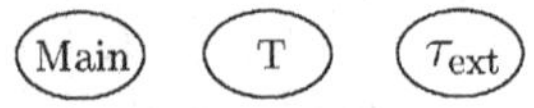

(a) Example CG

Fig. 5. Example: False Positive

3.3   False Positives

First we would like to note that dead code can lead to *false negatives* in our live lock analysis. In addition, performing *dead code analysis* before our algorithm significantly reduces the number of false positives.

As already mentioned above, detecting livelocks requires the detection of infinite loops in programs. Since this problem is undecidable, we cannot solve the livelock problem in the general case, i.e., we have to live with false positives.

Although Ada has the `loop ... end loop;` kind of statement that allows to explicitly[1] program infinite loops, general loop statements with exits make it necessary to develop heuristics to determine the iteration schemes needed by our approach. These heuristics are the primary source for false positives. We give an example for such a case below.

If +- and $\oplus$-loops are treated as *- and $\circledast$-loops, respectively, false positives may arise. For example consider the ERE $(\rho^x)^+$ which simplifies to ρ^+ if $x \in \{+, \oplus\}$ and ρ^* if $x \in \{*, \circledast\}$.

It should however be noted that most Ada multitasking programs are supposed to use the `loop ... end loop;`-construct for infinite loops which is easy to spot. In addition, we do not expect complex loop structures (exit, ...) in safety related or embedded programs.

3.4   Reducing the Number of False Positives

Theorem 2 is a conservative approximation of the set of programs that may produce a livelock. It requires the CG of a program to be weakly connected, which holds if every task τ (including the program's environment task) meets the following constraints.

1. Every task τ must contain a loop l with a "+" iteration scheme,
2. on every path through the body of l task τ must communicate with the external task τ_{ext} (or with a task that communicates with τ_{ext} and so on...), and
3. every path through the CFG of τ must contain loop l.

---

[1] In contrast to the `while true loop ... end loop;` style of other programming languages.

The above constraints are so strict that many non-livelocking programs occurring in practice fail to meet them. (i.e., their CGs are disconnected despite the programs being non-livelocking). Fig. 5 contains a program with two tasks that fail to produce a weakly connected CG (the CG is depicted in Fig. 5 (a)). Task T communicates with the external task τ_{ext}, but not within a "+" iteration scheme, and the environment task (corresponding to the body of "Main") contains a program path that does not contain the "+" iteration scheme (i.e., if variable X is false).

To reduce the number of false positives, we lower the abstraction level of our analysis from tasks to loop bodies. Informally, livelocks are caused by infinite loops. Lowering the abstraction level from tasks to loops allows for a more fine-grained analysis and excludes tasks without loops altogether. Deviating from Def. 2, we move the basic blocks of the CFG to the CFG edges (cf. [2]). We defer discussion of nested loops to a latter part of this section and focus our analysis on acyclic program paths through loops. In what follows, the term "loop" denotes the ERE corresponding to the argument of a "*" or "+" ERE operator. Exhaustive application of the rewrite rules

$$(R_1 \mid R_2) \cdot R_3 \Rightarrow (R_1 \cdot R_3) \mid (R_2 \cdot R_3) \tag{1}$$
$$R_1 \cdot (R_2 \mid R_3) \Rightarrow (R_1 \cdot R_2) \mid (R_1 \cdot R_3) \tag{2}$$

to a loop l results in an ERE $p_1 \mid \cdots \mid p_3$ where each p_i denotes an acyclic program path through the body of l (recall that the discussion of nested loops is deferred). Predicate $\text{Com}\tau_{ext} : \text{ERE} \rightarrow \{true, false\}$ is $true$ iff every path through the ERE provided as argument contains a communication with the external task τ_{ext} (e.g., a read/write operation on memory mapped I/O, etc.). Predicate $\text{Com} : \text{ERE} \times \text{ERE} \rightarrow \{true, false\}$ is $true$ iff a synchronous communication (i.e., a rendezvous) between the two argument EREs R_1 and R_2 occurs on every path through R_1 and R_2. Note that for the sake of exposition the above predicates are defined on EREs; for our analysis we will apply them only to single acyclic program paths.

Our analysis is based on the observation that not all paths through a loop need to generate communication patterns that contribute to a livelock. As an example, consider Fig. 6. It depicts three loops $l_1 \cdots l_3$. For each loop the acyclic program paths p_i are depicted (a single post-body node collects acyclic program paths; a single back edge connects the post-body node with the loop header; back edges are depicted with dashed arrows). Lines connecting paths p_i and p_j denote intertask communication, i.e., $\text{Com}(p_i, p_j) = true$. Loops l_1 and l_3 livelock at runtime only iff l_1 enters an infinite execution sequence along path p_3, and l_3 enters an infinite execution sequence along path p_7. Path p_8 of loop l_3 contains communication with itself, which is possible with task types. Two tasks entering an infinite execution sequence along path p_8 constitute another livelock. No other paths across loops $l_1 \cdots l_3$ can contribute to a livelock.

Eq. (3) defines a predicate to determine paths that cannot contribute to a livelock. Informally, a path p_1 cannot contribute to a livelock if no communication occurs on p_1, or if p_1 communicates with the external task τ_{ext} or with another

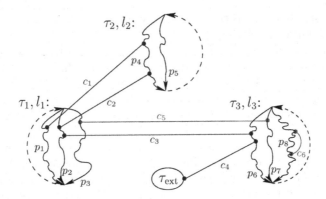

Fig. 6. Example: Communication Behavior of Three Loops $l_1, \ldots, l_3$

path that communicates with τ_{ext}. A path that cannot contribute to a livelock is called a *safe* path, otherwise the path is *unsafe*.

$$\text{Safe}(p_1) \Leftrightarrow \big(\forall p_2 : \neg \text{Com}(p_1, p_2)\big) \\ \vee \text{Com}\tau_{\text{ext}}(p_1) \vee \big(\exists p_3 : \text{Com}(p1, p_3) \wedge \text{Safe}(p_3)\big) \tag{3}$$

Returning to the example in Fig. 6, all paths except p_3, p_7 and p_8 are safe.

Fig. 7 depicts the algorithm that we use to detect unsafe paths. The algorithm proceeds in two steps: (1) across all CFGs of all task (types) it computes the set $\mathcal{L}$ of loops, and (2) determines if the paths through those loops are safe. Procedure Slice uses a pattern matching algorithm to determine EREs that constitute loops (see [4]). Procedure Rewrite applies the rewrite rules of Eq. (1) and Eq. (2). Procedure Com*(p) uses the transitive closure on predicate Com and returns a set containing all paths that path p communicates with. Each such set constitutes a set of unsafe paths that may produce a livelock at run-time.

Nested Loops. Consider a loop l with path expression R. Assume that $R_1 = (a|b)^*$ is a subexpression of R. To determine the communication behavior of l, a conservative approximation of communication with τ_{ext} assumes that R_1 is executed zero times or once. For a loop with a "+" iteration scheme, the conservative approximation is to assume one iteration. The following rewrite rules replace nested loops with their conservative approximations.

$$R^* \Rightarrow (\epsilon \,|\, R) \qquad R^\circledast \Rightarrow (\epsilon \,|\, R) \qquad R^+ \Rightarrow (R) \qquad R^\oplus \Rightarrow (R) \tag{4}$$

These rules are added to procedure Rewrite. Procedure Slice returns a loop body for every "*" and "+" operator across all loop nesting levels (cf. [4]). These loop bodies contain possible nested loops. As an example, consider a loop l with path expression $a \cdot ((b^* \,|\, ((c \cdot (d)^*)^*)$. The sliced loop bodies are $\{b, c \cdot (d)^*, d\}$.

Input:
  set $\mathcal{G}$ of CFGs of the input program's task (types)
Output:
  set $\mathcal{U}$ containing sets of acyclic paths across loops that generate livelocks
Algorithm:

COMPUTE UNSAFE PATHS $(\mathcal{G})$
1   $\mathcal{U} := \{\}, \quad \mathcal{L} := \{\}$
2   **for** *all CFGs $g \in \mathcal{G}$* **do**
3   *compute ERE $R = R(g)$*
4       $\mathcal{L} := \mathcal{L} \cup \text{Rewrite}(\text{Slice}(R))$
5   **endfor**
6   **for** *all loops $l \in \mathcal{L}$* **do**
7   **for** *all paths $p \in \text{Pathset}(l)$* **do**
8   **if** $\neg \text{Safe}(p)$ **then**
9               $\mathcal{U} := \mathcal{U} \cup \text{Com}^*(p)$
10   **endif**
11   **endfor**
12 **endfor**

Fig. 7. Detection Algorithm for Unsafe Paths

Implementation Considerations. The practicality of the path-based approach depends critically on the number of acyclic paths across loops. This number grows exponentially in the number of if- and case statements and nested loops. In [4] we conducted a study on the complete SPEC95 benchmark suite with over 5000 CFGs. The purpose of this study was to determine the number of acyclic paths across loops for large real-world applications. For 90% of all surveyed CFGs this number was below 4000, which means that our approach is tractable for real-world applications.

4   Related Work

There is a vast amount of work about the detection of deadlocks, but surprisingly few publications to livelock detection in concurrent programming languages like Ada and Java. Livelocks are mostly mentioned as a sideline while treating deadlocks. A variety of work has been done for detecting or avoiding livelocks in routing algorithms and client/server architectures. In this section we focus on the related work concerning detection of livelocks in concurrent non-distributed software.

Examples for early work on livelock and liveness properties in general are [20,21,27]. Recent work on liveness and fairness we are aware of include [36].

Techniques for the detection of livelocks in concurrent software are based on petri-nets, model-checking, or CSP.

Petri-Nets. Cheng and Ushijima use extended Petri nets to represent Ada multitasking programs [9]. This representation of a program is analyzed with linear algebra methods to statically detect deadlocks and livelocks. The model includes no cycles and therefore is not strongly connected which is a convenient property for their livelock analysis. If an infinite firing sequence in the Petri net exists a livelock is detected. The existence of a tasking deadlock and/or livelock is shown when a matrix equation has a positive integer solution. The approach cannot handle dynamic creation of tasks, abort statements, and exception handling. Like our approach it also detects some spurious livelocks. Because this method is based on an extended Petri net, it is fundamentally different to our work. It can only detect the effect not its cause. The authors state that much work has to be done to establish a practical static analysis for livelock detection.

Model Checking. The abstraction imposed by models derived from the actual source code generally results in differences between the model and the real program implementation. Thus results given by model checking are in general non-transferable to the real program. Static analysis like our approach do not have this drawback because the application source code is used directly.

In the model-checking tool Spin [17,16] the models are build in a language called *Process Meta Language* (Promela). Spin enables analyzing liveness properties like non-progress cycles (i.e. livelocks). The detection of livelocks relies on special labels. Therefore such labels have to be placed by the user. Thus it is not fully automated. Both, *Java PathFinder* (JPF) [37] and Bandera [10], act as a front-end enabling model checking concurrent Java software (e.g. livelock checking).

Model checking approaches addressing livelock detection we are aware of include [1,24,22,12,8].

The indirect approach in [19] addresses generally starvation in Ada programs and is based on the finite delay property of [21].

CSP. The following tools use CSP [15] as a basis to enable the detection of race hazards, deadlock, starvation and especially livelock. All these approaches have similar flaws like in model checking i.e. design specifications or (the other way round) abstractions may have differences to the actual software.

Deadlock Checker is a tool which performs various checks on parallel programs written in CSP in order to prove freedom from deadlock and livelock [25]. It acts as a design workbench for designers of safety-critical distributed systems. The approach is efficient because of certain simplifications and is thus incomplete.

Joël Ouaknine's *Slap* [18] is a conservative livelock checker for processes written in a subset of CSP. If Slap outputs "LIVELOCK-FREE" then the CSP model is livelock free. If the tool outputs "POTENTIAL LIVELOCK" then no definite conclusion can be made. Slap is currently in beta stadium and its source is available.

Failures-Divergence Refinement (FDR) [23,28] is a model-checking tool which enables CSP based proofs and analysis. FDR uses the so called "failures-divergences model" of CSP for detection of a set of traces after which a process may livelock. At present it is limited to analyzing systems of up to one hundred million global states.

Communicating Sequential Processes for Java (JCSP) [38], *Communicating Threads for Java* (CTJ) [13], and *Java2CSP* [31] can be used to enable a CSP-like verification of Java programs. Also C++CSP and JCSP.net for C++ and .net, respectively, are available.

An example using CSP for detecting livelocks in real applications is the work of Buth [6,7]. occam code from the International Space Station (ISS) is being converted to CSP using abstraction techniques. The resulting CSP model is checked using FDR. Nevertheless the presented technique needs some manual steps and knowledge. Thus it is far from being fully automated.

5 Conclusion

We have presented simple algorithms for detecting livelocks in Ada multitasking programs. Although their worst-case execution time is exponential, the algorithms can be expected to run in time $O(|V|^2)$, where $|V|$ denotes the number of nodes of the CFG of the analyzed program.

Since the problem is strongly connected to finding infinite loops, which is undecidable, our algorithms compute only an approximation to the real solution of the problem. As a consequence our algorithms compute false positives.

A future direction of our work will be to include data-flow in our approach which might result in a more fine-grained analysis.

Another future direction of our work will be to set up a symbolic framework (e.g., based on [5]) for livelock detection. Such a framework can be expected to use more resources (time and space) than the approach presented in this paper, but will be less amenable to false positives.

References

1. Abdulla, P.A., Jonsson, B., Rezine, A., Saksena, M.: Proving Liveness by Backwards Reachability. In: Baier, C., Hermanns, H. (eds.) CONCUR 2006. LNCS, vol. 4137, pp. 95–109. Springer, Heidelberg (2006)
2. Burgstaller, B.: Symbolic Evaluation of Imperative Programming Languages. Technical Report 183/1-138, Department of Automation, Vienna University of Technology (June 2005), Available at http://www.auto.tuwien.ac.at/~bburg/reports.html
3. Burgstaller, B., Blieberger, J., Mittermayr, R.: Static detection of access anomalies in Ada95. In: Pinho, L.M., González Harbour, M. (eds.) Ada-Europe 2006. LNCS, vol. 4006, pp. 40–55. Springer, Heidelberg (2006)
4. Burgstaller, B., Scholz, B., Blieberger, J.: Tour de Spec — A Collection of Spec95 Program Paths and Associated Costs for Symbolic Evaluation. Technical Report 183/1-137, Department of Automation, Vienna University of Technology (June 2004) Available at http://www.auto.tuwien.ac.at/~bburg/reports.html
5. Burgstaller, B., Scholz, B., Blieberger, J.: Symbolic Analysis of Imperative Programming Languages. In: Proceedings of the 7th Joint Modular Languages Conference. LNCS, pp. 172–194. Springer, Heidelberg (2006)

6. Buth, B., Peleska, J., Shi, H.: Combining Methods for the Livelock Analysis of a Fault-Tolerant System. In: Haeberer, A.M. (ed.) AMAST 1998. LNCS, vol. 1548, pp. 124–139. Springer, Heidelberg (1998)
7. Buth, B., Peleska, J., Shi, H.: Deadlock- und Livelock-Analyse für die Internationale Raumstation ISS (August 2006)
8. Cassidy, T., Cordy, J., Dean, T., Dingel, J.: Source Transformation for Concurrency Analysis. In: Proc. LDTA 2005, ACM 5th International Workshop on Language Descriptions, Tools and Applications, Edinburgh, Scotland, April 2005, pp. 26–43 (2005)
9. Cheng, J., Ushijima, K.: Analyzing Ada Tasking Deadlocks and Livelocks Using Extended Petri Nets. In: Christodoulakis, D.N. (ed.) Ada: The Choice for '92. LNCS, vol. 499, pp. 125–146. Springer, Heidelberg (1991)
10. Corbett, J.C., Dwyer, M.B., Hatcliff, J., Laubach, S., Păsăreanu, C.S.: Bandera: Extracting Finite-state Models from Java Source Code. In: Proceedings of the 22nd International Conference on Software Engineering, Limerick, Ireland, June 2000, pp. 439–448 (2000)
11. Cormen, T.H., Leiserson, C.E., Rivest, R.L.: Introduction to Algorithms. MIT Press, Cambridge, MA (1989)
12. Godefroid, P.: Software Model Checking: The VeriSoft Approach. Form. Methods Syst. Des. 26(2), 77–101 (2005)
13. Hilderink, G.H., Broenink, J.F., Bakkers, A.W.P.: Communicating Threads for Java. In: Cook, B.M. (ed.) Proceedings of WoTUG-22: Architectures, Languages and Techniques for Concurrent Systems, Keele, UK, March 1999, pp. 243–261 (1999)
14. Ho, A., Smith, S., Hand, S.: On deadlock, livelock, and forward progress. Technical Report UCAM-CL-TR-633, University of Cambridge, Computer Laboratory (May 2005)
15. Hoare, C.A.R.: Communicating Sequential Processes. Prentice Hall, London (1985)
16. Holzmann, G.J.: Proving Properties of Concurrent Systems with Spin (invited tutorial). In: Lee, I., Smolka, S.A. (eds.) CONCUR 1995. LNCS, vol. 962, Springer, Heidelberg (1995)
17. Holzmann, G.J.: The Spin Model Checker – Primer and Reference Manual. Addison-Wesley, Reading, Massachusetts (2003)
18. Ouaknine, J.: SLAP tool (Version 0.1): A Static Livelock Analyzer for CSP Processes, http://web.comlab.ox.ac.uk/oucl/work/joel.ouaknine/software/slap.html
19. Karam, G.M., Buhr, R.J.A.: Starvation and Critical Race Analyzers for Ada. IEEE Transactions on Software Engineering 16(8), 829–843 (1990)
20. Kwong, Y.S.: On reductions and livelocks in asynchronous parallel computation. PhD thesis (1978)
21. Kwong, Y.S.: On the Absence of Livelocks in Parallel Programs. In: Kahn, G. (ed.) Semantics of Concurrent Computation. LNCS, vol. 70, pp. 172–190. Springer, Heidelberg (1979)
22. Leue, S., Ştefănescu, A., Wei, W.: A Livelock Freedom Analysis for Infinite State Asynchronous Reactive Systems. In: Baier, C., Hermanns, H. (eds.) CONCUR 2006. LNCS, vol. 4137, pp. 79–94. Springer, Heidelberg (2006)
23. F.S.E. Ltd. Failures-Divergence Refinement, FDR 2 User Manual (2005), www.fsel.com
24. Martin, J.M.R., Huddart, Y.: Parallel Algorithms for Deadlock and Livelock Analysis of Concurrent Systems. In: Welch, P.H., Bakkers, A.W.P. (eds.) Communicating Process Architectures, September 2000, pp. 1–14 (2000)

25. Martin, J.M.R., Jassim, S.A.: A Tool for Proving Deadlock Freedom. In: Proc. WoTUG20: Parallel Programming and Java, April 1997, pp. 1–16. IOS Press, Amsterdam (1997)
26. Mogul, J.C., Ramakrishnan, K.K.: Eliminating Receive Livelock in an Interrupt-Driven Kernel. ACM Transactions on Computer Systems 15(3), 217–252 (1997)
27. Owicki, S., Lamport, L.: Proving Liveness Properties of Concurrent Programs. ACM Trans. Program. Lang. Syst. 4(3), 455–495 (1982)
28. Roscoe, A.W.: The Theory and Practice of Concurrency. Prentice-Hall, Englewood Cliffs (1997)
29. Rosen, K.H.: Discrete Mathematics and its Applications, 3rd edn. McGraw-Hill, New York (1995)
30. Scholz, B., Blieberger, J.: A New Elimination-Based Data Flow Analysis Framework using Annotated Decomposition Trees. In: Proc. ETAPS 2007, Braga, Portugal, March 2007, LNCS (2007)
31. Shi, H.: Java2CSP: A System for Verifying Concurrent Java Programs. In: Schellhorn, G., Reif, W. (eds) FM-TOOLS 2000, number 2000-07 in Ulmer Informatik-Berichte, pp. 111–115 (2000)
32. Stallings, W.: Operating Systems: Internals and Design Principles. Prentice Hall, Englewood Cliffs, NJ (2001)
33. Tai, K.-C.: Definitions and Detection of Deadlock, Livelock, and Starvation in Concurrent Programs. In: ICPP, August 1994, vol. 2, pp. 69–72 (1994)
34. Tarjan, R.E.: A unified approach to path problems. J. ACM 28(3), 577–593 (1981)
35. Tarjan, R.E.: Fast algorithms for solving path problems. J. ACM 28(3), 594–614 (1981)
36. van Glabbeek, R.J., Voorhoeve, M.: Liveness, Fairness and Impossible Futures. In: Baier, C., Hermanns, H. (eds.) CONCUR 2006. LNCS, vol. 4137, pp. 126–141. Springer, Heidelberg (2006)
37. Visser, W., Havelund, K., Brat, G., Park, S.: Model Checking Programs. In: IEEE International Conference on Automated Software Engineering (ASE), Grenoble, France (September 2000)
38. Welch, P.H., Martin, J.M.R.: A CSP Model for Java Multithreading. In: PDSE '00: Proceedings of the International Symposium on Software Engineering for Parallel and Distributed Systems, Washington, DC, USA, vol. 114, IEEE Computer Society Press, Los Alamitos (2000)

Towards the Testing of Power-Aware Software Applications for Wireless Sensor Networks[*]

W. K. Chan[1], T. Y. Chen[2], S. C. Cheung[3], T. H. Tse[4], and Zhenyu Zhang[4]

[1] City University of Hong Kong, Kowloon Tong, Hong Kong
wkchan@cs.cityu.edu.hk
[2] Swinburne University of Technology, Hawthorn, Australia
tchen@ict.swin.edu.au
[3] The Hong Kong University of Science and Technology, Clear Water Bay, Hong Kong
sccheung@cse.ust.hk
[4] The University of Hong Kong, Pokfulam, Hong Kong
{thtse,zyzhang}@cs.hku.hk

Abstract. The testing of programs in wireless sensor networks (WSN) is an important means to assure quality but is a challenging process. As pervasive computing has been identified as a notable trend in computing, investigations on effective software testing techniques for WSN are essential. In particular, energy is a crucial and scarce resource in WSN nodes. Programs running correctly but failing to meet the energy constraints may still be problematic. As such, testing techniques for power-aware applications are useful; otherwise, the quickly depleted device batteries will need frequent replacements, hence challenging the effectiveness of automation. Since current testing techniques do not consider the issue of energy constraints, their automation in the WSN domain warrants further investigation.

This paper proposes a novel power-aware technique built on top of the notion of metamorphic testing to alleviate both the test oracle issue and the power-awareness issue. It tests the functions of programs in WSN nodes that are in close proximity, and uses the data consolidation criteria of data aggregation in programs as the basis for verifying test results. The power-aware transmissions of intermediate and final test data as well as the computation required for verification of test results are directly supported by the WSN programs. Our proposed technique has been strategically designed to blend in with the special features of the WSN environment.

Keywords: Wireless sensor network, WSN application, power awareness, test oracle, metamorphic testing, software testing, test automation.

1 Introduction

A wireless sensor network (WSN) is an ad hoc computer network formed by many sensor devices interconnected by wireless channels. Each sensor device, known as

---

[*] This work is supported in part by a grant of the Innovation and Technology Commission in Hong Kong (Project No. ITS/076/06), a grant of City University of Hong Kong (Project No. 7200079), a discovery grant of the Australian Research Council (Project No. DP 0771733), and CERG grants of the Research Grants Council of Hong Kong (Project Nos. 612306 and 717506).

N. Abdennahder, F. Kordon (Eds.): Ada-Europe 2007, LNCS 4498, pp. 84–99, 2007.

a sensor node or simply a *node*, is built with sensors to capture data (such as temperature and light intensity) from its physical environment. Because of physical and environmental limitations, such nodes should satisfy various constraints regarding battery power, computation capacity, unforeseeable communication restrictions, and others. A popular class of sensor nodes are those that, once deployed, will be operational until the depletion of their batteries. In other words, the lifetime of the sensor nodes depend critically on power management.

In certain WSN, many nodes are deployed in proximity to perform the same function, such as sensing a change of temperature for the detection of any passing hot object. A few nodes, equipped with relatively plentiful resources, are selected as base stations that bridge other nodes and target client stations. These nodes are normally known as *data aggregators*. They consolidate the data from sensory nodes and send the consolidated results to other nodes. For example, they eliminate duplicated copies of data or compute statistics from the data received according to defined evaluation criteria. In this paper, we refer to such criteria as *data consolidation criteria*. In this way, the data consolidation feature of a WSN application would save transmission energy by propagating the computed results instead of simply relaying received data [10].

Power efficiency is critical to many WSN applications. A power-aware application should "enable users to work for longer periods of time before having to reconnect to recharge the system battery. ... an anti-virus scanner would run in a full-featured fashion, providing file scanning on all files opened and also running periodic system-wide scans. When on battery power, the scanner could defer the system-wide scans until a later time and continue processing safely, analyzing just the open files." [1] For example, according to http://www.tinyOS.net, the de facto site for important news release for tinyOS, researchers advocate to design WSN artifacts to be power-aware.

On the other hand, the nodes in a typical WSN must coordinate among themselves and the transmission of data across nodes in the network is a typical feature in a WSN application — but data communication is the most energy-demanding aspect among communication, sensing and computation. [2]

The development of automated testing techniques for WSN applications with the above properties is further complicated by the following:

(a) The outputs from an individual node are often unstable, unreliable, and dependent on hardware quality and unforeseeable physical environmental conditions. One way to overcome these limitations is to test software components on a node simulator, such as TOSSIM [3], which emulates simplified situations of WSN applications. In practice, however, such an approach requires elaborated studies of possible application-specific environments. Testing on a real platform is another alternative. Unfortunately, the results of an application in the unforeseeable WSN environment are determined not only by *what* test cases are selected, but also *where*, *when* and *how* they are executed.

---

[1] http://solveit.jotxpert.net/WikiHome/Articles/277366.

[2] M. Srivastava. Wireless sensor and actuator networks: challenges in long-lived and high-integrity operation. ASI Lecture, City University of Hong Kong, December 4, 2006. Available at http://www.cs.cityu.edu.hk/ asi06/program.shtml.

[3] http://www.cs.berkeley.edu/ pal/research/tossim.html.

(b) As the power-aware aspect is a key feature of WSN applications, the testing of both functional correctness and power-awareness is necessary for quality assurance. In particular, applications in sensor nodes are often designed for a particular range of workload such as sleeping for 99% of its time and working actively for the remaining 1%. Using excessive resources in sensor nodes to conduct testing activities may change the workload pattern, which directly alters the energy consumption and, hence, the power-awareness test results. The testing of applications in the WSN environment is, therefore, a research and practical challenge.

As such, we identify at least two testing research directions for assuring WSN applications: (1) the formulation of effective testing techniques for power-aware applications, and (2) the development of energy-efficient testing techniques for WSN. This paper is our first step towards these goals.

As we have mentioned earlier, data communication is unavoidable in WSN and consumes most of the energy. It inspires us to use the existing data communication of the application to transmit test results to data aggregators (which have relatively plentiful resources) to conduct the checking of test results. We explore this observation to develop our testing proposal.

This paper proposes a novel test automation strategy to alleviate the test oracle issue associated with power management concerns in a WSN environment. The backbone of our test verification technique is metamorphic testing [7]. Our strategy consists of three elements: (a) The test inputs are sensed data of isotropic physical phenomena of sensor nodes that are in proximity. (b) We then use the data consolidation criteria supported by the data aggregators of WSN applications as a basis for verifying results according to the metamorphic approach [8]. (c) We enhance current techniques of metamorphic testing, such as [8,9,17], to address non-functional concerns. For any given test case, apart from verifying the functional output from the sensor node, we also check the energy consumption that has been used to compute the functional output. By comparing and contrasting the energy consumptions, we verify whether an abnormal amount of energy has been consumed.

The main contributions of the paper are two-fold: (i) To our best knowledge, it is the first research to alleviate the test oracle problem for the testing of software applications running on top of wireless sensor networks. (ii) It is also the first attempt to address the testing of power-aware concerns for these applications.

The rest of the paper is organized as follows: It first reviews related work in the next section, followed by metamorphic testing in Section 3. In Section 4, we shall develop a software testing model that helps testers alleviate the test oracle problem in the presence of power management concerns. In Section 5, we discuss issues of other potential options, and portray directions for future work. We conclude the paper in Section 6.

2   Related Work

To support high-quality automated software testing, a reliable and automatic test oracle should be developed. Binder [6] extensively reviews many popular types of test oracle and casts them in the context of object-oriented testing. A simple and intuitive mechanism for automatic test oracles is program assertion, as supported by JUnit [2]. This approach may also be applied to the testing of programs in sensor nodes. However, sensory computing is intrinsically imprecise. The use of program assertions in imprecise WSN computation warrants further research.

Some practitioners recommend adopting the techniques in Graphical User Interface (GUI) testing to embedded systems testing [11]. Berstel et al. [5] use a formal specification approach to verify GUI specifications. They work at the specification level; whereas we propose a technique that works at the implementation level. Xie and Memon [19] empirically study the effect of a number of selected test oracle approaches on GUI applications. They find in their experiments that, for effective identification of failures, test oracles should be strong, or else the failures for some test cases may not be identifiable by the test oracles. Our approach proposes to use data aggregation criteria of the application to serve as the mechanism to define test oracles. Their work complements ours.

Chen et al. [9] evaluate the failure-detection capabilities of different metamorphic relations for the same applications. They find that different forms of metamorphic relations have diverse strengths in detecting failures even for the same set of source test cases. We also utilize the knowledge of domain experts specified in the data consolidation criteria for eliminating duplicated data entries by the data aggregator of the application.

Tse et al. [16] report on an approach, which is close to metamorphic testing, to tackle the test oracle issue for embedded software in bonding machines. They do not consider the power-awareness issue. Kapfhammer et al. [12] propose to unload not-in-use test components to ease the memory constraints of testing activities. Our approach, on the other hand, directly uses application code to detect failures.

Some researches improve the infrastructure to support testing. For example, testers may use emulators of wireless sensor networks [13,18] to selectively track whether their applications have executed as intended. These emulators simulate the hardware environments to facilitate the development and checking software applications.

The emulator approach is quite laborious since extensive prior profiling is required. An alternative is to use verification patterns [15] that implement test scenarios collectively as test templates so that different initializations of test scripts can share the same test infrastructure. There are approaches that propose some kind of conformance testing framework to test embedded software formally [14].

The effectiveness and tradeoffs of these approaches are, however, not examined. Although WSN applications are gaining popularity, their testing problems have not yet been adequately studied.

3   Metamorphic Approach

Metamorphic testing [7,8] was proposed as a property-based approach to alleviate the test oracle problem. It has been applied to unit testing as well as integration testing. These studies illustrate the notion of metamorphic testing via functional testing. Since our proposal is closely related to the notion, we review it in this section.

3.1   Concept

A test oracle is a mechanism to determine whether a test case has passed or failed. It is difficult to establish (automated) test oracles for some programs. Examples are software for optimal routing, shortest paths, and partial differential equations. This is known as the test oracle problem. Although human may serve as manual test oracles in some cases, it is costly and error-prone.

In such circumstances, metamorphic testing aims at selecting follow-up test cases based on source test cases, and check whether their results satisfy necessary conditions relating the expected solutions of the source and follow-up test cases. These necessary conditions are known as metamorphic relations [7,8].

3.2   Metamorphic Relation

Informally, a metamorphic relation consists of two components. The first relies on a relation, known as a source relation, which defines the relationship between source test cases, their outputs, and follow-up test cases. This effectively provides a specification for developers or test drivers to select follow-up test cases. The second component defines the relationship among the target functional outputs of the source test cases and follow-up test cases, and the test cases themselves. Such a metamorphic relation can be used to verify test results to alleviate the test oracle problem.

A metamorphic relation is vital to the application of metamorphic testing. We adapt the definition of metamorphic relation from [8] as follows:

> Let f be a target function and let P be its implementation. Intuitively, a metamorphic relation is a necessary condition over a series of inputs $x_1, x_2, \ldots, x_n$ and their corresponding results $f(x_1), f(x_2), \ldots, f(x_n)$ for multiple evaluations of f.

Definition 1 (Metamorphic Relation). [8] *Let $x_1, x_2, \ldots, x_k$, where $k \geq 1$, be a series of inputs to a function f and let $\langle f(x_1), f(x_2), \ldots, f(x_k) \rangle$ be the corresponding series of results. Suppose $\langle f(x_{i1}), f(x_{i2}), \ldots, f(x_{im}) \rangle$ is a subseries, possibly an empty subseries, of $\langle f(x_1), f(x_2), \ldots, f(x_k) \rangle$. Let $\langle x_{k+1}, x_{k+2}, \ldots, x_n \rangle$, where $n \geq k+1$, be another series of inputs to f and let $\langle f(x_{k+1}), f(x_{k+2}), \ldots, f(x_n) \rangle$ be the corresponding series of results. Suppose, further, that there exist relations $r(x_1, x_2, \ldots, x_k, f(x_{i1}), f(x_{i2}), \ldots, f(x_{im}), x_{k+1}, x_{k+2}, \ldots, x_n)$ and $r'(x_1, x_2, \ldots, x_n, f(x_1), f(x_2), \ldots, f(x_n))$ such that r' must be true whenever r is satisfied. We say that*

$$MR = \{ (x_1, x_2, \ldots, x_n, f(x_1), f(x_2), \ldots, f(x_n)) \,|$$
$$r(x_1, x_2, \ldots, x_k, f(x_{i1}), f(x_{i2}), \ldots, f(x_{im}), x_{k+1}, x_{k+2}, \ldots, x_n)$$
$$\rightarrow r'(x_1, x_2, \ldots, x_n, f(x_1), f(x_2), \ldots, f(x_n)) \}$$

is a metamorphic relation. When there is no ambiguity, we simply write the metamorphic relation as

$$MR: \text{ If } r(x_1, x_2, \ldots, x_k, f(x_{i1}), f(x_{i2}), \ldots, f(x_{im}), x_{k+1}, x_{k+2}, \ldots, x_n),$$
$$\text{then } r'(x_1, x_2, \ldots, x_n, f(x_1), f(x_2), \ldots, f(x_n)).$$

Furthermore, $x_1, x_2, \ldots, x_k$ are known as *source test cases* and $x_{k+1}, x_{k+2}, \ldots, x_n$ are known as *follow-up test cases*.

Consider an implementation of a hash function f, which computes the hashed values of input vectors $a_1, a_2, \ldots, a_m$. A necessary condition for its correctness is that the hashed values of the input elements of an input vector should not change even if we rearrange their positions in the input vector. In other words, given a correct implementation, the hash total of the outputs from a source input vector should be the same as that of the outputs from a permuted input vector.

Based on the above concept, a tester may first find a reliable permutation program π to rearrange input vectors. The tester then sets up a source relation $\langle b_1, b_2, \ldots, b_m \rangle = \pi(\langle a_1, a_2, \ldots, a_m \rangle)$ to select a follow-up test case $\langle b_1, b_2, \ldots, b_m \rangle$ from any source test case $\langle a_1, a_2, \ldots, a_m \rangle$. Thus, the tester can define a metamorphic relation for the hash function as follows:

MR_{hash}: If $\langle b_1, b_2, \ldots, b_m \rangle = \pi(\langle a_1, a_2, \ldots, a_m \rangle)$,

then $\sum_{i=1}^{k} f(\langle b_1, b_2, \ldots, b_m \rangle)[i] = \sum_{i=1}^{k} f(\langle a_1, a_2, \ldots, a_m \rangle)[i]$,

where $[i]$ refers to the i-th index of the array.

3.3 Metamorphic Testing

We also adapt the definition of metamorphic testing from [8] as follows:

This [metamorphic] relation must be satisfied when we replace f by P; otherwise P will not be a correct implementation of f.

Definition 2 (Metamorphic Testing). [8] *Let P be an implementation of a target function f. The* metamorphic testing *of metamorphic relation*

MR: *If* $r(x_1, x_2, \ldots, x_k, f(x_{i1}), f(x_{i2}), \ldots, f(x_{im}), x_{k+1}, x_{k+2}, \ldots, x_n)$,
then $r'(x_1, x_2, \ldots, x_n, f(x_1), f(x_2), \ldots, f(x_n))$.

involves the following steps: (1) *Given a series of source test cases* $\langle x_1, x_2, \ldots, x_k \rangle$ *and their respective results* $\langle P(x_1), P(x_2), \ldots, P(x_k) \rangle$, *select a series of follow-up test cases* $\langle x_{k+1}, x_{k+2}, \ldots, x_n \rangle$ *according to the relation* $r(x_1, x_2, \ldots, x_k, P(x_{i1}), P(x_{i2}), \ldots, P(x_{im})$, $x_{k+1}, x_{k+2}, \ldots, x_n)$ *over the implementation P.* (2) *Check the relation* $r'(x_1, x_2, \ldots, x_n,$ $P(x_1), P(x_2), \ldots, P(x_n))$ *over P. If r' is false, then the metamorphic testing of MR reveals a failure.*

Let us use the above hash function example for an illustration. Suppose the input vector $\langle 1, 2, 3 \rangle$ is hashed to $\langle -1234, 98, 36 \rangle$, and the input vector $\langle 3, 2, 1 \rangle$, constructed according to the implementation of the above source relation, is hashed to $\langle 36, 98, 1234 \rangle$ by the implementation under test. A test driver will then compute the sum of $-1234, 98$, and 36, which is -1100. It will also compute the sum of $36, 98$, and 1234, which is 1368. Since the two resultant values differ, the metamorphic relation is violated. The two test cases collaboratively reveal a failure.

4   Our Approach

In this section, we first clarify its relationship with metamorphic testing. Next, we discuss the software environment in which the notion of metamorphic testing can be adapted to reveal functional and non-functional problems of an application. Section 4.3 gives an example application scenario, and describes the types of fault. Finally, we shall illustrate the use of our approach to identify these faults in Section 4.4.

4.1   Relationship with Metamorphic Testing

Consider a program P under test that supposedly implements a target function f. Metamorphic testing, as reviewed in the last section, relies on the formulation of a necessary condition of f. It ignores the software environment of P. On the other hand, we observe that the deployment of P in different environments has substantial impacts on its non-functional properties. Putting P on a low-voltage platform, for example, may cause the power consumption to be different from that on a standard PC platform. We suggest that the software environment should also be taken into consideration for necessary conditions related to non-functional properties.

In addition, the generic notion of metamorphic testing needs to be enhanced to address at least the following two areas in the testing of WSN applications: (a) How to implement a metamorphic relation in wireless sensor networks? (b) Where to evaluate the test results, since most WSN nodes have very limited storage, memory, bandwidth, and so on?

In the rest of this section and Section 5, we shall investigate and elaborate on our proposal to address these concerns and beyond.

4.2   Software Environment

In this section, we present an overview of our test model of WSN software applications. A WSN is modeled as a set of nodes. We assume that one software component is deployed in each node.[4] Hence, one may refer to a software component by simply referring to a node. In the sequel, we shall use the terms "node" and "software component" interchangeably unless otherwise stated.

Each software component has its own function. We have studied a variety of third-party TinyOS [4] applications as well as the tutorial applications of TinyOS to come up with the following observation. We note that each software component will accept an input, complete the required processing, and output a result before accepting another input. Furthermore, in nesC applications, for instance, there are sub-components within a software component such that the output of one sub-component is piped to another sequentially. We maintain the concept of sequential programs in our model because typical sensor nodes have little resources, and concurrency models found in conventional operating systems are still poorly developed in, say, TinyOS and nesC [3]. Thus, a temperature sensor node may behave as follows: It obtains the

---

[4] It is not difficult to extend our model to allow more than one software component to be deployed in a node.

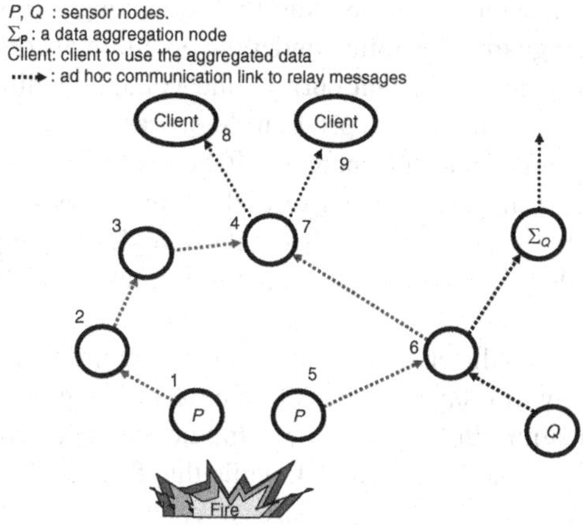

Fig. 1. Example scenario of software application of wireless sensor network, which monitors whether there is any wildfire

current and voltage readings from its temperature sensor and computes the value of the temperature. It then identifies its surrounding nodes and sends the computed value to a destination node such as a data aggregation node or a base station.

We assume the following network property based on the characteristic that nodes in a wireless sensor network are deployed in large scale for a particular application, such as temperature monitoring in a nontrivial area zone.

> Assumption: *Every node has at least one adjacent node whose software component performs the same function as the node itself.*

Since energy is a critical resource for WSN nodes, each node is equipped with a residual energy-level scan function. We model it as a *utility function* that returns the instant energy level of the node. Hence, a test driver may inquire about the energy level of a node before and after the execution of a software component in a software environment and determine the energy ϕ consumed by the execution of a test case. From this, software testers can track the energy spent on the execution of one test case in one particular node.

4.3   Example Software Application Scenario

We describe an example temperature monitoring application that aims to identify incidents of wildfire and forward alerts to the clients concerned. Figure 1 depicts a blueprint of the application.

Description of the software application.   A cluster of wireless sensor nodes is deployed in a fire control zone. Some of them, such as nodes 1 and 5, are deployed with the same software component P that computes the ambient temperature. These nodes determine a raw temperature reading as follows: The resistance of the conductor in a sensor normally varies with temperature, causing changes in current and voltage according to Ohm's Law plus or minus detailed practical deviations.

For the ease of discussion, let us assume that the change in resistance is directly proportional to the change in temperature under the operational conditions of the sensor nodes. Thus, by comparing the instant current and voltage readings from the sensors with those of reference temperatures, program logic can be implemented to estimate the present temperature from the current and voltage readings.

Suppose a wildfire breaks out near sensor nodes 1 and 5, as shown in Figure 1. The ambient temperature rises and, hence, triggers these nodes to gauge the environment. As described above, the software component P will interpret the current temperature based on the readings.

Each of the two nodes will send the computed temperature values to their respective adjacent nodes, which will relay the values to the data aggregation device, node 7, for further data summarization. In Figure 1, the computed temperature value from node 1 is forwarded to node 7 via nodes 2, 3, and 4, while that from node 5 is routed via nodes 6 and 7. (We note that nodes 4 and 7 are aliases of each other.)

Data aggregation is essential for wireless sensor networks [10]. It merges duplicated data from distinct sources to save energy in data transmission. This is mostly application-oriented. In other words, data consolidation criteria should have been implemented in WSN applications to cater for resource constraints. In our example, the data from nodes 1 and 5 are consolidated at node 7, so that clients at nodes 8 and 9 will receive a consolidated result.

Program. Embedded system developers frequently implement their software to meet resource-stringent constraints. They use application-specific heuristics to develop the program logic.

In the example application, the temperature sensors attached to nodes 1 and 5 have the following specific property: In certain temperature ranges, the current or voltage reading has a linear relationship with the temperature. See, for instance, the linear portions of the two sample plots in Figure 2. On the other hand, the temperature range applicable to the linear portion of the current-temperature plot may not overlap with the temperature range applicable to that of the voltage-temperature plot [1]. Furthermore, the relationship among temperature, current, and voltage may be non-linear and much more complex outside these temperature ranges.

Thus, when a program finds that it cannot determine the temperature value using a simple calculation based on the instant current reading, it will try to compute the temperature based on the instant voltage reading. When both approaches are not applicable, it will use a more sophisticated and computationally expensive formula. This three-way policy serves to save energy. There is also some environment-specific calibration in the program to initialize the temperature variable.

Consider the following annotated self-explanatory example code fragment of software component P to compute the temperature.[5]

---

[5] The data types of the variables are integers instead of floating point numbers, because floating-point calculation is expensive and seldom used in embedded system computations. For the ease of presentation, a current of "I mA" is written as "$10000 \times I$" in the sample code. The treatment of voltage V is similar. We also show numbers in the format of, say, "$53 - 48$" instead of "5", to enable readers to cross-reference with the example code fragment.

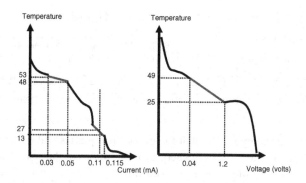

Fig. 2. Example plots of variations in temperature against variations in current (left) and voltage. (Not to scale.)

```
P (clb_I, clb_V: integer) { // environmental specific calibrations
                            // for current and voltage.
      V, I, T: integer;     // voltage, current, and temperature
      T = 300;              // environment-specific initialization
      ...
      V = sensor_channel1( );
      I = sensor_channel2( );
      ...
      if (I >= 300 and I <= 500)
s0:       T = 53 - (( I - 300 ) * (53 - 48)) / (500 - 300) + clb_I;
      else if (I >= 1100 and I <= 1150)
          // [Hard] Fault (a): The correct version should be:
          // T = 27 - (( I -  1100 ) * (27 - 13)) / (1150 - 1100) + clb_I;
s1:        T = 27 - (( I -  1150 ) * (53 - 48)) / (1150 - 1100) + clb_I;
          // [Soft] Fault (b): The "else" keyword is missing.
          // The correct version should be:
          // else if (V >= 400 and V < 12000) ...
      if (V >= 400 and V < 12000)
s2:       T = 49 - (( V - 400 ) * (49 - 25)) / (12000 - 400) + clb_V;
      else ...
          // the general and sophisticated approach to compute T.
          return T;
      }
```

In the code fragment above, clb_I and clb_V are the input parameters of the program *P*, denoting calibrations of voltage and current. Since the qualities of the hardware of different nodes may vary, these parameters are used to offset the differences.

Faults. Two faults occur in the above program. **Fault (a)** affects the correctness of the program. For instance, if clb_I is 0 and I is 1100, the faulty statement s1 will compute T to be 13 instead of the expected value of 27. **Fault (b)** will cause statement s2 to re-compute T (after being computed once by statement s0 or s1) if the voltage reading fulfills the guard condition. Suppose that each of statements s0, s1, and s2 consumes

Table 1. Example test cases, their test outputs, and MT results that indicate failures

Test case	At node	Temperature of environment	Input components of test case		Computed result of $P(0,0)$	Expected result of $P(0,0)$	Computed by	Metamorphic testing result that indicates failure
			Sensed I	Sensed V				
t_1	1	27	0.110 mA	–	13	27	$s1$	"MR_A: If $r(T_1, T_2)$, then $\approx_P(T_1, T_2)$" is
t_2	5	27	–	1.15 V	27	27	$s2$	violated because $13 \neq 27$.
t_3	1	49	0.047 mA	0.04 V	49	49	$s0, s2$	"MR_B: If $r(T_3, T_4) \wedge \approx_P(T_3, T_4)$, then $\phi_3 = \phi_4$"
t_4	5	49	0.060 mA	0.05 V	49	49	$s2$	is violated because $2\omega \neq \omega$.

the same amount of energy ω, and that the energy for queries and condition checking is negligible. Then, we have different energy consumptions of the sensor node although the functional correctness of the program is not affected. We should add that, in practice, the code is much more complex than the statements s0, s1, and s2 in the example.

To help readers follow our illustration, we note that many physical events have life cycles, in which an event initializes, occurs, evolves, and then fades out. Different sensors may simultaneously observe the same event at the same stage in their life cycles, probably with slight differences in reading, which will be used as input parameters to the WSN applications such as the example program above. For similar input parameters, if two executions of the same program consume excessively different amounts of energy, it may indicate an anomaly in the program.

4.4 An Illustration of Our Testing Approach

To adapt metamorphic testing to software applications on wireless sensor networks, testers should determine a source relation r and the encompassing metamorphic relation. In the sequel, we first illustrate them using the example application scenario. Next, we will describe how to use them to detect faults (a) and (b).

Source relation. The use of isotropic physical conditions as metamorphic relations has been proposed by Tse et al. [17]. For the testing of WSN applications, however, we need to determine how to obtain such physical conditions. Consider again our application scenario, where a wildfire sends heat to sensors nearby. As sensor nodes are typically deployed in a massive scale, readings sensed by adjacent nodes or nodes in proximity, such as nodes 1 and 5 in Figure 3, should be close enough to be considered equivalent. As we shall explain in the next paragraph, a sense of equivalence is determined by the application itself and we propose to use this important feature of WSN applications as the basis for metamorphic relations.

As shown in the column "Temperature of environment" in Table 1, for example, the temperatures at nodes 1 and 5 are equivalent during the first two scenarios (T_1 and T_2 as depicted in Figure 3), and again equivalent during the last two scenarios. Testers can control their test cases by controlling the location of the fire and the locations of the sensor nodes. In this way, nodes can be set up to monitor the same physical phenomenon. This source relation is represented by $r(T_1, T_2)$ above the dotted line linking nodes 1 and 5 in Figure 3.

Metamorphic relations. Two metamorphic relations are proposed:
Data aggregation is essential to software applications for wireless sensor networks [10]. As we have explained in Section 4.2, a major property of data aggregators is to eliminate

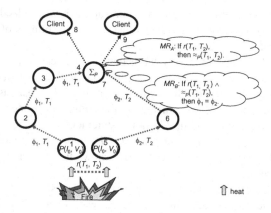

Fig. 3. Example metamorphic testing in wireless sensor network.

duplicated data. A data aggregator may have a data consolidation criterion $\approx_P()$ to determine whether two data sets resemble each other. In our example, since any two sensory inputs fulfilling the isotropic physical condition r should trigger the program under test to give "equivalent" estimated temperatures, the data consolidation criterion should decide whether two estimated temperatures are close enough to be treated as duplicated data. For the ease of illustration, we shall use simple identity as the data consolidation criterion for the equivalence of temperatures. The resulting metamorphic relation is as follows, and if a pair of test cases and their execution results do not satisfy MR_A, it indicates a functional failure.

$$MR_A:\text{ If } r(T_1, T_2), \text{ then } \approx_P (T_1, T_2).$$

Let us now consider non-functional testing. In the absence of a test oracle, we cannot isolate functionally passed test cases from failed ones. We resolve to make use of test cases that do not indicate functional failures in terms of metamorphic relations such as MR_A. Since equivalent temperature values are determined from the application-specific data consolidation criterion $\approx_P()$ based on an isotropic physical condition r, if they need non-equivalent amounts of power for computation, it should indicate a failure. We express this idea as a metamorphic relation.

$$MR_B:\text{ If } r(T_1, T_2) \text{ and } \approx_P (T_1, T_2), \text{ then } \phi_1 = \phi_2.$$

Testing. In defining the above metamorphic relations, we recommended to make use of the data consolidation criteria of data aggregation supplied by the application, together with the isotropic physical conditions of sensor nodes in close proximity. A sketch of the scheme is depicted in Figure 3.

We propose to place the task of test result evaluations in the data aggregator component of the application, because the data consolidation criteria constitute part of the logic of the data aggregator. This also relieves sensor nodes from having to evaluate the test results, which would deplete the batteries faster than the original plan of the application designers. Moreover, by utilizing the implementation provided by the application, any failure detected via our approach will indeed indicate a fault in the application. In the sequel, we shall illustrate the usefulness of our proposal in identifying such failures.

To identify a failure due to fault (a), let us consider test cases t_1 and t_2 in Table 1.[6] Suppose that the input current and voltage calibrations are both zero as indicated in the column captioned "Computed result of $P(0,0)$" in the table. Test case t_1 causes P to output 13 via the statement s1 (as indicated in the column captioned "Computed by") while test case t_2 cause P to output 27 via the statement s2. Since 13 and 27 are not equivalent, it violates the metamorphic relation MR_A and, hence, reveals a failure. The column captioned "Expected result of $P(0,0)$" shows the expected result of the test case for readers' reference.

To identify a failure due to fault (b), let us consider the test cases t_3 and t_4 in Table 1. Test case t_3 executes both statements s0 and s2, each of which suffices to give the correct result; however, the amount of energy consumed by the test case is 2ω. Test case t_4 executes statement s2 only and, hence, the energy consumed is ω. As a result, they consume different amounts of energy. According to MR_B, this indicates a failure related to the energy consumption of the temperature monitoring software application.

5   Discussions

In our model, we place the implementation of a metamorphic relation in a data aggregation node. There may be other alternatives. In general, one may deploy a piece of software to a resource-stringent existing node (or cluster), to an existing node (or cluster) with ample resources, or to a new node (or cluster). Our approach lies with the first option.

The second option further routes the data to a device with an ample amount of resources, such as the server or a client workstation. However, the data communication will consume a lot of energy. Sending all the test verdicts from a massive number of devices to a specific monitoring device may exhaust the batteries of the devices easily. It is, therefore, a less attractive approach.

One may suggest using simulations such as TOSSIM [13] for TinyOS applications, so that simulated batteries can be replenished easily for simulated data communications whenever necessary. However, simulators need profile settings in order to emulate various initial testing conditions. The effort to set up testing profiles to cover different test cases and the respective simulation results would be nontrivial.

The third option requires setting up a new device (or cluster) that may communicate with the existing wireless sensor network. Since existing devices would discover and communicate with the new device (or cluster), this may affect, say, the scheduling and routing of the existing network and, hence, the original configuration to be verified. Our proposal also suffers from a similar limitation, but intuitively to a lesser extent. The impact of these issues warrants further investigation.

Our current proposal does not support streaming data, and has not explored the potential of using other generic characteristics of WSN applications to define

---

[6] Source test cases can be generated randomly or via test case selection methods. Discussions on test case generation are beyond the scope of this paper.

metamorphic relations. We are identifying representative applications for case studies and further investigation.

6 Concluding Remarks

We share the view of other researchers that there is a mega-trend in computing that many computational units will be shifted to pervasive devices. Software applications running on top of wireless sensor networks are emerging. It is a fast changing field where a mature software development methodology is yet to be defined. This is particularly the case for the testing of such applications, which must be carefully conducted before deployment in real life. Our work is the first research attempt to adapt a testing technique to the wireless sensor network environment.

Unlike their counterparts in conventional computing, wireless sensor networks applications are subject to additional non-functional constraints (such as energy constraint) that may have critical impacts on the behaviors of the software. For example, a functionally correct execution can still be anomalous if it consumes an abnormal amount of energy. In this paper, we have studied the correctness issue in the presence of power-awareness concerns. We have investigated techniques to apply test cases and verify test results related to power-awareness in a WSN environment. In short, our testing technique has been strategically designed to blend in with the special features of the WSN environment.

A sensory node reports readings by gauging the environment. It is, therefore, intuitive to apply test cases in sensory nodes. However, these nodes are typically resource-stringent, such as being equipped with limited amounts of memory and battery power. Executing all the test activities in sensory nodes is impractical. This paper proposes to execute automated test result evaluations in data aggregation nodes instead. The power-aware transmissions of intermediate and final test data are supported directly by WSN programs. Since the data aggregation feature of WSN programs should be power-aware, it further makes our technique attractive.

Our technique takes advantages of such built-in functionality of data aggregation. We believe in the design rationale held by software engineers when they implement the data aggregation functionality onto WSN nodes in their applications. As such, we propose to use the data consolidation criteria of data aggregators to verify the test results of isotropic physical phenomena of WSN applications in nodes in close proximity to such data aggregation nodes. Since either the original application code or the built-in equality check of the programming language is used to implement metamorphic relations, any failure revealed should be due to a fault in the WSN application under test.

We use a temperature monitoring application scenario to illustrate how to formulate metamorphic relations based on the data consolidation criteria, and to tackle both functional faults and power-related faults. We have taken an initial step to extend the notion of metamorphic testing to deal with non-functional quality aspects. We have also discussed the limitations and alternative approaches in the paper. Future work includes the study of test case selection techniques, further optimization of oracle checks, and the debugging of software applications. We shall report such findings and conduct more empirical evaluations in the future.

Acknowledgment

We thank the anonymous reviewers for their invaluable advice to improve the paper.

References

1. FHSST physics electricity: nonlinear conduction. Wikibook. `http://en.wikibooks.org/wiki/FHSST_Physics_Electricity: Nonlinear_conduction`
2. JUnit. `http://www.junit.org`
3. nesC. `http://nescc.sourceforge.net`
4. TinyOS. `http://www.tinyOS.net`
5. Berstel, J., Reghizzi, S.C., Roussel, G., San Pietro, P.: A scalable formal method for design and automatic checking of user interfaces. ACM Transactions on Software Engineering and Methodology, 14(2), 124–167 (2005)
6. Binder, R.V.: Testing Object-Oriented Systems: Models, Patterns, and Tools. Addison Wesley, Reading, Massachusetts (2000)
7. Chan, F.T., Chen, T.Y., Cheung, S.C., Lau, M.F., Yiu, S.M.: Application of metamorphic testing in numerical analysis. In: Proceedings of the IASTED International Conference on Software Engineering (SE 1998), pp. 191–197. ACTA Press, Calgary, Canada (1998)
8. Chan, W.K., Chen, T.Y., Lu, H., Tse, T.H., Yau, S.S.: Integration testing of context-sensitive middleware-based applications: a metamorphic approach. International Journal of Software Engineering and Knowledge Engineering 16(5), 677–703 (2006)
9. Chen, T.Y., Huang, D.H., Tse, T.H., Zhou, Z.Q.: Case studies on the selection of useful relations in metamorphic testing. In: Proceedings of the 4th Ibero-American Symposium on Software Engineering and Knowledge Engineering (JIISIC 2004), pp. 569–583. Polytechnic University of Madrid, Madrid, Spain (2004)
10. Heidemann, J., Silva, F., Intanagonwiwat, C., Govindan, R., Estrin, D., Ganesan, D.: Building efficient wireless sensor networks with low-level naming. In: Proceedings of the 8th ACM Symposium on Operating Systems Principles (SOSP 2001), pp. 146–159. ACM Press, New York (2001)
11. Kandler, J.: Automated testing of embedded software. International Conference on Software Testing Analysis and Review (STAREAST 2000), Orlando, Florida (2000), Paper available at http://www.stickyminds.com/s.asp?F=S2049_ART_2
12. Kapfhammer, G.M., Soffa, M.L., Mosse, D.: Testing in resource constrained execution environments. In: Proceedings of the 20th IEEE/ACM international Conference on Automated Software Engineering (ASE 2005), pp. 418–422. ACM Press, New York (2005)
13. Levis, P., Lee, N., Welsh, M., Culler, D., TOSSIM,: TOSSIM: accurate and scalable simulation of entire TinyOS applications. In: Proceedings of the 1st ACM Conference on Embedded Networked Sensor Systems (SenSys 2003), ACM Press, New York (2001)
14. Sanvido, M.A.A., Cechticky, V., Schaufelberger, W.: Testing embedded control systems using hardware-in-the-loop simulation and temporal logic. In: Proceedings of the 15th IFAC World Congress on Automatic Control, Barcelona, Spain (2002)
15. Tsai, W.-T., Yu, L., Zhu, F., Paul, R.: Rapid embedded system testing using verification patterns. IEEE Software 22(4), 68–75 (2005)
16. Tse, T.H., Lau, F.C.M., Chan, W.K., Liu, P.C.K., Luk, C.K.F.: Testing object-oriented industrial software without precise oracles or results. Communications of the ACM (to appear)

17. Tse, T.H., Yau, S.S., Chan, W.K., Lu, H., Chen, T.Y.: Testing context-sensitive middleware-based software applications. In: Proceedings of the 28th Annual International Computer Software and Applications Conference (COMPSAC 2004), vol. 1, pp. 458–465. IEEE Computer Society Press, Los Alamitos, California (2004)

18. Werner-Allen, G., Swieskowski, P., Welsh, M.: MoteLab: a wireless sensor network testbed. In: Proceedings of the 4th International Conference on Information Processing in Sensor Networks (IPSN 2005), pp. 483–488. IEEE Computer Society Press, Los Alamitos, California (2005)

19. Xie, Q., Memon, A.: Designing and comparing automated test oracles for GUI-based software applications. ACM Transactions on Software Engineering and Methodology (to appear)

An Intermediate Representation Approach to Reducing Test Suites for Retargeted Compilers

Gyun Woo[1], Heung Seok Chae[1], and Hanil Jang[2]

[1] Dept. of CSE, Pusan National Univ., Busan 609-735, Republic of Korea
{hschae,woogyun}@pusan.ac.kr
[2] SureSoft Technologies Inc., Banpo, Seocho, Seoul, 137-808, Republic of Korea
hijang@suresofttech.com

Abstract. Reducing test suites is crucial for reducing the test cost, for the test cost is directly proportional to the size of test suites. Reducing the test cost is particularly important when we need to urgently develop a stable compiler for a newly developed processor. In this paper, we propose a framework to reduce test suites for retargeted compilers using intermediate representations of test input programs. We describe that redundancy of test cases at the level of source codes exists from the viewpoint of intermediate representation and, thus, testing efficiency can be improved by excluding those redundant test cases. We also conduct a case study with RTL where we found that test suite can be considerably reduced. In addition, we show that the fault detection capability can be maintained with the reduced test suites by means of mutation testing.

1 Introduction

Software testing is one of the most commonly used techniques for validating software quality [1]. Testing compilers is even more critical activity because defects of compilers directly result in incorrect codes of applications generated by them. Therefore, there are many works [2–11] addressing compiler testing.

Recently, embedded software has been widely used in our lives [12]. The main task of embedded software is to engage the physical world, interacting directly with sensors and actuators. Typically, such software must be extremely reliable. Even a simple failure of software can lead to a catastrophic consequences. Therefore, the quality of compiler for embedded systems is even more important.

In addition, retargetable compilers for embedded processors have received much interest recently. There are many needs of developing compilers for newly fabricated processors for embedded systems. By retargeting compilers, we can develop a new compiler for the processor by simply adapting some existing compilers instead of completely developing it from scratch. Therefore, retargeting compilers is an efficient approach to developing a new compiler.

In this paper, we propose a compiler testing approach based on intermediate representation of compilers, which is particularly efficient for testing retargeted compilers. The existing approaches to compiler testing are based on the source

N. Abdennahder, F. Kordon (Eds.): Ada-Europe 2007, LNCS 4498, pp. 100–113, 2007.

language. They are concerned with coverage criteria for determining testing adequacy and test case generation from the source language grammar. That is, the grammar of the source programming language is the basis of test case generation.

However, testing based on intermediate representation seems to be proper for testing retargeted compilers. The rationale for this approach are as follows. First, the machine code generated by a compiler directly depends on the intermediate code. Therefore, we have to perform a thorough testing with the intermediate code even though its source code was sufficiently tested. This is because some test cases adequate for source codes may not sufficiently cover test cases at the level of intermediate representation. That is, there may be some intermediate codes which are not covered by test cases in source language when they are generated without considering the intermediate language.

Second, it may happen that several test cases at the level of source code can be mapped to common test cases at the level of intermediate code. That is, some test cases at the level of source codes are redundant because they are already addressed by other test cases. Since applying a test case requires much effort such as determining the expected output, defining appropriate test data, and executing the test case, and finally evaluating the execution of the test case, it is highly desirable to minimize the size of test cases for reducing testing cost. In this respect, it is necessary to improve efficiency of test case generation approach by excluding redundant test cases.

Intermediate representation may be particularly important when compiler developers do not have enough time to adequately test the retargeted compiler. As the need of embedded processors continuously grows, there is also considerable need of rapid development of a stable compiler for the embedded processors. Moreover, it is usual to develop such retargeted compilers even within a limited time. In such case, our approach can be used as a guideline to selecting the more effective test cases for focusing on the back-ends of the retargeted compilers where actual modification mainly took place.

To improve existing compiler testing works, we propose a testing approach based on intermediate representation of programs. The final codes generated by compilers are the direct output from intermediate codes. We argue that the test cases should be based on the intermediate codes rather than on source codes, especially for the cases of retargeted compilers where the modifications during retargeting extensively take place at the back-ends of the compilers.

In this paper, we presents an efficient approach to compiler testing by excluding redundant test cases based on coverage at the level of intermediate representation. RTL [13] is used for intermediate representation and we give a detailed description on how to filter redundant test cases from the viewpoint of RTL. In addition, we have performed a case study with a C compiler. From the case study, we found that many redundant test cases can be generated according to existing compiler testing techniques and those techniques can be improved by adopting our intermediate representation based approach. We also applied mutation testing technique to show that the fault detection capability of the reduced test suite can be equivalent with that of the original ones.

The rest of the paper is organized as follows: Section 2 briefly describes compiler testing and RTL. Section 3 presents an efficient test case generation approach based on RTL. Section 4 describes the result of a case study. The related works and conclusion are given in Section 5 and 6, respectively.

2   Research Backgrounds

2.1   Compiler Testing

Testing is an activity performed for evaluating and improving software quality by identifying defects [1]. Software testing consists of the dynamic verification of the behavior of a program on a finite set of test cases, suitably selected from the usually infinite executions domain, against the expected behavior. The generation of test cases is the most important concern in software testing because the capability of testing mainly depends on the test cases. According to the information used for generating test cases, testing techniques are classified as white-box, also called glassbox, if the tests rely on information about how the software has been designed or coded, or as black-box if the test cases rely only on the specification given to the software. Since compiler is generally of very large scale and the generation of target code from source code is the only concern, black-box testing is more appropriate for compiler.

In compiler testing, a variety of source programs should be used as test data to examine if the compiler generates the correct target code. Actually, testing should consider infinite source programs. However, only a finite set of test cases, so called a test suite, are selected among them which is expected to locate the equivalent defects. That is, the efficiency of testing is also an important concern to perform testing with a reasonable effort.

The concept of testing coverage is generally accepted for defining testability and generating test cases in a systematic way. Since grammar of source language defines the structural organization of source programs, the grammar is the natural basis of test case generation. As a basic coverage for compiler testing, rule coverage means that a test suite exercises all rules of a grammar. That is, a test suite satisfies the rule coverage if there exists at least one test case for every rule of a grammar. Intuitively, rule coverage is the minimum criteria for evaluating compiler. That is, we should at least provide test suites where every rule is checked. It can be considered a minimal criteria for testing software [1, 7, 14].

2.2   RTL

RTL (Register Transfer Language) is an intermediate language adopted by GNU Compiler Collection (GCC). The syntax of RTL is similar to that of LISP, i.e. generalized list, and therefore, RTL is suitable for representing instruction patterns. The patterns in RTL are used in code generation phase and the RTL representation of a program is extensively transformed during optimization phases of GCC. Hence, understanding RTL is a crucial part when retargeting GCC to a whole new machine.

RTL is much closer to the target machine than the internal tree representation directly produced by the front-end of GCC. For instance, RTL deals with registers, as its name stands for, which are not generally dealt with in an intermediate language. However, the registers in RTL are not real, but pseudo-registers, which will be replaced by real registers during the register allocation phase. In fact, RTL can be still considered an intermediate language though it is closer to target machines.

An RTL program consists of several RTL expressions (RTX for short) which are doubly linked in sequence. Every RTX may contain several RTL objects and a kind of RTL objects, called expression code (RTX code), describe the machine operations. The machine operations recorded in a RTL program are called instruction patterns and the native machine code is generated by pattern-matching procedure utilizing these instruction patterns.

3   An Approach for Reducing the Number of Test Cases

In this section, we describe a framework to generate an efficient test suite for testing retargeted compilers. This framework utilizes the grammar rules for the intermediate language rather than those for the source language. This framework is based on the well-known concept of grammar coverage [6, 9–11], which will be briefly reviewed here.

3.1   Testing Retargeted Compilers

For compiler testing purpose, a *test suite* itself is a set of programs $T = \{p_1, p_2, \ldots, p_n\}$. It is mandatory that every program $p \in T$ should be well-formed according to the grammar, i.e. *syntactically correct*. Further, it is desirable to be *semantically correct*, i.e. for a semantic function of L, say an interpreter $[\![.]\!]_L$, and a valid input x, the test program $p \in T$ should produce a meaningful output $[\![p]\!]_L x$.

The compiler correctness can be defined in terms of semantic functions. Since a compiler $\mathcal{C}$ translates a program t in a source language L into a machine language M, $\mathcal{C}$ is said to be correct if $\forall p \in L : [\![\mathcal{C}[\![p]\!]]\!]_M = [\![p]\!]_L$ where $[\![.]\!]_M$ is a semantic function for the machine language M. In reality, the behavior of the semantic function $[\![.]\!]_M$ is determined by the operations of the target machine.

Considering all the valid programs is practically impossible. Hence, only a subset of the valid programs, called test suite, are generally considered. In this case, the compiler $\mathcal{C}$ is said to be *correct for a test suite* T if $\forall p \in T : [\![\mathcal{C}[\![p]\!]]\!]_M = [\![p]\!]_L$. Note that this is a functional equivalence meaning that the equality should be hold for all the valid input data.

When a retargeted compiler is being developed, the original compiler can be used as an oracle for testing the newly developed compiler. Strictly speaking, the semantic function should be used as an oracle for testing a compiler. But, the semantic function of a language is rarely defined and further, considering the life cycles of the newly developed embedded processors, it is practically impossible to use the semantic functions as an oracle. Therefore, the reference compiler is assumed to be sufficiently stable and will be used as an oracle in this framework.

Considering an reference compiler, the success of the test of a retargeted compiler can be defined in terms of this oracle compiler. A retargeted compiler $\mathcal{C}$ for M is said to be *correct for a test suite T w.r.t. a reference compiler $\mathcal{C}_{ref}$* if $\forall t \in T : [\![\mathcal{C}[\![t]\!]]\!]_{\text{M}} = [\![\mathcal{C}_{ref}[\![t]\!]]\!]_{\text{M}_{ref}}$. Note that the compiler $\mathcal{C}$ is a retargeted compiler from machine M_{ref} to machine M.

3.2 Grammar Coverage Concepts

Now, let's consider the grammar coverage. A grammar is a formal definition to describe the set of well-formed programs. A grammar consists of a set of rules which will be used to generate well-formed programs. This generation steps are called *derivation*. If a grammar rule is used for generating a program, it is called *covered* with the program. Therefore, considering the test suite which covers all the grammar rules seems to be the least requirement for testing a compiler.

Harm and Lämmel extensively discussed the grammar coverage [4, 6]. They defined the coverage criteria and studied grammar conversion to reduce the number of rules to facilitate the testing the grammar itself. Based on their discussion, some definitions are developed addressing the grammar coverage. This paper particularly considers both of the source grammar and the intermediate language grammar.

Definition 1. *For a grammar G and a program $p \in L(G)$, the covered rules $R_G(p)$ is a set of productions used for generating p. The function R_G can be naturally extended for a set of programs T: $R_G(T) = \cup_{p \in T} R_G(p)$.*

Using coverage concept, the adequacy of a test suite can be defined. A test suite T is said to be *adequate* according to a grammar G if the set of covered rules by T is same to the set of all the productions of G. A test suite should be adequate according to the grammar of the source language. But, generating an adequate test suite blindly can make the number of the generated test cases explode. Hence, it is important to generate an efficient test suite without losing the adequacy.

3.3 Grammar Coverage Considering Intermediate Language

An intermediate representation (IR), or an intermediate code, is the result of the front-end of a compiler. Originally, IR concept is introduced to enhance the portability of an existing compiler. Nowadays, IR takes an important role for optimizing compilers because a lot of optimization phases are implemented on top of IR. Owing to this trend, an intermediate language (IL) is commonly defined for a nontrivial compiler.

For the ease of explanation, let's consider the front-end function $\mathcal{F}_\mathcal{C}$ of a compiler $\mathcal{C}$. For a given source program $p \in L$, $\mathcal{F}_\mathcal{C}$ generates an IR p' written in the intermediate language I: $\mathcal{F}_\mathcal{C}[\![p]\!] = p' \in I$.

Introduced the intermediate language I, the grammar G' for I can also be defined. And, the coverage definition can be extended to G'. Though a source program is not written in I, the covered rules of G' can be considered, too. Given a front-end $\mathcal{F}_C$, the grammar G' for an IL, and a source program p, the *covered rules* $R_{G'}(p)$ is a set of productions used for generating $\mathcal{F}_C[\![p]\!]$. We assume that the function $R_{G'}$ can be extended for a set of programs T: $R_{G'}(T) = \cup_{p \in T} R_{G'}(p)$.

Our goal is to find a smaller test suite without losing the IL grammar coverage. The comparison of the sizes of test suites can be defined in terms of grammar coverage. A test suite T_1 is *smaller than* T_2 *w.r.t. the source grammar* G if the covered rules of the test suites are same $(R_G(T_1) = R_G(T_2))$ but the size of T_1 is smaller than T_2 $(|T_1| < |T_2|)$, i.e. the number of test cases of T_1 is lesser than T_2[1]. Further, T_1 is *smaller than* T_2 *w.r.t. the IL grammar* G' if the covered rules of the test suites are same $(R_{G'}(T_1) = R_{G'}(T_2))$ but $|T_1| < |T_2|$.

The basic idea of this research is that we can find a *smaller* test set when we additionally considers the intermediate representation of a compiler. The main issue of grammar-covering test approach is to find a test suite which covers the productions of the source language grammar. However, the source program is somewhat far from the target program which actually determines the semantics of the program. Hence, it seems reasonable to determine the test set according to the intermediate language rather than the source language. This fact is especially important when retargeting a compiler because, during retargeting, only the back-end is modified.

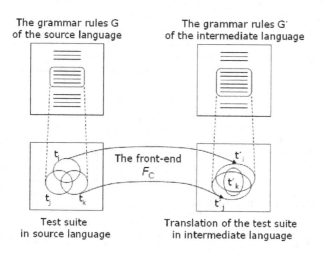

Fig. 1. The grammar coverage based on either G or G'

---

[1] Here, we assumed that the LOC's of the test cases are similar; hence, take the number of test cases of a test suite to the *size* of the test suite. However, if the LOC's vary in a large range, we can take the sum of LOC's of the test cases to the *size* of the test suite.

Fig. 1 illustrates the relationship between the grammar coverage based on the source language and the one based on the intermediate language. Each rectangle in the upper part indicates the set of grammar rules in G and G', respectively, where the line in the rectangle represents one production rule of the grammar.

According to the grammar coverage, a set of test cases (i.e., test programs) are generated from the grammar. In Fig. 1, there are three test programs, t_i, t_j, and t_k, which are generated from the grammar G of the source language. We can obtain the test programs t_i', t_j', and t_k' in intermediate language by applying front-end translation to t_i, t_j, and t_k. As seen from the figure, the test case t_k' is already covered by the union of the other two test cases t_i' and t_j'. This suggests that we can generate a reduced test suite by excluding such a test case as t_k' from the test suite.

3.4   RTL-Based Test Case Generating Framework

In this section, we describe the test case generation framework to support the test case generation based on the intermediate representation. Particularly RTL is chosen as an intermediate language because GCC is one of the popular compilers for retargeting [15]. The overall framework of this scheme is depicted in Fig. 2. We have implemented two tools, Test Case Generator and Test Case Filter, that provide major functions to reduce test suites based on the RTL.

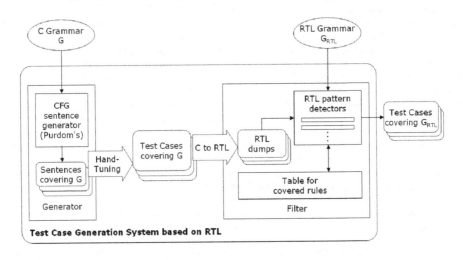

Fig. 2. The framework for RTL-based test case generation

 – **Test Case Generator.** The tool for generating the C programs as test cases according to the C grammar G. The original test programs are generated according to the grammar rules of C to cover the whole production rules of the grammar G.

Test Case Generator is implemented using a slightly modified Purdom's Algorithm. The Purdom's Algorithm cannot be directly applicable since it was devised to generate *one* big program to cover all the grammar rules. One big program is inadequate for debugging purpose since it is not helpful to locate compiler defects. Note that some of these test cases are redundant with respect to the RTL grammar rules.

The original test suites generated by the Test Case Generator are hand-tuned codes, for the sentence generated by the Purdom's algorithm are not well-formed. The reason for that is static semantics. Purdom's algorithm only considers the grammar rules but, to generate well-formed programs, the static semantics should be further considered. We used Purdom's algorithm to make the test cases covering the source grammar and tuned them by hand to reflect the static semantics without losing the covered rules.

- **Test Case Filter**. The tool for selecting the test cases according to the grammar rule of RTL G_{RTL}. The Test Case Generator module blindly generates the test cases without considering the RTL grammar.

Test Case Filter consists of a set of pattern detectors and a central table shared by these detectors. Each pattern detector is a program which analyzes the RTX code for a test case and determines whether the RTX code uses a certain RTL grammar or not. If it finds some RTL rules that are covered by the current test case, it looks up the central table to determine if some part of the rules has not been covered yet. In that case, the Filter passes the test case without filtering and the detector records the newly covered rules in the central table. Using this approach we can reduce the test suite with respect to the rule coverage of the RTL. The Test Case Filter assures that every test program which is not filtered should cover at least one new grammar rule of the RTL.

Implementing Test Case Filter, we tried to find the optimal coverage over RTL from the set of test cases. However, it turns out that the optimal coverage problem is a special case of finding minimum cover from the subsets of a set, which is NP-complete [16]. Hence, a simple sequential algorithm is used for Test Case Filter. It is highly expected that this sequential algorithm can be improved by making graph structures between the RTL sentences and the RTL patterns, yet this remains as future research.

4   Empirical Study

In this section, we describe a case study where a reduced test suites is generated from an original test suites based on the intermediate representation. Our case study is based on the retargeted GCC compiler and its RTL representation is considered. In addition, we also describe the result of mutation testing to show that the reduced test suites has still the similar fault detection capability to the original test suites.

4.1   Test Suites Reduction

To explore the effectiveness of our approach, we have conducted a case study using the test suite generation framework discussed in Section 3.4.

Initially, we generated a set of test cases using the Test Case Generator. Since the initial test suites can contain invalid C programs [17], we manually augment them so that they can be used as inputs to the Test Case Filter. We used GCC version 3.3.5 to transform hand-tuned test cases into RTL code. The Test Case Filter was fully implemented and used to exclude some redundant test cases from the viewpoint of RTL grammar coverage.

Well-defined grammars are needed to construct the Test Case Generator and the Test Case Filter. For Test Case Generator, the Standard C grammar of ISO: 9899 [18] is used. For Test Case Filter, we have constructed an RTL grammar from scratch since we could not find an appropriate one. The GCC documentation was much helpful for this grammar construction procedure. Leroy reported an RTL grammar [19] but it is too abstract to use for this filter.

The experimental result is summarized in Table 1. From the Test Case Generator following some augmentation, 91 C programs were generated that can cover all the Standard C grammar rules. And, from these 91 C programs, the Test Case Filter filtered 76 C programs whose corresponding RTL codes can be covered by some other test cases. According to the experimental result, 83.5% of the test cases are filtered out from the initially generated test cases. This means that only 16.5% of C programs that fully cover the source grammar rules are enough to cover the RTL rules.

Table 1. The RTL-Covering Test Suite is smaller than the C-Covering Test Suite without losing the rule-covering range

	Test Cases	LOC
C-Covering Test Suite	91	610
RTL-Covering Test Suite	15	101
Reduction	16.5%	16.6%

To verify the back-end of retargeted compiler, it is crucial that the test cases should cover all the RTL grammar rules. However, we discovered that some RTL rules are never covered even by the test cases that can fully cover C grammar rules. This indicates that source grammar based test case generation may not be sufficient to test the retargeted compiler since the back-end is extensively modified and RTL is the input to the back-end.

4.2   Fault Detection Capability

In this section we compare the reduced test suites with the original ones in terms of fault detection capability. That is, we describe the result of an experiment to show that the reduced test suites can detect as many faults as the original test suites.

Mutation testing, originally proposed by DeMillo et al. [20] and Hamlet [21], is a fault-based testing technique that can be used to measure the effectiveness of test cases, finally that of test case generation techniques. In mutation testing, simple faults are intentionally injected into the program by creating a set of faulty versions, called mutants. These mutants are created from the original program by applying mutation operators, which describe syntactic changes to the original program.

Each mutant is executed with test cases, expecting that it will produce an output different from the original program. When a mutant produces a different output, the mutant is said to be killed; otherwise it is a live mutant. A test suite that leads to the more killed mutants is considered to be effective since the test suite can find more faults in the program. Therefore, we can investigate the fault detection capability of two test suites by comparing the number of killed mutants.

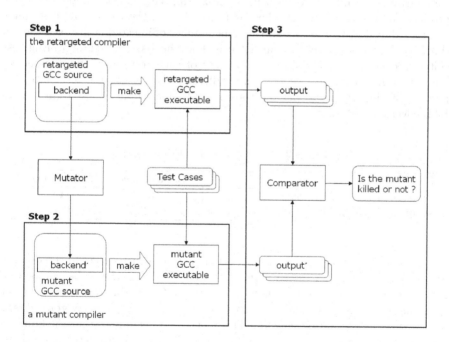

Fig. 3. Mutation analysis for comparing fault detection capability

To examine the fault detection capability of the test suites, a number of mutant compilers are generated. Since our framework is for testing retargeted compilers, only the back-end is changed for mutation testing. The overall procedure for this mutation test is depicted in Fig. 3. Firstly, the retargeted compiler is built (Step 1). This compiler will be used as a reference compiler. And then,

Mutator alters the back-end of the reference compiler to generate a number of mutant compilers (Step 2). Finally, every test case of the test suite is processed by the reference compiler and a mutant compiler to produce the result to be compared by Comparator (Step 3). Comparator compares the assembly output of the compilers to determine whether the mutant should be killed or not.

We adopted a weak mutation method [22] in implementing Mutator. Specifically, the mutation operator used is the replacement of a 'variable reference', which is suggested by Howden [23] as one of five basic types of program components. The mutants are generated by changing the *operand* variables in RTX-functions; The number of mutants generated is 573. Each mutant has exactly one faulty RTX-function which also contains exactly one fault.

Inserting multiple faults for each RTX-function is also possible. This is a kind of strong mutation approach. But it is hardly practical because a strong mutation will produce a tremendous amount of mutant compilers (over $40,000^2$).

We have performed this mutation test with the original C-covering test suites and then with the reduced RTL-covering test suites. The experimental result is summarized in Table 2. As seen in Table 2, Applying two kinds of test suites produce the same number of killed mutants; that is, the C-covering test suites and its reduced test suites detect the same number of injected faults even though the C-covering test suites is much more than the reduced RTL-covering test suites (see Figure 1). Considering the sizes of each test suite, the numbers of killed mutants per test case are quite different. For C-covering test suite, the number of killed mutants per test case is 0.14 which is much less than that of RTL-covering test suite.

Table 2. The number of killed mutants

Test Suite	C-Covering	RTL-Covering
Number of Killed Mutants	13	13
Number of Killed Mutants per Test Case	0.14	0.87

For some killed mutants, the numbers of test cases which detect injected faults are shown in Table 3. Here we only presented the cases where the numbers of test cases are different. Notice that the number of C-covering test cases is bigger than that of RTL-covering cases. Note also that some mutants, say gen_addsi3 or gen_cmpsi3, are more easily killed than others. This implies that the faults in these mutants are easier to detect than others; in other words these operations, adding single-precision integers or comparing single-precision integers, are more frequently used than other operations.

5   Related Works

There are several works concerning compiler testing. Recently, major testing methods and test case generation approaches were surveyed in [2, 3]. Boujarwah

Table 3. The number of test cases which detect the defect of each killed mutant. Only the cases where the numbers are different are shown.

	The Number of C-Covering Test Cases	The Number of RTL-Covering Test Cases
gen_addsi3	13	8
gen_cmpsi3	5	1
gen_divmodsi3	2	1
gen_movsi	91	15
gen_split_936	2	1

and Saleh compared various compiler testing techniques with respect to some selected criteria including type of grammar, data definition coverage, syntax coverage and semantic coverage [2]. Kossatchev and Posypkin described compiler testing methods for generating, running, and checking the quality of compiler test suites based on formal specification of programming language syntax and semantics [3].

Several authors described grammar-based approaches to the testing of the implementation of language syntax and static semantics [4–6]. They proposed coverage criteria for attribute grammars and coverage oriented test case generation strategies. Zelenov et. al presented approach based on grammar transformation for testing compilers and other formal text processors [8]. Kalinov et. al proposed compiler testing approaches based on Abstract State Machine [9–11]. In addition to syntax, their approaches also mentioned test case generation from semantics of a grammar which is defined in Montages [24]. They proposed several coverage criteria based on the syntax and semantics of mpC language. In addition, several works addressed the problem of the implementation of an oracle for compiler testing [25–27].

All the testing approaches mentioned above are based on some grammar of source programming language. However, our approach focuses on testing the back-end of compiler which is the target of the modification when retargeting compilers for embedded processors. By generating test cases from the intermediate representation, we can construct an efficient test suite which can directly address the back-end of compilers.

Recently, Hennessy and Power proposed an approach to generating minimal test suites for grammar-based software [28]. They applied a test suite reduction algorithm originally proposed by Jones et al. [29] in order to reduce test suites on the basis of rule coverage. Like other works mentioned above, their approach is based only on the grammar of a source language.

6 Conclusion and Future Work

Since defects in a compiler directly lead to incorrect target code developed with the use of the compiler, testing should be performed to reveal hidden defects in the compiler. In black-box techniques, many compiler testing approaches consider the grammar of source language for the basis of test case generation; that is, testing coverage criteria is defined on the basis of the grammar of source language.

We have proposed an approach to compiler testing based on intermediate representation, which supports more efficient generation of test cases. Our test suite only include the set of test cases which can cover different cases at the level of intermediate representation. The proposed approach becomes more important for testing retargeted compilers, where the back-end is extensively modified according to a specified processor without change in the front-end. Through the case study, we showed that the size of test suites can be significantly reduced while maintaining the fault detection capability. Although RTL is considered for intermediate representation, our approach can be straightforwardly extended to other intermediate representations.

We plan to support automation of the proposed approach. By now, some of tasks in the approach are performed manually. By automating the whole approach, we will enhance its applicability. The proposed approach will be extended to support other intermediate representation such as SUIF [30]. In addition, we will propose coverage criteria based on intermediate representation. We believe that adequate and efficient test case generation is possible using coverage criteria based on intermediate representation not on source language.

References

1. Beizer, B.: Software Testing Techniques. John Wiley & Sons, Inc, New York (1990)
2. Boujarwah, A., Saleh, K.: Compiler test case generation methods: a survey and assessment. Information and Software Technology 39, 617–625 (1997)
3. Kossatchev, A., Posypkin, M.: Survey of compiler testing methods. Programming and Computer Software 31, 10–19 (2005)
4. Harm, J., Lämmel, R.: Two-dimensional approximation coverage. Informatica (Slovenia), vol. 24 (2000)
5. Hannan, J., Pfenning, F.: Compiler verification in LF. In: Scedrov, A. (ed.) Proceedings of the Seventh Annual IEEE Symposium on Logic in Computer Science, pp. 407–418. IEEE Computer Society Press, Los Alamitos (1992)
6. Lämmel, R.: Grammar Testing. In: Hussmann, H. (ed.) ETAPS 2001 and FASE 2001. LNCS, vol. 2029, pp. 201–216. Springer, Heidelberg (2001)
7. Gargantini, A., Riccobene, E.: ASM-based testing: Coverage criteria and automatic test sequence. JUCS: Journal of Universal Computer Science, vol. 7 (2001)
8. Zelenov, S.V., Zelenova, S.A., Kossatchev, A., Petrenko, A.: Test generation for compilers and other formal text processors. Programming and Computer Software 29, 104–111 (2003)
9. Kalinov, A., Kossatchev, A., Posypkin, M., Shishkov, V.: Using ASM specification for automatic test suite generation for mpC parallel programming language compiler (2002)
10. Kalinov, A., Kossatchev, A., Petrenko, A., Posypkin, M., Shishkov, V.: Coverage-driven automated compiler test suite generation. Electr. Notes Theor. Comput. Sci. vol. 82 (2003)

11. Kalinov, A., Kossatchev, A., Petrenko, A., Posypkin, M., Shishkov, V.: Using asm specifications for compiler testing (2003)
12. Lee, E.A.: What's ahead for embedded software? IEEE Computer 33, 18–26 (2000)
13. Stallman, R.M.: Using and porting the GNU compiler collection (2001)
14. Miller, K.W.: A modest proposal for software testing. IEEE Softw. 18, 98–100 (2001)
15. Leupers, R., Marwedel, P.: Retargetable compiler technology for embedded systems: tools and applications, Norwell, MA, USA. Kluwer Academic Publishers, Dordrecht (2001)
16. Garey, M.R., Johnson, D.S.: Computer and Intractability: A Guide to the Theory of NP-Completeness, vol. New York. W.H.Freeman and Company, New York (1979)
17. Malloy, B.A., Power, J.F.: An interpretation of purdom's algorithm for automatic generation of test cases. In: Proceedings of 1st Annual International Conference on Computer and Information Science (2001)
18. ISO/IEC: Programming languages–c. ISO/IEC international standard 9899:1990 (e) (1990)
19. Bertot, Y., Grégoire, B., Leroy, X.: A structured approach to proving compiler optimizations based on dataflow analysis. In: Filliâtre, J.-C., Paulin-Mohring, C., Werner, B. (eds.) TYPES 2004. LNCS, vol. 3839, pp. 66–81. Springer, Heidelberg (2006)
20. DeMillo, R.A., Lipton, R., Sayward, F.: Hints on test data selection: Help for the practicing programmer. IEEE Computer 11, 34–41 (1978)
21. Hamlet, R.G.: Testing programs with the aid of a compiler. IEEE Trans. Software Eng. 3, 279–290 (1977)
22. Offutt, A.J., Lee, S.D.: An empirical evaluation of weak mutation. IEEE Transactions on Software Engineering 20, 337–344 (1994)
23. Howden, W.E.: Weak mutation testing and completeness of test sets. IEEE Transactions on Software Engineering SE-8, 371–379 (1982)
24. Kutter, P.W., Pierantonio, A.: Montages specifications of realistic programming languages. JUCS: Journal of Universal Computer Science 3, 416 (1997)
25. Jaramillo, C., Gupta, R., Soffa, M.L.: Comparison checking: An approach to avoid debugging of optimized code. In: ESEC / SIGSOFT FSE, pp. 268–284 (1999)
26. Necula, G.C.: Translation validation for an optimizing compiler. ACM SIGPLAN Notices 35, 83–94 (2000)
27. McNerney, T.S.: Verifying the correctness of compiler transformations on basic blocks using abstract interpretation. SIGPLAN Notices 26, 106–115 (1991)
28. Hennessy, M., Power, J.F.: An analysis of rule coverage as a criterion in generating minimal test suites for grammar-based software. In: ASE '05: Proceedings of the 20th IEEE/ACM international Conference on Automated software engineering, pp. 104–113. ACM Press, New York (2005)
29. Jones, J.A., Harrold, M.J.: Test-suite reduction and prioritization for modified condition/decision coverage. IEEE Trans. Softw. Eng. 29, 195–209 (2003)
30. Wilson, R.P., French, R.S., Wilson, C.S., Amarasinghe, S.P., Anderson, J.A.M., Tjiang, S.W.K., Liao, S.W., Tseng, C.W., Hall, M.W., Lam, M.S., Hennessy, J.L.: SUIF: An infrastructure for research on parallelizing and optimizing compilers. SIGPLAN Notices 29, 31–37 (1994)

Correctness by Construction for High-Integrity Real-Time Systems: A Metamodel-Driven Approach

Matteo Bordin[1] and Tullio Vardanega[2]

Department of Pure and Applied Mathematics,
University of Padua,
via Trieste 63, 35121 Padova, Italy
{[1]mbordin,[2]tullio.vardanega}@math.unipd.it

Abstract. Current trends in software engineering promote the contention that the use of model-driven approaches should prove as beneficial to high-integrity systems as they have to business applications. Unfortunately, model-driven approaches as they presently stand focus more on attaining greater extents of automation than on warranting absolute end-to-end correctness for the target development process. This paper presents some elements of a novel approach that centres on a correctness-by-construction philosophy rooted on a domain-specific metamodel designed to formally define and constrain the design space and prove the allowable model transformations down to automated code generation.

Keywords: Model-Driven Architecture, Metamodelling, Correctness by construction, Ravenscar Profile.

1 Introduction

In recent years, model-driven development has arisen as one of the main innovation vectors in engineering. In the software arena in particular, model-driven engineering has taken *de facto* the name of the OMG Model-driven Architecture (MDA) initiative. Model-driven architecture aims to represent the matters of interest (the "system") using a precise formalism and to facilitate its realization by means of a set of automatic transformations. The system is formalized as a model, which is the designer's representation of a particular aspect of a concrete reality: it is expressed by, and thus conforms to, a precise language, which is its *metamodel*. To some extent, a metamodel is for a model what a grammar is for a programming language.

The main advantages of a model-drive approach are: (i) the separation of platform-neutral aspects from platform dependent implementation; (ii) the precise definition of aspects of interest viewed at different levels of abstraction; and (iii) the possibility to express rules that drive transformations across models.

The model-driven architecture approach leverages a considerable extent of automation to attain a more efficient development process. A model is usually designed at a higher and platform-independent abstraction level and it is automatically transformed into a model that targets a specific execution platform, some computational model, some

N. Abdennahder, F. Kordon (Eds.): Ada-Europe 2007, LNCS 4498, pp. 114–127, 2007.

middleware, and so forth. This transformation is thus said to produce a platform-specific model (PSM) from a platform-independent model (PIM).

Model-driven approaches often regard correctness as a consequence of a highly automated development process: a verified transformation or code generation engine is supposed to produce a correct output. We contend that this view is at best naïve, for models and even more so metamodels can themselves be a very powerful tool indeed to enforce and warrant correctness *before* model transformation. The aim of this paper is to show how a model (or better still a metamodel)-driven approach can be coupled with the principles of the correctness-by-construction paradigm to define a process designed for the correct and fully automated production of software artifacts.

1.1 The Correctness by Construction Approach

Correctness by construction (C/C) is a software engineering practice championed among others by Praxis High-Integrity Systems [1]. The primary goal of C/C is to develop a safer, cheaper and more reliable system by easing the early detection and removal of development errors. In practice, this ambitious goal is attained by the combined application of six different strategies [1]:

1. Use of formal and precise tools and notations for any product of the development cycle, it being a design document or a piece of source code.
2. Use of tool support to validate the product of each step: since formal tools have been used to develop every artifact (cf. point 1), it is possible to constructively reason on their correctness.
3. Divide the development in smaller steps to defeat error persistence: products of every step must be verified against their formal specification as soon as possible.
4. Say things only once, to avoid any contradictions and repetitions.
5. Design software that is easy to validate, for example using safer language subset or explicit coding and design patterns
6. Do the hard things first: this includes thorough requirement analysis and the development of early prototypes.

1.2 Domain-Specific Metamodelling

Domain-specific metamodelling, along with the definition of domain specific languages, joins in the path of Language Oriented Development (LOP, [4]). The goal of LOP is to develop highly-specialized problem-oriented languages specialized to express domain-specific semantics. Domain specific languages are an easy and attractive means to increase design abstraction, for they promote an intentional (declarative) specification of a software system, shifting the burden of the imperative implementation to tools like code generator engines and compilers. The typical example of a domain-specific language is SQL; in contrast, the most common domain-specific metamodels are UML profiles.

A domain-specific metamodel is somewhat similar to a DSL, as it also is a language tailored for a precise domain of interest. However, a model entity is defined along with its own semantics, whereas a grammar literal has no intrinsic meaning. A metamodel is usually designed using object-oriented tools: elements of a metamodel are then *metaclasses*, which can be thus reused and specialized to suit particular domain-specific needs.

The approach we propose revolves around the development of a domain-specific metamodel precise enough to constrain the design freedom to a set of finite and well defined choices that are expressed declaratively in a platform-independent model. A platform-specific model that contains the imperative specification of the system can then be generated by automatic model transformation. A constrained and formal design space coupled with the high degree of automation typical of model-driven approaches should then guarantee a development process that truly enforces correctness by construction.

1.3   The Overall Picture

The work described in this paper is only a little part of a complex tool infrastructure developed within the ASSERT project (cf. the Acknowledgments section at the bottom of this paper). The ultimate goal of the project is to develop an integrated model-driven development environment capable of addressing functional and non-functional requirements, attributes and properties of high-integrity real-time systems, while providing automated, model-based schedulability and sensitivity analysis [7]. The functional behavior of the system is designed using the reuse-oriented approach described in [5], while the approach taken to automate model-based schedulability and sensitivity analysis is the subject of separate publications. Round-trip engineering is implemented by directly feeding the result of timing analysis back into the model: in this manner, the design can be tuned according to the predicted performance of the system. This paper focuses on the metamodel and model transformations that lay at the heart of both the design environment and the envisioned development process. The overall design environment is due for release as an Eclipse plug-in by the end of Q1 2007.

2   Metamodelling Geared to Correctness by Construction

Employing the correctness by construction paradigm via a metamodel requires a precise and formal specification of the "legal" design space, both in terms of allowed semantics and abstraction levels.

The envisioned metamodel has two distinct abstraction levels [9]: *application level* (AP-level) and *virtual machine level* (VM-level). Design entities living at AP-level resemble UML components and take the name of AP-level containers: they publish services through a cohesive provided interface. The sequential operational behaviour of individual provided interface is defined by means of classes and state charts; the concurrent semantics attached to the invocation of provided interfaces is expressed declaratively instead of imperatively: the specification defines *what* the concurrent behaviour attached to an invocation is meant to be, but not *how* it is realized, leaving the burden of realizing the full imperative specification of it to lower abstraction levels. AP-level containers are platform independent, because they neither specify their execution platform nor the computational model they rely upon.

Entities living at VM level are instead called VM-level containers: they are run-time entities that express an intended concurrent semantics. The term "virtual machine" indicates an execution platform that warrants and actively preserves the expected run-time behaviour for legal containers. VM-level containers are platform specific, because they clearly relate to a target computational model and to specific run-time semantics. Every AP-level container requires one or more VM-level container to realize its declared semantics on the chosen target platform/computational model. The transformation of AP-level containers to VM-level containers represents, in MDA terms, the transition from a platform independent model to a platform specific one.

Given the domain of interest, a metamodel-driven enforcement of the correctness by construction paradigm follows these steps:

1. We choose a computational model that we trust to guarantee static analyzability in the space and time dimensions. The design space (the metamodel) for VM-level containers is then constrained to only and exclusively employ entities that abide by the chosen computational model.

2. We define a language to design AP-level containers using a mathematical formalization. Since AP-level containers must be transformed to VM-level ones, we constrain this language to use semantics that provably and constructively implies the creation of "legal" VM-level containers only. The metamodel then becomes an emanation of the chosen language: in this manner the design freedom is limited to legal choices only. Deriving a metamodel from a mathematical notation guarantees that the metamodel is formal, precise and without any inconsistencies or ambiguities.

3. We formally specify a deterministic transformation that translates an AP-level container to a set of interconnected VM-level containers. The correctness of the transformation is proven using the language defined at item 2 above. Since the creation of VM-level containers can be completely automated, there is nothing to be gained in letting the designer handle the low-level, platform-specific representation of the system: the only available design space thus is the one populated by AP-level containers.

2.1 Choosing a Computational Model

Step 1. above is taken care of by adopting the Ravenscar Computational Model. The Ravenscar Computational Model is a theoretical abstraction of the well-known profile for the Ada programming language [8], which renders a concurrent architecture amenable to static analysis and allows for a highly efficient, reliable and certifiable implementation of the underlying kernel. As our metamodel is a direct emanation of the Ravenscar Computational Model, we nicknamed it RCM.

VM-level containers are then Ravenscar compliant *a priori* because they are expressly defined with this particular computational model in mind. VM-level containers represent the basic building blocks (in fact, the genuine archetypes) for the construction of real-time systems the way we envisage it.

VM-level containers come into four flavours[1]:

- *Cyclic VM-level containers*, which represent the semantics of a periodic execution. Each such container includes a periodic Thread that responds to a single, clock-generated activation event.
- *Sporadic VM-level containers*, which are similar in nature to cyclic containers but whose threads are released in response to a single software-generated event with a guaranteed (and preserved) minimum inter-arrival time.
- *Protected VM-level containers*, which are monitor-like structures providing for concurrent read access (read-lock) and/or mutually-exclusive write access (write-lock) to shared data. Protected VM-level containers use the immediate priority ceiling protocol [11] to guarantee a deadlock-free execution.
- *Passive VM-level containers*, which are simple wrappers of functional code and state with no access protection facilities.

2.2 An Algebra for AP-Level Containers

Services of AP-level containers are described by use of an algebraic approach [9]: services are then elements of a well-defined space and the connection between them is formalized as a set of relations and operators. The formalization of the description of RCM provided services as algebraic elements allows us to attain a high level mathematical abstraction especially useful to:

- provide a formal language to declaratively express the functional and concurrent semantics of a service
- prove that the metamodel implementation is as expressive and constraining as the formalized theory.

We name the algebraic notation for services of AP-level containers *RCM grammar*.

An RCM service is a channel interposed between a caller and a callee and it is defined as a point in the space defined by:

$$s \in (P \times S \times W \times V)$$

P is the service profile, which includes: its computational cost (*C*); its parameter profile ($\varnothing$| *in* | *out* | *inout*) and the affected state (*State*). The state affected by a service is the set of static variable accessed during its execution.

S is the synchronization protocol, which specifies whether the service provides a controlled access to the container's data. A synchronization protocol may be void ($\varnothing$), horizontal or vertical. A horizontal protocol is valued h_r or h_w depending on whether it is to provide for read-lock or write-lock protection respectively. The protocol is said to be vertical (*v*) when it is meant to model conditional synchronization, in which case it must also specify the Boolean guard (*G*) that is to govern the synchronization condition.

W is the concurrent weight of an invocation. A concurrent weight equal to 0 identifies an immediate call, while a value of 1 characterizes deferred invocations, which are services executed by a Thread of control operating on behalf of the callee. As the number of Threads in an RCM system is statically fixed, it will typically be the case that any single Thread should operate as the designated executor of multiple

---

[1] Readers aware of HRT-HOOD [10], will certainly be able to tell where we come from.

deferred invocations. To address this issue we stipulate that an RCM Thread might execute either a nominal or an alternate operation out of a statically defined range of alternatives, depending on whether the activation event delivered by the deferred invocation was tagged as either nominal or modifier. It is up to the designer to decide whether the effect of a modifier invocation on the operation of the target Thread should be permanent (as it would be in case of a mode change) or just one off. To represent this particular semantics, deferred invocations (W=1) are sub-typed: value 1_c denotes a clock-generated nominal activation event; value 1_t denotes a software-generated nominal activation event; value 1_v denotes a modifier activation event intended to deflect from a given nominal operation. For this reason, any deferred invocation must be specified to be part of a given enumeration denoted ε that specifies which deferred invocations should be targeted to one and the same Thread of control within the container. Any such enumeration ε must include a single nominal invocation (W = 1_c | 1_t), and may include any number of modifier invocations. In a way, a modifier models the effect of a deferred asynchronous transfer of control (ATC) without incurring the intrinsic nondeterminism of "pure" ATC [8].

A deferred invocation is also characterized by a deadline (D) and a period (T). The deadline stipulates the latest completion time allowable for the execution of the deferred operation. The period specifies the minimum separation time that must elapse between any two subsequent releases.

Finally, V specifies the visibility of the service, which in its simplest form, may be public (pu) to all containers or restricted (pr) if it is visible to a limited set of containers only.

Not every point in the (P S W V) space denotes a legal service in RCM: for example, the realization of a deferred service requires a non-void synchronization protocol. The legal combinations may thus be expressed in terms of the following literals:

$$\text{Unprotected} = \{P=\{*, C, \{\text{State} \mid \quad\}\}, S=\{\quad, \quad\}, W=0, V=*\} \tag{1}$$

$$\text{Protected} = \{P=\{*, C, \{\text{State}\}\}, S=\{h_r \mid h_w, \quad\}, W=0, V=*\} \tag{2}$$

$$\text{Entry} = \{P=\{*, C, \{\text{State}\}\}, S=\{v, G\}, W=1_c \mid 1_t, V=pr\} \tag{3}$$

$$\text{CER} = \{P=\{\quad, C, \{\text{State}\}\}, S=\{h_w, G\}, W=\{1_c, D, P, \varepsilon\}, V=pr\} \tag{4}$$

$$\text{START} = \{P=\{\quad, C, \{\text{State}\}\}, S=\{h_w, G\}, W=\{1_t, D, P, \varepsilon\}, V=*\} \tag{5}$$

$$\text{Modifier} = \{P=\{\quad, C, \{\text{State}\}\}, S=\{h_w, \quad|G\}, W=\{1_v, D, P, \varepsilon\}, V=*\} \tag{6}$$

Literal (1) identifies an immediate service with any parameter profile, any visibility and void synchronization protocol.

Literal (2) identifies an immediate service with any parameter profile and any visibility, which provides a (read or write) protected access.

Literal (3) identifies an entry invocation conditioned to the value of a Boolean guard G. The entry has a non-null concurrent weight (thus it is deferred) because the opening of the conditioning guard results in the release of a Thread inside the container. The entry service interface has a visibility restricted to internals of the providing container's only on account of the Ravenscar profile constraint that requires not more than a Thread to wait at a closed entry [8].

- Literal (4) identifies a cyclic deferred operation: CER stands for Cyclic Execution Request. It is not visible to any container and it cannot have any parameter because it is invoked by the system clock (via the execution platform). Since CER is a nominal activation it also is attached to a unique ε. The CER literal provides a controlled access (h_w) for the invocation must be allowed to modify the guard G that conditions the entry.
- Literal (5) identifies a sporadic deferred activation. Since START denotes a nominal activation it is attached to a unique ε. Similarly to CER, it requires a controlled access since its invocation must be allowed to modify the guard G that conditions the entry.
- Literal (6) identifies a modifier: its ε value must be the same as that of a nominal activation included in provided interface of the container. It is worth noting that a modifier can only affect the guard G that conditions the activation event for sporadic Threads.

A further constraint applies across all legal combinations of grammar values: literals that present a non-void synchronization protocol cannot share any state with literals that do not protect access to it. The wisdom of such a constraint should be obvious to the reader: the presence of a synchronization protocol to protect a state is vain if another service can modify that state in an unprotected way.

2.3 Mapping AP-Level Containers

To date we already developed a prototype tool to describe Ravenscar-compliant services and we thus arguably demonstrated the feasibility of the RCM-grammar based approach to the specification of container interfaces. It still remains to be seen whether the expected degree of semantic accuracy and formalization can be drawn from the realization of a domain-specific metamodel. We contend that this is a key prerequisite to showing that the correctness by construction paradigm can effectively be enforced through a metamodel-driven process.

In developing the RCM metamodel, we deliberately opted for the development of a stand-alone metamodel instead of relying on the UML profiling mechanism. Our choice guarantees that the design space can be modelled exactly the way it is described by the RCM grammar. An important drawback of our choice however is that we cannot rely on any existing UML development tool as a design environment for RCM: however, the number of productive software frameworks to develop design environment based on a domain-specific metamodel is rapidly increasing (hopefully along with their quality); consider for example the Graphical Modeling Framework (GMF, cf. www.eclipse.org/gmf/)

Since AP-level containers represent the sole design entities availed to the user, here we discuss their metamodel implementation only.

In RCM, the functional aspect of a service is represented by a class method: its operational profile and computational cost are then implicit in its specification. The state affected by an operation is a subset of the members (Property) of the owning class: to map this semantics, an instance of the metaclass Operation is connected to a set of Property belonging to the owning class (cf. figure 1). The proposed approach presents a clear difference with UML: the RCM metamodel forces the designer to be precise and formal and represents the whole semantics as a set of interconnected model elements that can be analyzed and subject to transformation in full automation. An AP-level container aggregates several classes to provide its services: it publishes their methods through a cohesive *provided interface*. Each method is published through a port, which represents a distinct interaction point between a container and the surrounding environment [13].

The concurrent semantics of a service is specified in its port by setting the *"kind"* attribute to a given set of enumeration values. The chosen value for the *kind* attribute of a port determines the VM-level containers required to represent the AP-level container in terms of run-time implementation entities abiding by the Ravenscar Computational Model. It is then necessary to avoid any inconsistency or conflict with the chosen concurrency model: Ravenscar compliance must be guaranteed at all time during the design of the model (*a priori*), and not by a separate verification process (*a posteriori*).

The only allowable values for the *kind* attribute are then *"CER"*, *"START"*, *"Modifier"*, and *"Protected"*, and *"Unprotected"*. It is important to note that it is not possible to define a port that publishes a service and has *kind* equal to *"Entry"*. The reasons for this restriction are manifold. Firstly, the Entry literal must always be present if a CER or START literal is present too: we maintain it would be an error-prone and useless repetition to force the designer to explicitly say something that is implicit in her actions. Secondly, a Barrier literal must be private to a single Thread

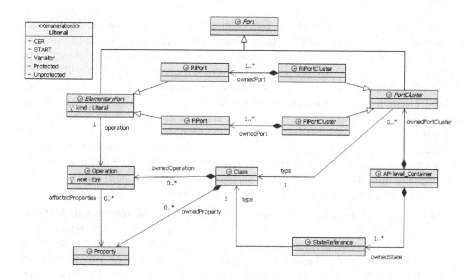

Fig. 1. RCM metamodel: the figure represents a simplified vision of the metamodel implementation. Since in RCM a port can provide or require a single service, the Port metaclass is subtyped in PiPort (providing a service) and RiPort (requiring a service). Ports publishing methods of the same class are grouped in subtypes of PortCluster. The functional states embedded in an AP-level container are called StateRefence and are characterized by a type specifying their inner structure and the services to access them. Diagram designed with the TOPCASED Ecore editor (cf. www.topcased.org).

only, which is the one behind the associated CER of START literal: letting the designer decide if and when to put a Barrier can only incur the risk of inconsistencies.

In setting the *kind* value, another constraint must be contemplated: the metamodel implementation includes on-line checks to avoid that an operation attached to a port marked as Unprotected may share its state with an operation provided by a port with a *kind* value equal to CER, START, Modifier or Protected.

In designing AP-level containers, the correctness by construction paradigm is then not only supported but actively enforced by avoiding any useless repetition of implicit or necessary design decisions and by constraining the designer to dodge erroneous models a priori.

The implemented metamodel is a direct representation of the algebraic formalization of services for AP-level containers: RCM presents a design space that enforces formal precision in describing a model and constrains the designer to use Ravenscar compliant semantics only. The design environment dynamically changes the allowed design freedom in response to the designer choices: for example, if a port is marked as Unprotected, then ports providing services affecting the same state can be marked as Unprotected only. Correctness by construction is then achieved mainly by constructively limiting the design freedom to a finite and formalized set of choices inevitably ending in easy to verify semantics.

3 RCM Model Transformations

The last step to achieve correctness by construction is to automate the development process to the maximum possible extent. Transformations can be applied if and only if the model is complete in every detail: it doesn't make sense to progress the development forward if any previous steps were not completed yet. In addition, the highly constrained design space allowed by RCM permits to know in advance which are the possible legal combinations of model elements input to a transformation: under this condition, the realization of the transformation is considerably easier. Compared to usual model-driven approaches, the proposed process focuses on the use of a formal notation (the RCM grammar for us) to prove the correctness of the applied transformations. In our vision, a transformation is said to be correct if and only if it preserves the intended design semantics across every individual step.

Three transformations have been implemented in support to the RCM metamodel:

- A *vertical* transformation generating a set of interconnected VM-level containers from a model made up of interconnected AP-level containers: its implementation permits to design a system independently of the target technology and relieves the designer of the burden of coping with the intricacies of the concurrency model employed on the target. The transformation is implemented using the Atlas Transformation Language (ATL, cf. www.eclipse.org/m2m/atl/).

- A *horizontal* transformation working on the classes that enclose the sequential functional behaviour of the system. The horizontal transformation automatically decomposes classes in a cohesive set of methods all sharing the same and only functional state. Also this transformation is implemented with ATL.

- A *code generation* targeting (at present) Ada 2005 limited to the Ravenscar profile ratified in the language standard [15]. The chosen execution platform is the Open Ravenscar Kernel (ORK) developed at the Technical University of Madrid [14]. The mapping is based on the definition of a set of archetypes implementing VM-level containers on a Ravenscar-compliant platform. While the complete approach will be the subject of a future publication, its driving ideas can be found in [6]. Code generation is implemented with MOFscript (cf. www.eclipse.org/gmt/mofscript).

The vertical and horizontal transformations are model-to-model transformations that use one and the same underlying metamodel: their correctness can then be formally proved using the RCM grammar and showing that the semantics is preserved across every transformation step. Unfortunately, it is not possible to use a formal tool to prove the correctness of the code generation logic because there is no single underlying metamodel between the source and the target of the transformation. The only viable option is then to relate the intended semantics to the language standard.

As a simple demonstration of the use of the RCM grammar, we illustrate the following example. Consider a START and a Protected public literals that share the *same* functional state; the model is represented by the following grammar phrase:

$$\text{START}_{\{\text{State = S, V= pu }\}}; \text{Protected}_{\{\text{State = S, V = pu}\}}$$

It is important to note that, since the state is accessed by at least two different threads (the one behind the START literal and the client(s) of the Protected service), the overall functional state must be protected against concurrent invocations. The vertical transformation provides then for the generation of two VM-level containers: a sporadic one that derives from by the START literal, and a protected one. The latter provides the original public Protected service and an additional Protected restricted

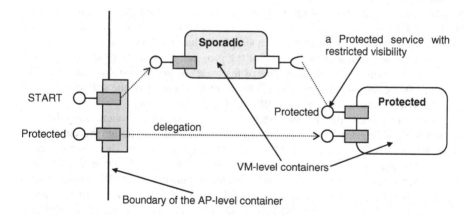

Fig. 2. A graphical representation of the grammar production used as an example (expressed with UML2-like graphical syntax). The functional state is embedded in the protected VM-level container and accessed by the sporadic VM-level container through a Protected service with restricted visibility. The services of the AP-level container are delegated to the VM-level containers accordingly with the declared concurrent semantics.

(in terms of visibility) service used by the sporadic VM-level container to access the shared functional state. The sporadic VM-level container exhibits then a required interface towards the restricted Protected service of the protected VM-level container. The grammar production is then the following:

$$\text{START}_{\{\text{State} = \text{S}, \text{V}= \text{pu}\}}; \text{Protected}_{\{\text{State} = \text{S}, \text{V} = \text{pu}\}} ::= \\ (\text{START}_{\{\text{State} = \text{S}, \text{V}= \text{pu}\}}); (\text{Protected}_{\{\text{State} = \text{S}, \text{V} = \text{pu}\}}; \text{Protected}_{\{\text{State} = \text{S}, \text{V} = \text{pr}\}})$$

plus a connection between the required interface of the START service and the provided restricted Protected service, which can also be expressed with the RCM grammar (not shown here): figure 2 is a graphical representation of the grammar production. This simple example shows how apt the RCM grammar may be to formalize, prove and analyze the transformation from AP to VM –level containers.

4 Current Results

The metamodel, transformations and code generation engine discussed in this paper have been tested in the development of a test case application covering a subset of an on-board software system, in particular some basic elements of the telemetry and telecommand communication system for a satellite. The application targeted ORK [14] running on the Leon-2 processor (cf. www.gaisler.com). Our comparison was finalized with the help of the main industrial partner of the ASSERT project (see the Acknowledgements section at the end of the paper). While the developed application was comparatively simple, the process suggested by the use of the RCM metamodel has proved to be quite effective and flexible, especially when compared to traditional design methodologies as HRT-HOOD [10]. Thanks to the restricted and formalized design space, the developer designs a Ravenscar-compliant system from the very beginning, but without being even aware of it. In the same way, automatic model transformations greatly speed up the development: if we compare this aspect with the HRT-HOOD approach, we may observe that all architectural (de)composition is automatically performed starting from a simple declarative specification.

We performed an initial assessment of the pros and cons of the proposed approach in the development of the aforementioned test case. In the analysis we addressed two axes: (1) the development time; and (2) the industrial quality of the software product; in comparison to using a traditional HRT-HOOD based process.

The time required to develop the concurrent architecture of the system using the RCM metamodel and the related tools is comparable to what it takes to design the same system using the top-level elements of an HRT-HOOD design hierarchy. There is a saving on our side however, for we need *not* design the inner structure of the system architecture, which we produce automatically by model-to-model transformations. We may thus argue that the gain from using our approach is then directly proportional to the system complexity, without any perceivable loss in the expressive power availed to the designer. In the long term, the seamless encapsulation of the sequential behaviour inside object-oriented constructs (classes) will guarantee a higher degree of reuse and adaptation of existing models: this is a step forward in respect to HRT-HOOD, since the method presents an evident overlapping of functional and non-functional specification in the design space. The reuse possibilities are increased even further thanks to the use of a declarative specification of concurrent behaviour: reuse of the same functional model with different concurrent semantics requires virtually no effort, mainly thanks to the vertical transformations. In our process the modeling of the sequential functional behaviour uses state machines and a high-level action language [5]. In our current experience those techniques are effective enough to describe systems which do not completely rely on low-level, highly-optimized algorithmic code (like CPU-intensive computations), but may require quite some element of hand coding and verification otherwise. An interesting asset of our process is that it provides for fully automatic code generation for the concurrent view of the model. Since the correctness of the transformation may be proved *a priori* and Ravenscar compliance permits automatic *model-based* static analysis [16], we then gain from not having to perform any further verification of the timing behaviour of the system: this feature has proven to be of interest for the industrial partners in the project. Finally, RCM models are more scalable than those designed with HRT-HOOD, thanks to the transition from an object-centric design space to a class-centric one: the RCM metamodel allows to design several instances of the same entity (AP-level container), each one with its own characteristics (as real-time attributes).

As for the industrial quality of the product, we have observed that the executable code that we currently produce is larger in size than current standards: we suspect that this downside may be due to the overhead of some memory-intensive object-oriented constructs (for example virtual tables) and to possibly excessive reliance on Ada generic packages in the generation strategy (The memory footprint of macro-expanded generic packages tends of course to grow linearly with the number of instantiations). However, the quality of the generated code has proven to be comparable to industrial standards: object-orientation doesn't prevent the designed application from being analyzable for timing constraints, as the design space and transformations avoid all the possible inconsistency related with the literal use of object-oriented semantics.

Overall we must admit that some difficulties and hurdles still remain to be addressed. First of all, the allowed decomposition level is too shallow and thus inadequate for complex applications: we are confident that this issue may be fixed with the next release of the metamodel and related development tools. Furthermore, while a design space changing in response to designer's actions works great and can effectively enforce correctness by construction, it does require quite a sophisticated tool support to be put to practice. Finally, the internal process of the tool infrastructure is quite muddled as it required a complex integration of different tools (transformation and code generation engines, timing analysis tools, etc) in a single design environment.

5   Conclusions and Future Work

One of the main lessons we learned from the experiment at this point in the project is that a metamodel-driven development process can be a very effective conduit to the correctness by construction paradigm that we seek to follow. In this paper we argued that, starting from an algebraic and hence formal representation of the design space, we can derive a metamodel that is as restricted and semantically characterized as the formal notation. The design space does not only prevent the user from venturing into illegal concurrent semantics[2], but it also "completes" the designer's specification, provably with no semantic distortion, in all parts that are disallowed to the direct expression of the designer, by leveraging on built-in knowledge of all legal transformations that can apply to a specification. In this manner, the design freedom allowed to the user is limited to a finite and well defined perimeter at every stage of the specification process.

The definition and implementation of model transformations turn the reliance on a rather cryptic formal notation to the user's benefit: they can in fact be defined using a high-level tool and developed knowing in advance all of the allowable combinations of model elements. The definition of a stand-alone metamodel opposed to a UML profile was a winning choice: the overall transformation process is truly simplified by the use of a design language directly mapping domain specific semantics. Moreover, the inclusion of an additional abstraction level (represented by VM-level containers) placed between the designed model and the generated code helps in keeping the code generator simpler and to imagine an easier transition process to alternative target platforms. In contrast with the OMG guideline for Model-Driven Architecture, the intermediate abstraction level is *not* in the editable design space: there is then no need to keep it synchronized with the higher abstraction model, avoiding one of the biggest hassles (especially for tool implementers) of "pure" MDA.

Current work focuses mainly on strengthening the current tool support infrastructure, in particular functional modelling, and on the extension of the formal notation and metamodel to encompass logical and physical distribution.

Acknowledgments. The research work from which this work has originated was carried out in part in the ASSERT project (IST-FP6-2004 004033) partially funded by the European Commission as part of the 6th Framework Programme. The views presented in this report are however those of the authors' only and do not necessarily engage those of the other members of the ASSERT Consortium.

The development of the RCM metamodel and related tools is the result of the collective effort of several people. The authors of this paper gratefully acknowledge: Daniela Cancila, Marco Panunzio and Marco Trevisan (at the University of Padua, Italy) for their valuable contributions respectively to the RCM grammar, the timing analysis and the RCM metamodel; Alessandro Pasetti and Ondrej Rohlik (at the Swiss Federal Institute of Technology Zurich) as the leading party on sequential modeling; Mathieu Le-Coroller and Gerald Garcia (at Alcatel-Alenia Space) for their help in the practical evaluation of the proposed approach; Stefano Puri (at Intecs) for his work in developing the design environment.

References

1. Chapman, R.: Correctness by construction: a manifesto for high integrity software. In: Proceedings of the 10th Australian workshop on Safety critical Systems and Software - Vol. 55 Sydney, Australia
2. Czarnecki, K., Eisenecker, U.W.: Generative programming: Methods, Tools and Applications. Addison-Wesley, Reading (2000)

---

[2] Illegal to the Ravenscar Computational Model, of course.

3. OMG : MDA Guide Version 1.0.1, available at www.omg.org/mda
4. Ward, M.: Language Oriented Programming. Software - Concepts and Tools 15, 147–161 (1994)
5. Cechticky, V., Egli, M., Pasetti, A., Rohlik, O., Vardanega, T.: A UML2 Profile for Reusable and Verifiable Software Components for Real-Time Applications. In: Morisio, M., et al. (ed.) ICSR 2006. LNCS, vol. 4039, pp. 312–325. Springer, Heidelberg (2006)
6. Bordin, M., Vardanega, T.: Automated Model-based Generation of Ravenscar-compliant Source Code. Proceedings of the 17th Euromicro Conference on Real-Time Systems, July 2005, pp. 69–77. IEEE Computer Society Press, Los Alamitos (2005)
7. Bini, E., Di Natale, M., Buttazzo, G.: Sensitivity Analysis for Fixed-Priority Real-Time Systems. In: Proceedings of the 18th Euromicro Conference on Real-Time Systems, Dresden, Germany (July 2006)
8. Burns, A., Dobbing, B., Vardanega, T.: Guide for the Use of the Ada Ravenscar Profile in High Integrity Systems. Technical Report YCS-2003-348, University of York (UK) (2003) Approved as ISO/IEC JTC1/SC22 TR 42718
9. Vardanega, T.: A Property-Preserving Reuse-Geared Approach to Model-Driven Development. The 12th IEEE International Conference on Embedded and Real-Time Computing Systems and Applications. (invited paper), IEEE, pp. 223–230 (August 2006)
10. Burns, A., Wellings, A.: HRT-HOOD: A Structured Design Method for Hard Real-Time Ada Systems. Elsevier, Amsterdam (1995)
11. Sha, L., Rajkumar, R., Lehoczky, J.P.: Real-time synchronization protocol for multiprocessors. In: Proceedings of the IEEE Real-time Systems Symposium (1988)
12. Raistrick, C., Francis, P., Wright, J., Carter, C., Wilkie, I.: Model-driven architecture with executable UML. Cambridge University Press, Cambridge (2004)
13. OMG: Unified Modeling Language: Superstrucutre – version 2.0.
14. The Open Ravenscar Kernel, cf. http://polaris.dit.upm.es/õrk/
15. Annotated Ada Reference Manual. ISO/IEC 8652:2007(E)
16. Panunzio, M., Vardanega, T.: A Metamodel-driven Process Featuring Advanced Model-Based Timing Analysis. In: Abdennahder, N., Kordon, F. (eds.) Ada-Europe 2007. LNCS, vol. 4498, pp. 128–141. Springer, Heidelberg (2007)

A Metamodel-Driven Process Featuring Advanced Model-Based Timing Analysis

Marco Panunzio and Tullio Vardanega

Department of Pure and Applied Mathematics
University of Padua, Italy
via Trieste 63, 35121 Padova, Italy
{panunzio,tullio.vardanega}@math.unipd.it

Abstract. In the development of high-integrity real-time systems it is arguably paramount that the engineering process should allow the designer to focus attention on all aspects of interest in a manner that warrants methodological correctness and some controlled form of separation of concerns. Model-driven engineering approaches strive to attain separation between concerns that are either independent or dependent of the platform. They however provide scarce support if any at all for round-trip engineering, which is a crucial asset for high-integrity real-time systems, where functional modelling can only be confirmed by proving feasible in the space and time domain. In this paper we discuss some elements of a development process based on a rigorous metamodel definition and on advanced model transformation techniques, which permits the execution of timing analysis *directly* on the system model.

1   Introduction

1.1   Metamodels and Domain Specific Metamodeling

In recent year model-driven engineering is a system development practice that has been gaining increasing reputation across industry at large. In particular, the Model-Driven Architecture (MDA) initiative promoted by the Object Management Group (OMG) [1] has caught the attention of important industrial leaders. The chief intent of the MDA approach is to permit systems to be described as *models* that are abstractions of the product under development. In the definition of the system model the designer may progressively focus attention on the matters of true importance at any particular stage of development and abstract away from the rest. In practice, the MDA approach promotes a strong separation between those aspects that are intrinsically *independent* of the implementation platform, which are described in a Platform Independent Model (PIM), and those that are *determined* by the implementation platform, which are addressed in possibly multiple Platform Specific Models (PSM).

The idea that underlies the MDA approach is to provide an architectural framework in which the designer may specify their model and which permits agile and *automated* transformations from PIM to PSM.

The description that the model provides about the system must conform to a specific formal language: the *metamodel*, which specifies the semantic rules that underlay the

N. Abdennahder, F. Kordon (Eds.): Ada-Europe 2007, LNCS 4498, pp. 128–141, 2007.

definition of the entities that may populate the model. A *domain-specific* metamodel then is a formal language designed for the specification of model entities in a particular domain of interest. From a given domain-specific metamodel one may derive conforming models capable of expressing:

1. concepts and notions that are specific to that domain.
2. attributes, properties and relations that characterise entities that may exist in the domain.
3. constraints on the nature of model entities and on the relations among them that emanate from the domain.

1.2   The Overall Process

This paper covers only a modest yet important segment of a composite and innovative process that the EC-funded ASSERT project is presently defining for the development of high-integrity real-time system (cf. the Acknowledgement section at the bottom of this paper). In the project vision the overall process shall be supported by a cohesive tool environment that:

- provides the designer with a modelling space which separates out PIM issues from PSM concerns while actively preserving consistency and coherence between all of the relevant views.
- limits the designer's freedom to legal choices only by virtue of the semantic rules fixed by the metamodel and actively policed the tool environment.
- permits the designer to perform static timing analysis of the model at PIM level relying on the automated production of the PSM view(s) that must be subject to analysis as well as on their back-propagation to the source PIM view.
- caters for fully automated code generation for the entirety of the system directly from the PIM level via the appropriate PSM transformations.

The PIM view primarily focuses on the functional description of the system. For the specification of this view the project adopts the reuse-oriented component-based approach discussed in [2]. In contrast, the semantic space currently allowed by our metamodel for the PSM view is mapped to the computational model that emanates from the Ada Ravenscar Profile [3]. We name that semantic space "Ravenscar Computational Model" (RCM for short). As a consequence of this choice the primary and most natural target for the automated code generation engine is the Ada Ravenscar Profile supported by Ada 2005 [4], while another candidate target that we are investigating is some Ravenscar-like profile of the Real-Time Specification for Java (RTSJ) (e.g.: [5]). The general strategy that the project employs for the automated code generation targeted to Ravenscar Ada is outlined in [6]. A more thorough description and critical assessment of it will be the subject of a separate future publication.

The use of the RCM coupled with a code generation strategy which abides by the coding restrictions typically enforced for high-integrity software (e.g., no recursion; unbounded loop allowed exclusively to permit a thread structure to issue jobs with the desired timely behaviour; ...) guarantees that models designed in compliance with it are by definition amenable to static timing analysis, which is a crucial asset to our

PSM, and yet expressive enough to address the increasing complexity of systems in our target domains (space and aerospace, chiefly). Another distinct bonus to be gained from the choice is that RCM platforms may be realized by small, simple and efficient real-time kernels, which is attractive both for performance reasons and in regard of any prospective route to product certification. To date, implementations of the RCM exist in the incarnations of: ORK by the Technical University of Madrid (Spain) [7] and ObjectAda/Raven by Aonix [8] in the Ada domain; Aonix PERC Raven [9] and Ravenscar Java [10] from the RTSJ domain.

2   The Design Space

Before entering the core matter of this paper we need to provide a brief overview of the modelling space that we avail to the designer and the way we warrant the desired level of separation between PIM and PSM aspects.

2.1   A Multiple View Metamodel

Though ultimately and critically bound to unity, the design of embedded real-time systems permits (arguably even requires) some separation of concern between functional and non-functional modelling. Each such design space then requires a certain amount of semantics that is distinctly specific to the modelling view of concern. The process we envision rests on a *single* domain-specific metamodel which integrates in a coherent and cohesive space *all* of the aspects that are of concern to each and every view availed for modelling to the designer and yet offers them to the designer in separate views.

We are very well aware that there currently is mounting tension between those who favour reliance on the UML metamodel (which would permit to specialize UML into a domain-specific *profile*) and those who argue for the greater simplicity and productivity of defining their own domain-specific metamodel. In fact, we have followed the latter route but also attempted along the way to map every aspect of our domain-specific metamodel to a corresponding UML2 profile.

In order that the designer may focus their attention on specific matters of concern, whether in relation to functional modeling or to timing, sizing and concurrency issues, our metamodel provides for three separate and yet tightly integrated views to system design:

- a *functional view* in which the designer specifies the sequential functional behaviour of the system components by means of class diagrams, state charts and diagrams that can effectively be regarded as a distinct profile of UML2 (and to perform which one can thus use industrial-quality profiling and modelling tools).
- an *interface view*, which allows the designer to specify how functional components aggregate together and what interfaces they offer and require to one another. This modelling view is expressed using declarative specifications which decorate the interface of model components and the relations among them with attributes that specify the desired concurrent semantics within the expressive power availed by the underlying metamodel; the formalism we use at this level is a direct emanation of our domain-specific metamodel but we trust we will be able to relate it to a UML2 profile that also encompasses the functional view.

– a *concurrent view*, which "realizes" the concurrent semantics specified in the interface view by assembling and deploying entities that may legally exist at run time in the target platform that implements the Ravenscar Computational Model. Also this view is currently expressed in a domain-specific language which is however designed in a way to allow mapping to a UML2 profile.

The functional view and the interface view together constitute the PIM specification of the system, whereas the concurrent view does represent the PSM that in the current instance targets the Ravenscar Computational Model. The three views we offer address distinct and non-overlapping aspects of the system. Yet they are strictly and cohesively related to one another by the metamodel rules that determine what semantics attach to what model elements and how.

It is worth noticing in this regard that the computational model that must inform the PSM is chosen, the concurrency semantics that can be attached to interfaces of and relations among PIM components must strictly adhere to and comply with that computational model. In our particular case this compliance is warranted by embedding the required semantics and constraints in the metamodel, which in turn ensures that any view constructed in any allowable modelling space, whether PIM or PSM, can only be legal because of the active enforcement of the applicable constraints applied by the underlying metamodel.

2.2   Modelling Entities and Abstraction Levels

The modelling entities that the designer manipulates in the interface view are termed Application-level containers (APC for short). Those entities embed cohesive services and functional state and expose them controlledly through a provided interface (PI). If the execution of any provided service needs the support of other entities then that need is exposed in the form of a contract-based required interface (RI). Every individual provided service has a sequential behaviour specified in the functional view, whereas the concurrent semantics that effect the caller and the callee across the concerned provided interface is specified in the interface view.

The concurrency view is placed *outside* the control of the design, for it is generated automatically by transformation of the interface view. Models in the concurrency view are populated by entities termed Virtual Machine-level containers (VMC for short). Since the concurrency view represents the PSM part of the system the entities that populate models in that space must be direct emanations of run-time entities that may legally exist on the target execution platform, which in our case is a trustworthy implementation of the RCM.

It should be clear to the reader at this point that APC and VMC reside at distinct levels of abstraction in the design space. The former exist in the PIM space and in effect provide a platform-independent specification of reusable software components. The latter "implement" the former in manners that provably abide by the chosen computational model. The intent of this separation of concerns is to allow the designer to concentrate on the designing the abstract solution to the system problem at specification level leaving the concrete implementation of it to a transformation engine that is intimately aware and in control of the facilities provided by the execution platform and of the constraints posed on their correct use.

The space between the PIM and the PSM in our process is bridged by a form of transformation that we term "vertical" on account of the fact that it crosses multiple levels of (hierarchical) abstraction. The extent of this crossing is obviously very important and very critical. We dare say we can only make it by relying on the solid theory that governs the entirety of the transformation logic. In particular:

- APC and VMC are described using a dedicated algebra that determines their semantics, their allowable attributes and the theorems that permit to relate APC to VMC at their respective level of abstraction
- the metamodel is developed in full conformance to the above algebra as a consequence of which the entire modeling space (whether PIM or PSM) abides by construction to the semantic rules and propositions that define what APC and VMC are and how they can relate to one another; since our metamodel conforms to the transformation algebra and also to the RCM it then follows that the transformation logic is informed by an algebraic representation of the RCM
- transformations turn individual APC into a set of interconnected VMC while preserving the interconnections placed between RI and PI in the APC model; in force of the above reasoning, those transformations are deterministic, fully automatable and provable by algebraic reasoning.

A full description and discussion of the RCM algebra and the associated transformation logic fall outside the scope of this paper; the interested reader is refered to [11]. In this paper we shall limit ourselves to mentioning that the VMC which APC are transformed into may take one of the four forms enumerated below:

- *Cyclic VM-level container*: it is an aggregate of run-time entities that include a thread of control that activates jobs at a fixed rate. The event that triggers the activation of a job of that thread is produced by a system clock. At APC level this activation is represented by the invocation of a PI that is specified as a *deferred* service that must be activated periodically.
- *Sporadic VM-level container*: it is an aggregate of run-time entities that include a thread of control that activates job sporadically, that is to say with a stipulated minimum separation time. The event that triggers the activation of a job of that thread is produced by invocation of a PI delegated by transformation to a VMC in the PSM from the APC in the PIM that owns the original PI. The actual invocation is delivered through the interconnection in the PIM between that PI with an RI that requires a service with matching characteristics.
- *Protected VM-level container*: it is a primitive run-time entity with PI synchronization in the form of the "Priority Ceiling Protocol" (PCP) [12] (or equivalently the "Stack Resource Protocol" (SRP) [13]). The use of any of those synchronization protocols warrants freedom from deadlocks induced by cumulation of resources; minimisation of priority inversion; and occurrence of blocking time at most one time per thread activation.
- *Passive VM-level container*: it is a primitive run-time entity with PI void of any synchronisation protocol.

The reader familiar with HRT-HOOD [14] and all of the follow-on ramifications (e.g. HRT-UML [15]) will surely recognise where those entities come from.

3   Model-Based Timing Analysis

As we have seen thus far, the process we envision stipulates that the designer should operate at PIM level exercising control over the functional view and the interface view. The "product" of a PIM design is a set of interconnected APC. Vertical transformation turns the PIM design into a PSM centred around the concurrent view, where every individual APC is turned into a set of interconnected VMC which preserve all of the attributes set on the source APC and realise their intended run-time semantics, in accord with the RCM algebra. Since we want to achieve and preserve correctness by construction throughout the whole chain of model transformations, the designer does *not* hold control over the concurrent view. It is however obvious that static timing analysis (in particular for feasibility and sensitivity) can only be performed at PSM level where implementation decisions that have effect on the timing behaviour of the system are made. We must therefore make provisions so that the designer may invoke the execution of the desired forms of static timing analysis directly on the interface view at PIM level *and* may see an intelligible return of it propagated back into the APC model, in a most classical form of *round-trip engineering*. In order to help the reader better follow the logic of our machinations we shall accompany our discussion by progressing through the use of a simple example.

3.1   Information Flow

In the interface view the designer is required to attach attributes and properties to APC, which specify the intended concurrency semantics of those containers and of the interactions among them. Some of the choices made by the designer on some elements of the model may cause some attributes to be set on other parts of the model that are effected by those choices. The intent of this provision, which may take place in full automation without any explicit intervention by the user, is that the specification of the model should contain no parts that may be incur a semantic error during vertical transformation.

Individual methods in the PI of an APC may for instance be attached an attribute that specifies their execution to be *immediate* or else *deferred* with regard to the invocation. In the former case the execution at run time is taken care of by the thread of control of the caller. In the latter case instead the invoked method is executed by a thread of control placed on the side of the called container. That thread will then have to be provided for by the VMC that realises that particular portion of the original APC. The semantics of a deferred invocation on the caller will thus be similar to an asynchronous communication: the caller container will post an execution request in a notional mailbox attached to the invoked interface method and that posting will result into the activation of a job in the particular VMC designated as the executor of the request. Threaded VMC will therefore appear at PSM level in the concurrent view as the result of there being APC in the interface view at PIM level which feature deferred PI. A sporadic VMC will result from a deferred PI that is connected to at least one RI in the corresponding model view. A cyclic VMC instead will result from a deferred PI that is connected to the system clock. (For the sake of brevity, the relevant PI will be termed "clocked".)

If the RI of multiple APC were connected to one and the same immediate PI of a given APC and that PI owned a functional state (that is, a non-void set of static variables operated upon by the execution of the PI) then a *protection* attribute will then be automatically attached to that PI to equip it with a level of synchronisation control required to warrant mutual exclusion on access to its functional state. No such protection would be added instead if the PI was invoked by a single RI or if its functional state was void. Figure 1 shows the relation between user-defined and automatically calculated attributes of PI in APC.

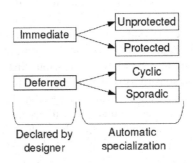

Fig. 1. Relation between user-defined and automatically calculated attributes of PI in APC in the interface view

At some point in the design process, all interfaces of APC in the interface view will have been decorated with all of the attributes that the designer is allowed to set. Table 1 enumerates those attributes.

Table 1. Real-time attributes attached to APC interfaces (PI and RI); Abstract attributes are underlined; Cy: cyclic operation, Sp: sporadic operation, Pr: protected operation, Un: unprotected operation, RI: required interface

Attribute	Attached to
Criticality	Cy,Sp
Period	Cy
Minimum Interarrival Time (MIT)	Sp
Worst Case Execution Time (WCET)	Cy,Sp,Pr,Un
Deadline	Cy,Sp
Maximum Allowed Execution Time (MAET)	RI
Resource Access Protocol	Pr

Since we want to attach attributes to APC entities that live in the PIM dimension, we must be careful not to mingle with attributes that instead strictly belong in the PSM dimension and which are meant to be invisible to the designer. Since vertical transformation must provide a realisation of the semantics intended in the interface view onto the chosen execution platform with no allowed distortion, it goes by itself that the

PSM-level attributes can only propagate, whether directly or indirectly, from PIM-level ones. Static timing analysis on the concurrent view under the RCM for instance requires that priority attributes are set on run-time entities that compose VMC. Priority attributes however may *not* be set directly at PIM level for they are very much specific to the target execution platform. We however enable the designer to influence the determination of the priority attribute at PSM level by expressing an *abstract* attribute that specifies the criticality that the designer attaches to the execution of any deferred operation (i.e., those that yield threads of control upon transformation).

Attributes not only specify the intended run-time semantics but also allow the modelling infrastructure to determine the legality of interconnections between RI and PI beyond purely syntactic considerations. For instance, RI may be attached a Maximum Allowed Execution Time attribute whereby they will only be permitted to match PI with a Worst-Case Execution Time (WCET) attribute no greater than that.

Let us now suppose that a designer is modelling the two APC shown in Fig. 2. The APC named *APC_0* publishes two deferred clocked services in its PI, respectively named *Op0* and *Op1*. Both of those operations invoke, via a specific RI, the immediate service *Op2* published in the PI of the other APC named *APC_1*. As a single immediate PI is invoked by more than one RI each of which attached to an independent thread of control, *Op2* may automatically be attached the attribute that equips its execution with mutual exclusion guarantees.

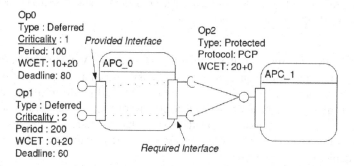

Fig. 2. PIM level view of the example system. Abstract attributes are underlined

The WCET attribute attached to a PI is automatically calculated as the execution cost of the part of the execution which is local to that PI summed to the execution cost of all of the operations invoked across RI that emanate from it. This calculation is comparatively straightforward, for the functional view specifies the local cost of each provided operation and the RI that its execution needs to invoke, while the interface view permits the designer to interconnect those RI to legally matching PI published by some APC in the PIM.

In the example shown in Fig. 2 the WCET cost calculated for *Op0* results from summing up the 10 units off its local execution cost to the 20 units specified as the local cost of *Op2*. As *Op1* performs no other action than just invoking *Op2* then its WCET attribute evaluates to 20.

When APC are transformed into VMC that transformation propagates the attributes set at APC level (on PI, RI and their respective interconnections) onto attributes and properties of VMC. The RCM algebra presides over that propagation to ensure that no semantic distortion may occur in the transformation. As we have just seen, a significant segment of that transformation *calculates* attributes that can only exist at VMC level from automated reasoning on attributes set by the designer at APC level.

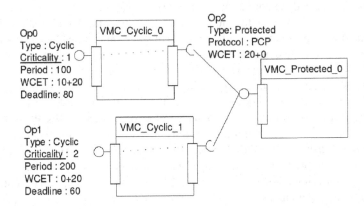

Fig. 3. PSM level view of the example system, which results from model vertical transformation of the PIM level design. Abstract attributes are underlined.

Figure 3 shows the result of the vertical transformation. At this point before being able to perform static timing analysis we need further information that specify the way the designer intends to deploy the system on the physical platform of execution. We capture that information in what we call **deployment view**, which complements the system design with respect to its intended physical characteristics. In the current implementation of our process, the deployment view is expressed using a subset of AADL [16]. The deployment view provides:

1. a description of the hardware components that make up the system (processors, interconnection networks, etc.)
2. a description of timing characteristics of the run-time support that realises the RCM on the target hardware
3. the mapping of logical partitions to physical nodes and of APC to logical partitions. VMC that derive from the vertical transformation of an APC are automatically deployed on that partition.

Logical partitions are architectural entities which are isolated in the spatial and temporal domain from one another. In our current design process we model partitions according to the priority-band architecture [17]. Current partitioned architectures, such as the ARINC 653 ([18]), though obviously fit for their intent, may be argued to be rigid, inflexible and hard to re-configure. Moreover they do not permit to distinguish among partitions, which all exist in a "flat space" (even if their respective criticality may be reflected in their time budget allocation). With the adoption of priority-band architecture, we achieve a considerably more flexible isolation mechanism, with much easier re-configuration (which in fact is achieved by simple changes in the configuration pragmas). Furthermore we can estabilish a total order between partition deployed on the same computational node, which may better reflect their relative importance.

Upon mapping APC (and consequently VMC) to the partitions specified to exist in the physical system we can finally resolve the abstract criticality attribute into a concrete attribute that designates the level of priority that our transformation engine considers an appropriate semantic representation of it. Higher priorities are assigned to threaded VMC deployed on higher-importance partitions; the priority of VMC deployed on one and the same partition is assigned respecting the relative order imposed by the criticality attribute (for example mapped to deadline monotonic considerations).

Let us suppose that our illustrative example be mapped to a target platform equipped with a single processing node that supports priorities in the $[0..63]$ range; we then estabilish a single partition (to which then all the software priorities are delegated to) and assign all APC to it. A mapping function transforms abstract criticality levels to execution priorities, for instance criticality level 1 to priority 0 and criticality level 2 to priority 1. After assigning priorities to threaded VMC, tracing the use relation from their RI to the PI of protected VMC we can automatically determine appropriate ceiling values to assign to the latter. A conservative choice, one that consumes as little priority levels as possible, would possibly assign a ceiling level of 1 to $VMC\_Protected\_0$ in Fig. 3 on account of it being the highest priority owned by a user VMC in the system.

3.2   Catering for Timing Analysis

To realise the tool required to perform static timing analysis in the context of our process and conjugated in the form of feasibility and sensitivity analysis we could either develop one from scratch or else extend an existing one. The former solution would have allowed us to develop a tool perfectly fitting our needs, yet at the cost of a development cycle that should have mandatorily included thorough validation of its design and implementation. The latter solution instead, on the condition of basing upon a tool with a solid pedigree, would only incur the cost of developing and validating the additional features required to fit our specific needs, of proving non regression and of integrating with our process infrastructure. On the whole, we reckoned that the latter choice was the best option for us since we could rely upon the MAST tool [19] developed by the Real-Time Group at the University of Cantabria in Spain. MAST is an open-source tool designed to model event-driven (as opposed to time-triggered) real-time systems and statically analyse them for schedulability.

The most part of theories for static timing analysis base upon various extensions of the "Periodic Task Model" [20], the original version of which provided a simplified and rather restricted abstraction of concrete real-time system. The way MAST describes the system is considerably richer in expressive power, for it permits to draw much more complex relations and dependences among tasks than they could be represented by strictly abiding by the pure periodic task model. In force of the greater expressive power of MAST, any system in the latter set may be directly represented in terms of a MAST event-driven model. The same obviously goes for our PSM level view of the system, which is made up of interconnected VMC decorated with real-time attributes.

As part of our ambition to provide a modelling infrastructure geared to the correctness-by-construction paradigm, we want to arrive at a formal proof that the whole chain of transformations starting from a model composed of APC to a MAST model is semantically correct. The first step of the chain (transformation of APC to VMC) may be proven correct via the RCM Algebra, while we are currently working on the final step (which govern the transformation from a PSM composed of VMC to a MAST model). However we are confident that we will attain that objective soon, leaning on the greater generality of the MAST real-time model.

The benefits of basing the PSM semantics on the RCM become especially tangible when it comes to static timing analysis, for RCM platforms are easily characterised for their run-time behaviour and the associated timing overhead (cf. e.g., [21] for a description of an RCM run-time platform).

In order to meet the project objectives we have extended MAST by incorporating new forms of timing analysis. The resulting tool is internally named MAST+. Table 2 summarises the analysis capabilities to be featured by MAST+. MAST supports feasibility analysis for monoprocessor and distributed systems with fixed priority or EDF dispatching and MAST+ obviously retains that capability. Furthermore, on account of the inclusion of the notion of priority band in the Ada 2005 standard (cf. [17]), we have a very attractive approach to allow an RCM system to include hierchical scheduling. In order to benefit from that important feature of Ada 2005 [4] we have decided to equip MAST+ with support for the analysis of hierarchical scheduling. To that end we have devised an adaptation of the analysis theory inspired on [22] and [23]. Moreover we have extended MAST with the ability to perform sensitivity analysis based on the theoretical approach described in [24], which applies to monoprocessor systems under fixed priority dispatching. The whole analysis framework we use is described in a separate publication [25] which is presently available on request.

With the help of MAST+ we will thus be able to report back to the designer at PIM level information on the timing feasibility of the system with the current set of attributes as well as quantitative advice on what modifications could or should be performed to improve the real-time performance of the system. In particular we will provide sensitivity information on: the shortest period (or MIT) allowable for any single deferred PI; and the longest WCET allowable for any single PI; which do not effect the overall feasibility of the system.

Table 2. Forms of analysis supported by MAST+. Where the entry reads M then the relevant capability is featured by MAST; where it reads EXT it denotes a MAST extension presently realized in MAST+; where it reads W it denotes work in progress in MAST+.

System Type	Feasibility Analysis	Sensitivity Analysis
Single processor	M	EXT
Distributed	M	W
Single-node hierarchical system	EXT	W
Distributed hierarchical system	W	W

3.3 Completing the Round Trip

As we mentioned in Sect. 3, one distinctive feature of our process approach is that it aims to support round-trip engineering. One key issue with that objective certainly lays in devising seamless support for feeding the results of the static timing analysis performed on the PSM level view back on the PIM level view under the control of the designer. Interestingly, our current experience with the implementation of the infrastructural support for this level of round trip has encountered some (solvable) technical problems and almost no conceptual hurdles.

Table 3 reports the attributes that will be reflected back in the PIM level view for the attention of the designer. It is worth noticing that we plan to allow the user to "see" some calculated attributes (Ceiling and Priority in particular) which derive directly from the PSM level view. Though strictly speaking those attributes should not be visibile at PIM level, our current orientation is to show them up without however allowing the designer to operate on them.

Let us now return to our illustrative example and contemplate the effect of the round trip from the form of static timing analysis outlined in Sect. 3.2. Figure 4 shows the PIM level view of the system decorated with attributes propagated back from the round trip analysis.

The designer should arguably take considerable benefit from this round-trip report at PIM level, for they would be able to undertake any refinement or rectification to the system at the "right" level of abstraction, that is to say, where the designer is fully in control of the design space.

Once the design authority is satisfied that the system model is fine, then all that it remains to do is to invoke direct code generation from PIM. That processs will of course first generate the final PSM level view, with the final attributes and then launch

Table 3. AP-level attributes after the round trip. Cy: cyclic operation, Sp: sporadic operation, Pr: protected operation, Un: unprotected operation, RI: Required Interface. Abstract attributes are underlined. The results of the round trip are in italics.

Attribute	Attached to
Criticality	Cy,Sp
Priority	Cy,Sp
Period	Cy
Minimum Interarrival Time (MIT)	Sp
Minimum Feasible Period or MIT	Cy,Sp
Worst Case Execution Time (WCET)	Cy,Sp,Pr,Un
Maximum Feasible WCET	Cy,Sp
Deadline	Cy,Sp
Worst Case Response Time	Cy,Sp
Worst Case Blocking Time	Cy,Sp
Maximum Allowed Execution Time (MAET)	RI
Resource Access Protocol	Pr
Ceiling	Pr

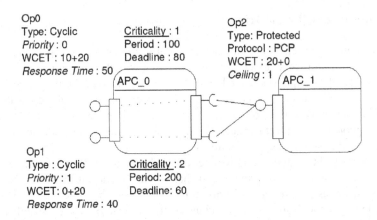

Op0
Type: Cyclic
Priority : 0
WCET : 10+20
Response Time : 50

<u>Criticality</u> : 1
Period : 100
Deadline : 80

Op2
Type: Protected
Protocol : PCP
WCET : 20+0
Ceiling : 1

APC_0

APC_1

Op1
Type : Cyclic
Priority : 1
WCET: 0+20
Response Time : 40

<u>Criticality</u> : 2
Period: 200
Deadline: 60

Fig. 4. Effect of the round trip analysis on the PIM level view of the example system. Abstract attributes are underlined. Round-trip results are in italics.

automated code generation from it, which will produce source code that can be directly submitted to an RCM compliant cross compiler for the target platform of choice.

4   Conclusion

In this paper we have provided a forcedly partial overview of some of the distinctive features of a novel process for the development of high-integrity real-time systems, which centred on a correctness-by-construction paradigm. The focus of this paper was placed on illustrating the provisions we made to allow for advanced forms of static timing analysis to be performed and reflected back on a platform independent view of the system, in a genuine instance of round-trip engineering. The final steps of implementation of the modelling infrastructure aimed to support this process are in progress at the time of this writing. The current prototypes have proven their effectiveness on representative test cases and thus have given us confidence in the soundness and prospects of our vision.

Acknowledgments. The research work from which this paper has originated was carried out in the ASSERT project (IST-FP6-2004 004033) funded by the European Commission as part of the 6th Framework Programme. The views presented in this paper are however those of the authors' only and do not necessarily engage those of the other members of the ASSERT Consortium.

References

1. The Object Management Group (OMG), http://www.omg.org
2. Cechticky, V., Egli, M., Pasetti, A., Rohlik, O., Vardanega, T.: A UML2 Profile for Reusable and Verifiable Software Components for Real-Time Applications. In: Morisio, M. (ed.) ICSR 2006. LNCS, vol. 4039, Springer, Heidelberg (2006)

3. Burns, A., Dobbing, B., Vardanega, T.: Guide for the Use of the Ada Ravenscar Profile in High Integrity Systems. University of York (UK), Technical Report YCS-2003-348 (2003)
4. Ada, Language Reference Manual. (2005), http://www.adaic.org/standards/ada05.html
5. Real-Time Specification for Java (RTSJ), https://rtsj.dev.java.net/
6. Bordin, M., Vardanega, T.: Correctness by Construcution for High-Integrity Real-Time Systems: a Metamodel-driven Approach. In: Abdennahder, N., Kordon, F. (eds.) Ada-Europe 2007. LNCS, vol. 4498, pp. 114–127. Springer, Heidelberg (2007)
7. de la Puente, J.A., Ruiz, J.F., Zamorano, J.: An Open Ravenscar Real-Time Kernel for GNAT, Reliable Software Technologies - Ada-Europe (2000)
8. Aonix Object-Ada Real-Time Raven.
   http://www.aonix.com/objectada_raven.html
9. Aonix PERC-RAVEN. http://www.aonix.com/perc.html
10. Kwon, J., Wellings, A., King, S.: Ravenscar Java: A High-Integrity Profile for Real-Time Java. University of York (UK), Technical Report YCS 342 (May 2002)
11. Bordin, M., Vardanega, T.: Correctness by Construction for High-Integrity Real-Time Systems: a Metamodel-driven Approach. Reliable Software Technologies - Ada-Europe 2007 (to appear, June 2007)
12. Goodenough, J.B., Sha, L.: The Priority Ceiling Protocol: a Method for Minimizing the Blocking of High Priority Ada Tasks. In: Proceedings of the 2nd International Workshop on Real-time Ada issues (1988)
13. Baker, T.P.: Stack-Based Scheduling of Realtime Processes. Real-Time Systems Journal 3(1), 67–99 (1991)
14. Burns, A., Wellings, A.J.: HRT-HOOD: a Structured Design Method for Hard Real-Time Systems. Real-Time Systems, Journal 6(1), (1994)
15. Bordin, M., Vardanega, T.: A New Strategy for the HRT-HOOD to Ada Mapping. In: Vardanega, T., Wellings, A.J. (eds.) Ada-Europe 2005. LNCS, vol. 3555, pp. 51–66. Springer, Heidelberg (2005)
16. Architecture Analysis & Design Language, SAE Standard AS-5506 (2006),
    http://www.aadl.info/
17. Pulido, J.A., Urueña, S., Zamorano, J., Vardanega, T., de la Puente, J.A.: Hierarchical Scheduling with Ada 2005. In: Reliable Software Technologies - Ada-Europe 2006 (2006)
18. ARINC. Avionics Application Software Standard Interface: ARINC Specification 653-1. (October 2003)
19. MAST: Modeling and Analysis Suite and Tools. http://mast.unican.es
20. Liu, C.L., Layland, L.: Scheduling Algorithms for Multiprogramming in a Hard Real-Time Environment. Journal of ACM, vol. 20 (1973)
21. Vardanega, T., Zamorano, J., de la Puente, J.A.: On the Dynamic Semantics and the Timing Behavior of Ravenscar Kernels. Real-Time Systems. Kluwer Academic Publishers, Dordrecht (2005)
22. Davis, R., Burns, A.: Hierarchical Fixed Priority Preemptive Scheduling. Technical Report YCS-2005-385, University of York (2005)
23. Lorente, J.L., Palencia, J.C.: An EDF Hierarchical Scheduling Model for Bandwidth Servers. 12th IEEE International Conference on Embedded and Real-Time Computing Systems and Applications (2006)
24. Bini, E., Di Natale, M., Buttazzo, G.: Sensitivity Analysis for Fixed-Priority Real-Time Systems. In: Proceedings of the 18th Euromicro Conference on Real-Time Systems, Dresden, Germany (July 2006)
25. Panunzio, M., Vardanega, T.: An Integrated Framework for the Timing Analysis of Hierarchical Systems. submitted to 19th Euromicro Conference on Real-Time Systems

ArchMDE Approach for the Development of Embedded Real Time Systems

Nourchène Elleuch[1], Adel Khalfallah[1], and Samir Ben Ahmed[2]

[1] Department of software engineering,
Higher Institute of Computer Science, El Manar,
2 Rue Abou Raihan El Bayrouni-2080 Ariana, Tunisia
`nourchene.elleuch@gnet.tn`, `adel.kalfallah@fst.rnu.tn`
[2] National Institute of Applied Sciences and Technology,
Centre urbain nord de Tunis-B.P.676 Cedex Tunis- 1080 Tunisia
`samir.benahmed@fst.rnu.tn`

Abstract. The development of Embedded Real Time Systems (ERTS) is generally a complex task that requires high costs and long delays. New development tools should be elaborated in order to improve ERTS developers productivity. Model Driven Engineering (MDE) is an emerging paradigm that advances the idea to use models and models transformations to make the development process cost effective.

This paper introduces the Architecture-centric Model Driven Engineering (ArchMDE) approach that stresses architecture-based development and validation of ERTS. We have defined a set of architectural meta-models and a set of QVT transformation rules to automate the generation of architecture-specific models of ERTS.

Keywords: MDE, Meta-model, Model Transformation, Architectural Style, Embedded Real Time System, TURTLE.

1 Introduction

Software development techniques are evolving in order to reduce time, costs, error-proneness, and increase productivity. An important trend of software development is the Model Driven Engineering (MDE) [11]. MDE is expected to overcome software development and validation challenges by combining meta-modeling and models transformations. It adresses the modeling of systems from different viewpoints: Platform Independent Models (PIM) and Platform Specific Models (PSM). At early development phases, a domain model, referred to as Computational Independent Model (CIM) [16] is elaborated. This first model doesn't include functional requirements. A set of transformations may then be performed to make the system more platform-specific. The first transformation produces the PIM, which focuses on the system functionalities. The second transformation builds the PSM, which combines the PIM with technology-dependent features of platforms.

Embedded Real Time Systems (ERTS) engineering is a domain where MDE can be helpful, particularly in addressing the problems of platforms and environments evolution as well as the problems of systems properties validation. For

N. Abdennahder, F. Kordon (Eds.): Ada-Europe 2007, LNCS 4498, pp. 142–154, 2007.

instance, [4] and [6] describe how MDE can be used for the code generation of ERTS and [9] describes the possibility of ERTS validation by using test models. However, model driven development of ERTSs is still at its infancy and many problems have to be resolved. One of them (early introduced in [14]) is related to the expression of architectural design decisions. It is recognized that the use of architectural styles should improve the overall quality of models and help in adopting a product line approach to the development of a family of systems [8].

But how to represent architectural styles and how to enforce their use are unresolved problems. This paper addresses these questions. Its main contributions consist of a development process named "Architecture-centric Model Driven Engineering (ArchMDE)". In the context of this process, the following aspects have been detailed :

- A set of meta-models describing the most important architectural styles.
- A set of transformation rules allowing for the automated generation of models in conformance with a particular architectural style.

Furthermore, our approach introduces a validation subprocess that relies on existing works [1],[12].

This paper is structured as follows. Related work is discussed in Sect. 2. Sect. 3 presents the ArchMDE approach and focuses on the description of ArchMDE's development process. Since ArchMDE is based on model transformations, we detail in Sect. 4 the transformation rules applied to generate an architecture-specific model. Finally, in Sect. 5 we present the main conclusions and outline future work related to the implementation of model transformations.

2   Related Work

Many different methodologies for the development of ERTS have been proposed in the literature. We classify them into two categories: 1) Model-driven development approaches and 2) Model-based architecture-driven development approaches.

Model-driven development approaches. Several approaches may be defined as model-driven and some of them are already supported by off-the-shelf tools: HIDOORS [22], ROPES [7] with Rhapsody tool, ARTiSAN [15] with the ARTiSAN Studio and Accord/UML [9].

HIDOORS encompasses the possibility to automatically generate Java code from a design model (PIM). However, HIDOORS doesn't provide a way to refine the PIM because it doesn't take into consideration the possibility of PIM-to-PIM transformation. HIDOORS supports also the analysis and validation of real-time properties by using Worst Case Execution Time (WCET) analysis. Firstly, the HIDOORS model-checker verifies the compliance of PIM with the real-time constraints. After the transformation of PIM into executable java code, the checker verifies also that the execution time is consistent with WCET defined in the PIM.

The development processes of ROPES and ARTiSAN include three steps: The creation of the design model (using class diagrams and state machines diagrams); The creation of a tasks model defined by a class diagram that uses active objects only; The weaving of the design and task models. However, no mapping rules are defined to assist the weaving process. ARTiSAN allows also the transformation of PIM into C, C++ or java code and claims round trip engineering capabilities by synchronizing between the code and the models.

The Accord/UML methodology proposes an MDA-based approach for ERTS that is similar to our approach: both approaches are based on explicit transformations (model refinement and code generation). However, the rules are implemented with a proprietary language (J language). As the approach uses executable modeling [13] the validation process is based on simulation.

Practically, all approaches in this category (with the exception of Accord/-UML) allow for code generation and little automation of the design workflow is provided. Any of the approaches above addresses the problem of architectural styles explicit representation.

Model-based architecture-driven development approaches. The approach of SAE is based on the emerging standard AADL (Avionics Architecture Description Language) [10]. It provides a mean to specify both the software and hardware architectures, to analyze and map software into hardware elements (operational architecture) and to produce component implementations. This approach offers a support for all stages of system development. However, to our best knowledge, no experiences of architectural styles modeling using this approach have been published yet.

The development of system architectures requires strong experience and modeling skills. The use of architectural style can improve and make easier the development and the comprehension of software architecture. Architectural styles provide a mean for the composition and collaboration of software architecture elements.

For all these reasons, we define the ArchMDE approach that fully supports the concepts of MDA and provides a generic way to build the architecture of ERTS according to a specific architectural style.

3   ArchMDE Overview

We share the view of [14], who states that the architecture should be considered as "a first class modeling citizen" and can be specified independently of any platform implementation. Therefore, architectural considerations must be dealt with at the PIM level which is decomposed into two models: an Architecture Independent Model (AIM) and an Architecture Specific Model (ASM). The ASM layer allows for the automated transformation of AIM into PSM, but may raise traceability problem. To overcome this problem, we have to rely on a development environment that maintains traceability links or investigate reversible transformations.

AIM and ASM are system models that don't have any information about technology-specific implementation. AIM is a pure design model free of any architecture-related choices. ASM is a refined AIM in which technology-independent architectural consideration are introduced. The main purpose of the ASM layer is to make architectural styles, design patterns, and other important design decisions explicit in the model. The distinction between the two levels increases the reusability of the AIM and its adaptability: whenever a change occurs, either in system functionalities or in architectural choices its impact will be localized.

We found it necessary to introduce three types of architectural models:

1. Software Architecture-Specific Models (SASM): they describe the system functionalities projected on the software components;
2. Hardware Architecture-Specific Models (HASM): they describe the physical components of the system;
3. Integration Architecture-Specific Models (IASM): they describe the relationships between SASM and HASM.

We have chosen UML [17] extended with the TURTLE profile to design ArchMDE models. TURTLE extends two UML diagrams: class/object diagrams and activity diagrams. The class/object diagrams are enhanced with the concept of composition operators that are used to represent parallelism and synchronization between objects. The activity diagrams are extended with synchronization actions and temporal operators (see [1], [2] for more details).

3.1   ArchMDE Process

The ArchMDE process (Fig. 1) covers the development and the verification of ERTS. The development process is based on the model design and transformation. The starting point is the requirements model (CIM) from which the AIM is derived. The AIM, also called the design model, comprises the domain logic and the behavior of the ERTS. In a second step, the design model can be merged with an architectural style model to obtain the SASM that covers functional and architectural aspects. A merge with HASM features results in IASM. Finally, the PSMs are derived from the integration model from which source code can be generated.

ArchMDE verification subprocess relies on the following considerations:

– The use of model checking to validate behavioral and temporal properties of ERTS. We use RT-LOTOS [5] and RTL [20].
– The feasibility of AIM to RT-LOTOS and ASM to RT-LOTOS automated transformations.

The feasibility of transforming a TURTLE model into an RT-LOTOS formal specification has been developed in [12]. To benefit from these results, we have chosen TURTLE to express AIM models and RT-LOTOS/RTL as formal foundations. The transformation of ASM models into RT-LOTOS specification is actually a manual step.

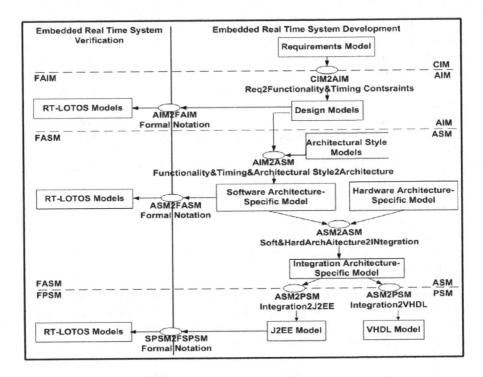

Fig. 1. ArchMDE Process Overview

3.2 ArchMDE Models

We illustrate ArchMDE by providing a simplified car speed regulator example, which is described in [3]. The car speed regulator maintains vehicle speed at a value selected by the driver in conformance with a regulation law. Pressing the ONButton will generate a start signal, which will activate the regulation system in concordance with speed constraints (min= 50km/h and max=130km/h). The driver regains control of the vehicle if one of the following situations occur: 1) he presses the brake pedal, 2) he pushes the ON/OFF button again, 3) he turns ignition OFF or 4) the car speed falls under 50 km/h. The shutdown time is 0.5 s when braking or turning ON/OFF and 100 ms when the car is stopped or speed drops to less than 50 km/h.

Requirements Model. The requirements model specifies the functional and non-functional requirements of the system. The functionalities describe the domain logic of the system. Whereas non-functional requirements may include constraints about the architectural style needed to build the system. The ArchMDE models functional requirements with TURTLE use case diagrams and TURTLE Interaction Overview Diagram (IOD). Both of them constitute our CIM. The IOD represents the relations among a set of scenarios, which are conceptualized by a sequence diagram. Temporal constraints appear at this step of the development

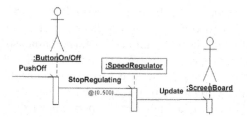

Fig. 2. Sequence Diagram (part of the IOD)

process. For example, an absolute time constraint has to be used in IOD to specify that the execution time of the regulation shutdown shouldn't exceed 500 ms when the OFFButton is pressed (Fig. 2).

Design Models. The design models describe the structure and the behavior of the system. ArchMDE also uses TURTLE for the design models, which include the description of the system structure and a set of behavioral descriptions for each entity in the structure model. The design models describe the system structure, which is free of architectural considerations. Figure 3 depicts a simplified Tclass diagram for the speed regulator.

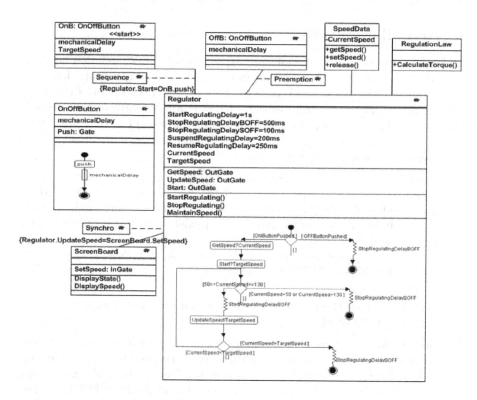

Fig. 3. Tclass Diagram

Software and Hardware Architecture-Specific Models. The TURTLE profile is not intended to cover the entire life-cycle of a complex system, but rather to address the high-level design and its formal analysis [1]. Certainly, the TURTLE profile is appropriated for real-time aspects modeling but it doesn't take into consideration the system architecture aspects. For this reason, we define software and hardware architecture meta-models. The purpose of those meta-models is the expression of a high level expert knowledge on hardware and software architectures. The SASM is built by merging the design model with a specific style. The SASM describes the distribution of the software artifacts generated by the design activities through a specific architecture configuration. The HASM illustrates the hardware components, which are characterized by frequency, memory size, bus protocol, etc...

Integration Architecture-Specific Model. The IASM holds the projection and the scheduling of the SASM on HASM. All the previously defined models, design, software architecture, hardware architecture and integration are platform independent. No component is associated with an execution or simulation technology. Once the components are associated with a specific real time middleware, the deployment is realized. A proposed transformation system will be developed to transform the integration model into a target software platform.

4   ArchMDE Models Transformations

ArchMDE Models transformations are expressed using QVT-relation language [18]. They require for their definition meta-models as input/output. Hence, we need to specify the meta-models of both the source and the target of the transformation. We use, in addition to the TURTLE profile, software architecture, hardware architecture and platform meta-models where all of them are MOF-compliant meta-models. ArchMDE transformation processes are classified into two major categories detailed as follow:

- Model transformations related to the main development workflow: they are composed of three groups: those used to build the design models (AIM), those needed to generate software or hardware architecture model (ASM), and finally those used for the integration models (ASM) and the generation of implementation (PSM).
- Model transformations related to the validation workflow: they translate different models into RT-LOTOS notation.

4.1   Building the Design Model: Transforming Requirements to Design (CIM2AIM)

The first ArchMDE transformation maps the ERTS requirements models into the design models. The transformation rules are defined as a mapping among the elements of TURTLE profile. This transformation is done by TURTLE Toolkit (TTool) [21], which will be used to generate automatically a TURTLE class diagram from IOD.

4.2   Creation of Architecture Models

Integrating Software Architectural Features (AIM2ASM). The design models (AIM) can be merged with architectural style models. ArchMDE provides meta-models for software architecture conforming to a specific architectural style like blackboard, C2, pipe-filter, etc. The transformation rules are based on ArchMDE meta-models and TURTLE profile.

Common Architecture Meta-models. The abstract syntax of software architecture is described by a MOF meta-model (Fig. 4). During the process of building a software architecture and hardware architecture meta-models, we noticed the existence of similarities among different concepts of the two meta-models that led us to group the concepts in the common architecture meta-model (Fig. 5). In both software and hardware architectures, components propose an interface materialized by their ports. The interfaces encapsulate the structure and the behavior of the components, and make them independent of their environment. The component can be composite or basic. The composite component is composed by the *ArchConnectors*, the ports and the components. The *ArchConnector* connects to either a component or an *ArchConnector*.

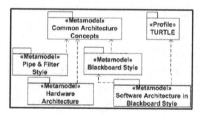
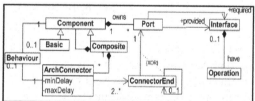

Fig. 4. Architecture Meta-models   **Fig. 5.** Common Architecture Meta-models

Software Architecture Meta-model for Blackboard Architectural Style. We enhance the AIM of the car speed regulator with the blackboard style elements [19] in order to illustrate our postulate. The blackboard architecture meta-model has been defined to describe the topological constraints in relation with the connectivity between components and connectors. Figure 6 depicts those relationships.

A blackboard architecture configures two components one called *Blackboard* and the other is termed *Administrator*. It also defines a dynamically changing set of components called *Users*. The *Blackboard* (respectively *Administrator*) has a port called *control* (respectively *board-control*), and several ports. The *Administrator* could be connected with a binary synchronous connector to the *control* of the *Blackboard*. Every *User* has a port called *board*, that is connected to a *Board-user-port* of the *Blackboard* by a connector. New *Users* are granted access by the *Administrator* as a consequence of *Register-operation* request. Similarly, the *Administrator* may remove *Users* by an *Unregister-operation*. The number of *Users* and *Board-user-ports* is identical, unless there are uncompleted register or unregister operations.

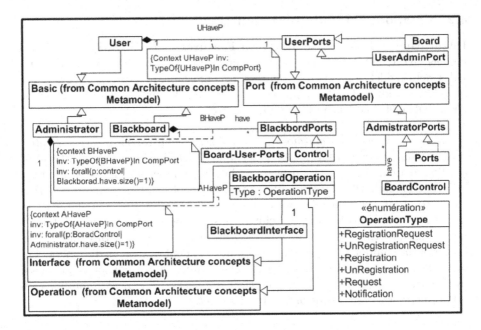

Fig. 6. Blackboard Metamodel

The blackboard style doesn't define constraints on the interactions of black-board architecture: any part may start or terminate interactions. But, It imposes certain configuration constraints in relation to the connectivity between different components, ports and connectors. We define a set of constraints expressed in OCL, which are defined below.

Constraint 1. A *BoardControl* port has a provided interface and hasn't a required interface. A provided interface has one operation and the operation type is *RegistrationRequest* or *UnRegistrationRequest*.

```
Context BoardControl inv:
    self.provided->size()=1
    self.required->size()=0
    self.provided->forall(bi:BlackboardInterface|bi.have->size()=1)
    self.provided->forall(bi:BlackboardInterface|
    bi.have.type=OperationType::Registration or
    bi.have.type=OperationType::UnRegistration)
```

Constraint 2. The *Blackboard* (respectively the *Administrator*) component has a dynamically changing set of ports called *Board-User-Ports* (respectively *Ports*).

```
Context Blackboard inv:
    forall(p:BoardUserPorts|Blackborad.BoardUserPorts.isnotEmpty())
Context Administrator inv:
    forall(p:BoardUserPorts|Administrator.Ports.isnotEmpty())
```

Constraint 3. Just one instance of blackboard metaclass is authorized.

```
Context blackboard inv: self.metaobject.allInstances.size = 1
```

Transformation Rules. The transformation rules describe which input concepts are used to produce output concepts. In the following, we present some of these rules that are expressed by MOF QVT-relation Language.

```
Transformation TurtleBlackboard (dm : TURTLE, sam:BlackboardStyle) {
    top relation ClassToBlackboard{//See Rule 1}
    top relation TobjectToAdministrator{//See Rule 4}
    top relation TclassToUser{//See Rule 2 and 3}
    relation GateToInterface{//See Rule 5}
    relation OperationToBlackboardOperation{//See Rule 5} ...}
```

The model named *dm* declares the TURTLE package as its meta-model, and the *sam* model declares the BlackboardStyle package as its meta-model. The transformation contains two kinds of relations: the top-level relation and the non-top-level relation. In the example above, ClassToBlackboard is a top level relation, whereas OperationTo-BlackboardOperation is a non-top-level relation. Figure 7 illustrates the SASM of car regulator obtained by applying transformation rules.

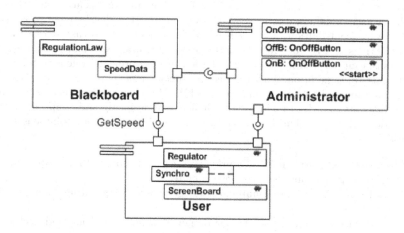

Fig. 7. SASM of a car speed regulator

Rule 1. All classes in the TURTLE diagram are transformed into one Blackboard Component named *"Blackboard"*.

Rule 2. The Tclasses that are linked to regular classes are translated into User component. Furthermore, all Tclasses that are linked with a Synchro composition operator with the preceding Tclasses are grouped in the same user component.

Rule 3. If two Tclasses are linked with a Parallel composition operator then they are mapped into two User components.

Rule 4. The Tobjects with their respective Tclasses are packed into the Administrator component.

Rule 5. A Tclass communicates with its environment using gates. The gates can be declared as private, protected or public. For each public gate that is not involved in an internal synchronisations, an Interface object provided by the port's component is created.

```
relation GateToInterface{
    checkonly domain dm t:TClass {gate=g:Gate
    {name=gn, visibility=VisibilityKind::public,
    synchronization=SynchronizationType::External}};
    enforce domain sam i:Interface{name=in};
    when {ClassToBlackboard (t,b); TobjectToAdministrator(t,a);
    TclassToUser(t,u);}
    where {in=gn; OperationToBlackboardOperation(t,b,a,u);}}
```

5   Conclusions and Future Works

In this work we have presented an approach (ArchMDE), which focuses on the ERTS development and verification. The combination of architecture-centric, model-driven paradigms and formal approaches are employed as an ERTS development process and constitute our contribution. ArchMDE is a development process that stresses validation and brings to the front models, a set of architectural meta-models and a set of QVT transformation rules. The transformation process provides a generic framework to automate the generation of an architecture-specific model.

We have proposed a way to transform the TURTLE elements into blackboard architecture elements in order to address the challenge of designing and adapting software architecture for ERTS. The introduction of the architectural viewpoint has several advantages.

– The architectural style for ERTS provides means for representing components and leads to a rigorous and clear software architecture.
– The software architecture is automatically generated by executing a mapping process.
– The software architecture allows for design decisions expression and enables the comprehension of the system at a higher level of abstraction.
– The introduction of a new layer can ease the transformation of AIM into PSM, but may raise traceability problem.

Formal verification increases the quality of software for ERTS by providing a way to check logical and time consistency. The validation is based on two major considerations: 1) Translating models into formal notation; and 2) Setting a validation action at each transformation step. This point is mainly assured by the integration of exiting analysis techniques and the adoption of timed model-checking tools.

Currently, we work on the definition of rules and meta-models for other architectural styles in order to define a framework for AIM/ASM transformation. We also work on giving a formal definition to the architecture meta-model concepts by using RT-LOTOS.

Acknowledgements

We would like to express our gratitude to Fabrice Kordon for his valuable remarks and comments who improved the quality of this paper. We thank also the anonymous reviewers for their feedbacks. Finally, we would like to thank Françoise Simonot-Lion and Xavier Rebeuf, for their comments and suggestions during the elaboration of the approach presented in this paper.

References

[1] Apvrille, L., Courtia, J.P., Lohr, C., De Saqui-Sannes, P.: A Real-Time UML Profile Supported by a Formal Validation Toolkit. In: IEEE Transactions on Software Engineering, vol. 30(7), IEEE Computer Society Press, Los Alamitos (2004)

[2] Apvrille, L., De Saqui-Sannes, P., Khendek, F.: TURTLE-P: a UML profile for the formal validation of critical and distributed systems. In: Software and Systems Modeling, Springer-Verlag, Heidelberg (2006)

[3] ATI-Wooddes project (2006), Visted on November http://wooddes.intranet.gr/ecoop2001/_private/Case-Study.ps

[4] Burmester, S., Giese, H., Schafer, W.: Model-Driven Architecture for Hard Real-Time Systems: From Platform Independent Models to Code. In: Hartman, A., Kreische, D. (eds.) ECMDA-FA 2005. LNCS, vol. 3748, pp. 25–40. Springer, Heidelberg (2005)

[5] Courtiat, J.P., Santos, C.A.S., Lohr, C., Outtaj, B.: Experience with RT-LOTOS, a temporal extension of the LOTOS formal description technique. Rapport LAAS No99133 Computer Communications 23(12), 1104–1123 (2000)

[6] Do Nascimento, F.A., Da, S., Oliveira, M.F., Wehrmeister, M.A., Pereira, C.E., Wagner, F.R.: MDA-based approach for embedded software generation from UML/MOF repository. In: Proceedings of the 19th Annual Symposium on integrated Circuits and Systems Design. SBCCI'06, Oliveira, pp. 143–148. ACM Press, New York (2006)

[7] Douglass, B.P.: Doing Hard Time: Developing Real-time Systems with UML, Objects, Frameworks and Patterns (4th Print), Boston, MA. Addison-Wesley, Reading (2001)

[8] Garlan, D.: Software Architecture: a Roadmap. In: Finkelstein, A. (ed.) The Future of Software Engineering, ACM Press, New York (2000)

[9] Gerard, S., Terrier, F., Tanguy, Y.: Using the Model Paradigm for Real-Time Systems Development: ACCORD/UML. In: Bruel, J.-M., Bellahsène, Z. (eds.) OOIS 2002. LNCS, vol. 2426, Springer, Heidelberg (2002)

[10] Hudak, J., Feiler, P.: Developing AADL models for control systems: A parctitioner's guide. Technical report. CMU/SEI-2006-TR-019. ESC-TR-2006-019 (October 2006)

[11] Kent, S.: Model Driven Engineering, Integrated Formal Methods. In: Butler, M., Petre, L., Sere, K. (eds.) IFM 2002. LNCS, vol. 2335, Springer, Heidelberg (2002)

[12] Lohr, C.: Contribution to real-time system specification relying on the RT-LOTOS formal description technique (in French). Ph.D.Thesis, Institut National Polytechnique de Toulouse (2002)

[13] Mraidha, C.: Modelisation executable et analyse de proprietes temps reel. Ph.D.Thesis, Universty of EVRY (2005)

[14] Mikkonen, T., Pitkanen, R., Pussinen, M.: On the role of architectural style in Model Driven Development. In: Oquendo, F., Warboys, B.C., Morrison, R. (eds.) EWSA 2004. LNCS, vol. 3047, pp. 74–78. Springer, Heidelberg (2004)
[15] Moore, A., Cooling, N.: Developing real-time systems using Object technology. Real-time Perspection: Foundation and overview version 1.3 (2000)
[16] OMG.: MDA Guide Version 1.0.1. omg document number omg/2003-06-01. (June 2003)
[17] OMG.: UML 2.0 Superstructure Specification (August 2003), http://www.omg.org/docs/ptc/030802.pdf
[18] OMG.: MOF QVT Final Adopted Specification. (November 2005), http://www.omg.org/docs/ptc/051101.pdf
[19] Pfleger, K.: hayes-Roth, B.: An Introduction to Blackbord-Style Systems Organization. Standford University technical Report KSL-98-03. Knowledge Systems Laboratory (1998)
[20] RTL.: RTL Tool (November 2006), Visited on http://www.lass.fr/RT-LOTOS
[21] TTool.: Turtle Toolkit. Visited on (January 2007), http://labsoc.comelec.enst.fr/turtle
[22] Ventura, J., Siebert, F., Walter, A., Hunt, J., HIDOORS,: HIDOORS - A High Integrity Distributed Deterministic Java Environment. Seventh IEEE International Workshop on Object-oriented Real-time Dependable Systems (WORDS), San Diego (January 2002)

Generating Distributed High Integrity Applications from Their Architectural Description

Bechir Zalila, Irfan Hamid, Jerome Hugues, and Laurent Pautet

GET-Télécom Paris – LTCI-UMR 5141 CNRS
46, rue Barrault, F-75634 Paris CEDEX 13, France
{bechir.zalila,irfan.hamid,jerome.hugues,laurent.pautet}@enst.fr

Abstract. High-Integrity distributed applications are used in many critical domains. They must be designed and built with a great deal of vigor, as a failure could mean loss of life. Thus, it is preferable that a significant part of their code be generated automatically from a model that describes their critical aspects. Automatic code generation eases the process of certification as well. In this paper we introduce the use of AADL as a modeling language for HI distributed systems. Then we present our Ravenscar Profile compliant Ada code generation rules from AADL models. Finally, we present our Ravenscar Profile compliant middleware, PolyORB-HI and the extension of the code generation rules for HI distributed applications.

1 Introduction

Designing High-Integrity (HI) distributed systems demands more attention and rigour compared to classical distributed systems as they are used in safety-critical domains such as space or avionics. The produced systems have to conform to many stringent functional and non-functional requirements from multiple contexts (runtime support for hardware, dependability, analyzability).

Ensuring all these requirements and features becomes very hard if the whole HI system is *hand-coded*. Thus, a part (as large as possible) of the application code should preferably be generated automatically from a verifiable and analyzable model. This makes easier the work of the developer and aids in code certification. Besides, producing a verifiable model (eg. *Petri Net*) from the application model using model transformation is simpler and safer than producing this model from source code.

AADL, which stands for "Architecture Analysis and Design Language" [SAE04] is an architecture description language that allows the modeling of distributed, real-time applications. AADL was first introduced to model the hardware and software architectures in the avionics domain, but was later retargeted to the general DRE (distributed real-time embedded) domain. This pedigree results in a language that is more amenable to static analysis and verification than other, more general-purpose modeling languages.

The Ravenscar Profile [BDV03] is a subset of rules and coding guidelines for Ada that ensure certain properties including static schedulability analysis, absence of deadlock and bounded execution times. These restrictions apply to multi-task applications that run on a single node.

N. Abdennahder, F. Kordon (Eds.): Ada-Europe 2007, LNCS 4498, pp. 155–167, 2007.
© Springer-Verlag Berlin Heidelberg 2007

In this paper we describe the Ada Ravenscar code generation for HI distributed applications from their AADL models. Section 2 introduces the AADL and the Ravenscar Profile. Section 3 gives an overview of the related works. In section 4, we present the rules to generate Ravenscar code for a single-node multitasking application. In section 5, we extend these rules in order to generate code for HI distributed applications and present our Ravenscar compliant middleware [HZP06]. Section 6 ends the article with our conclusions and an overview of future work.

2   AADL and Ravenscar

2.1   AADL

The AADL [SAE04] is an architecture description language for describing distributed, real-time embedded systems. An AADL system model consists of components, their interfaces, the connections between them and properties on various entities of the system model. The AADL standard defines a textual as well as graphical form of the language.

2.1.1   Components

Components represent an element offering and requiring services according to a certain specification. AADL divides components into three classes; software, execution platform and hybrid. *Process, thread, thread group, data* and *subprogram* are software components. *Processor, memory, bus* and *device* are execution platform (hardware) components. *System* is a hybrid component. Thus AADL allows describing an entire architecture (software and hardware).

Component definitions consist of a component type and zero or more component implementations. Component types define the interface that implementations must satisfy. Component implementations define the internals of a component. *Subcomponents* are component instances contained in a component. An implementation contains the subcomponents of a component and the connections between those subcomponents.

Process components represent a virtual address space which contains the code and data associated directly with the process and that of its contained threads and data

Thread components represent individual units of execution and schedulability. Every process component must contain at least one thread subcomponent

Thread groups logically group threads contained in processes. A thread group may contain threads, thread groups and data subcomponents

Data components represent a data type in the source text. Data subcomponents of processes and threads represent the instances of that data type within the said process/thread. Data components may declare subprograms as features, which may represent accessor procedures on that data type

Subprograms are an architectural abstraction of a procedure in imperative programming languages. Subprogram components may define parameters as features and contain data subcomponents

Processor components represent a CPU together with a scheduler. Process components are *bound* to a processor component. Thread and thread group components may also be bound to a processor component. Otherwise, they are mapped to the same processor their container process component is bound to.

Memory components represent a storage device (RAM/ROM or disk). Software components may be bound to memory components

Buses exchange control/data between processors, memories and devices

Devices represent hardware that can interface with the environment

Systems do not have any semantics and serve only to contain subcomponents

2.1.2 Features

Component types can declare interfaces (called *features* in AADL). Features of different components are connected together to enable them to communicate. There are several kinds of features:

Data ports are logical connection end-points between components that, when connected, represent a data flow. They are typed with a data component which specifies the type of data they transport. They also have directional qualifiers: in, out or in out. Data ports represent state variables, if an updated value is not read, it is lost. They are generally declared in thread, thread group or process components [1]

Parameters are notionally equivalent to data ports, applied to subprogram components

Event ports are logical connection end-points between components that, when connected, represent a pure control flow. They are similar to signals in operating systems. Incoming event ports have a queue. Event ports are generally declared in thread, thread group or process components [1].

Event data ports are logical connection end-points between components that, when connected, represent a control flow with auxiliary information. Incoming event data ports also have queues.

Required/provided data access signify that a component provides or requires access to a data component. It is used to model shared data among components

Subprograms features of a data component signify an accessor procedure

2.1.3 Properties

AADL allows the assigning of properties to most entities in the model (components, ports, connections etc.). Properties are name/value pairs that specify additional aspects of entities. Properties are used to describe the deadlines, periods and entry points for threads; concurrency control protocols for shared data; scheduling protocols for processors; queue sizes for event and event data ports etc. Property values may be integers, strings, floats, enumerations, component references or lists thereof.

Properties can be declared in a component's type, implementation or as part of its instantiation as a subcomponent. Thus a rich spectrum of refinement and overriding is possible for properties. In case a property is not defined in the standard AADL property set, project or tool-specific property sets can be defined. The semantics/processing of these user-defined properties is then the responsibility of the additional tooling.

2.1.4 Subprogram Call Sequences

AADL allows a finer description of threads and subprograms by giving the sequence of subprograms they call. A thread or a subprogram may have one or more call sequences.

---

[1] Out event [data] ports may also be declared as features of subprogram components.

A call sequence consists of the call to one or more subprogram(s). If there is only one call sequence then the work of the container thread or subprogram consists of calling the subprograms in the order they appear in the sequence. In the case of multiple call sequences, the AADL standard [SAE04] states that one of these sequences is chosen in an *indeterministic* way.

2.2   The Ravenscar Profile

The runtime of the Ada programming language provides extensive tasking capabilities. However, some of these are not suitable for safety-critical real-time systems. Rendez-vous, multiple entries on protected objects and `select` statements render execution time analysis very complex. The Ravenscar Profile [BDV03] is an effort to define a subset of Ada for use in HI systems; the major restrictions therein are detailed below.

Static tasking stipulates that the task-set be statically defined, there be no task terminations or aborts and no dynamic priorities

Static synchronization model enforces non-hierarchical protected objects, a static set of protected objects, no `select` statements and no entries on tasks

Deterministic memory usage states that there be no implicit heap allocation

Deterministic execution stipulates that there be a maximum of *one* entry per protected object, the queue length of said entry be one, there be no requeue statements, no asynchronous control of tasks and delays be absolute

Runtime configuration states that task dispatching be `FIFO_Within_Priorities`, the priority ceiling protocol [SRL90] be used for protected object access and that there be no suspendible code in a protected object procedure, function or entry

Only periodic and sporadic tasks are allowed. Periodic tasks are dispatched at regular time intervals (their *period*). Sporadic tasks are dispatched as a result of events, but with a specified minimum inter-arrival time between events. The behavior in case of violation of this rule is implementation dependant.

All inter-task communication must take place through protected objects or suspension objects. Protected objects (§ 9.4 and § 9.5 of [WG05]) provide task-safe access to shared data in a single address space. Protected objects offer three types of interfaces. *Functions* return a single value and cannot change the internal state of the object. *Procedures* may take input and output parameters and may change the internal variables of the object. *Entries* are similar to procedures but their execution is guarded by boolean entry barriers.

The concurrency control protocol is *"concurrent read"/"exclusive write"*, i.e.: multiple tasks can be in a function if none are in a procedure or an entry, or a single task can be in a procedure, or a single task can be in an entry.

The only potentially blocking operations that a task may call in its response loop are calls to protected object routines. Furthermore, no blocking operations are allowed in the code of protected objects. This aids in the schedulability analysis as well as the calculation of the upper-bound on blocking due to priority-inversion.

2.3 Rationale of the AADL to Ravenscar Profile Transformation

Coding a Ravenscar application by hand would prove to be a very tedious task. The collection of protected objects, suspension objects and tasks that use them for communication would make for a very complex topology.

AADL was first created to model HI applications in the avionics and space domain. As shown in 2.1, the syntax and the semantics of AADL enforce the developer to give many important architectural aspects of his application (number of threads, their properties, interaction between them...). The life of threads and protected objects is endless like in Ravenscar Profile. Thus, AADL proves to be a suitable design vehicle for Ravenscar applications. From a conceptual point-of-view we can note that AADL threads will be transformed to Ravenscar tasks. Data ports to data flow protected objects, event ports to suspension objects and event data ports to event (control) flow protected objects. AADL subprograms can be transformed to Ada procedures, data components to either local variables (if declared as subcomponent of a subprogram, a thread or a process) or as protected objects (if declared as subcomponent of a process).

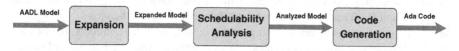

Fig. 1. Code generation process

The figure 1 shows Ada code generation process AADL: (1) the model is parsed and expanded to a second AADL model more suitable for analysis and code generation. (2) The expanded model is analyzed for schedulability using Cheddar [SLNM05]. (3) Finally, the Ada code is generated using Ocarina, our AADL toolsuite[2].

The expansion phase is important because it allows the separation of concerns (local application *vs* distributed application) by expanding the AADL model of a distributed application into several AADL models of local applications (corresponding to the nodes of the distributed application). The code generation rules for local applications (section 4) are applied on each one of these models to generate the *intra-node* part of the application. The code generation rules for distributed applications (section 5) are applied to generate the *inter-node* code.

This approach has been applied successfully on the AADL model given on figure 2. It describes a typical example of Telecommand/Telemetry application used in the space domain.

3 Related Work

Generating HI code from a model is not limited to AADL models. In [BV05], the authors state that generating code minimizes the risk of several semantic breaches when translating the model towards code. The manual coding exposes the developer to these

---

[2] Ocarina is freely available at http://ocarina.enst.fr

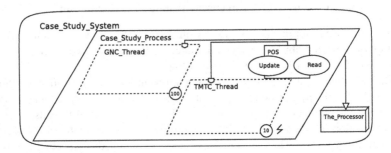

Fig. 2. Case study

breaches. They propose some guidelines to generate RCM compliant Ada code from HRT-UML. However, the excess of using generic instantiations introduces a considerable overhead in the executable code size (30%).

More closely to this paper's scope, the Annex D of the AADL language [SAE05] describes some coding guidelines to translate the AADL software components into source code (Ada and C). These rules are not complete mapping specifications, but they provide guidelines for those who want to generate code from AADL models. In our case, we took from these guidelines the rules that are compliant with the Ravenscar Profile.

More concretely, STOOD is a tool developed by Ellidiss Software [Sof]. It allows users to model their real-time applications using AADL or the HOOD method. STOOD allows the code generation from AADL to Ada by converting AADL models to HOOD models and then applying the HOOD to Ada mapping rules. However, the generated code does not rely on a middleware layer and works only for local applications.

4   Code Generation for a Single-Node Application

A single-node Ravenscar application is a system that is hosted on a single partition on a processor. This translates to an application with one Ada program having multiple tasks. The mapping rules for this case are given below.

4.1   Data Components

Data components are transformed to Ada data types, be they primitive types, arrays or records. Data component types and implementations represent Ada types in the source code; whereas data *subcomponents* of process, thread and subprogram components represent instantiations of said types.

Since the standard AADL properties do not allow fine-grained data type specification, we defined our own data type property set:

- Data_Type is an enumeration property that allows to define the primitive type of a data component (Integer, Boolean, Character...)
- Length is an integer property to specify the length of an array or the maximum length of a bounded string

– Element_Type is a data component reference property that indicates the element type of an array

To express the access policy to a data component, we use the standard AADL property Concurrency_Control_Protocol which takes its values from the set {None-Specified, Priority_Inheritance, Priority_Ceiling} . The set of values is extensible by the user. If the data subcomponent has a concurrency control protocol of Priority_Ceiling, then it is mapped to an Ada protected type having the priority pragma set to the correct value. In the case of a protocol not supported by the Ravenscar Profile (different from *priority ceiling* and none), the code generator complains and stops the code generation to ensure consistency.

If a data component implementation has data subcomponents, then it is mapped to an Ada record. Our code generator verifies the consistency of the properties and the component structure before generating the Ada code. The listing 1.1 shows a model for a protected data component and the listing 1.2 shows the mapped Ada protected type.

```
data POS
features
   Update  :  subprogram Update_POS;
   Read    :  subprogram Read_POS
properties
   Data_Type  =>  Integer;
   Concurrency_Control_Protocol =>
      Priority_Ceiling;
end POS;
```

Listing 1.1. AADL data component

```
protected type POS is

   procedure Update_POS;
   procedure Read_POS;

private

   Field  :  Integer;
end POS;
```

Listing 1.2. Ada generated type

```
thread Logger
features
   Failure          :  in event port;

   Engine_Fail  :  in event data port
      Boolean_Data ;

   Aileron_Fail :  in event data port
      Boolean_Data ;

properties
   Period => 10 Ms;
end Logger;
```

Listing 1.3. AADL Thread

```
type Logger_EIB
   (Port  :  <Appli_Name>_Event_Type
    := Logger_Failure)
is record
   case Port is
      when Logger_Failure =>
         null; — Event port
      when Logger_Engine_Fail =>
         Engine_Fail : Boolean_Data ;
      when Logger_Aileron_Fail =>
         Aileron_Fail : Boolean_Data ;
   end case;
end record;
```

Listing 1.4. Event Interface Block

4.2 Thread Features

Sporadic threads are dispatched at the reception of events. For each AADL application (monolithic or distributed), we declare an enumeration type that lists all the in event and in event data ports of all sporadic thread instances. This type is used to identify the event port that triggered the thread. Besides, it is used in the distributed case to statically fetch a request destination (section 5).

For each sporadic thread having one or more in event [data] port(s), we generate an *event interface block* (EIB) which is a discriminated record with a discriminant Port of the enumerated type described above and elements corresponding to the data types of the `in event [data]` ports. We use this record in order to be compliant with the Ravenscar Profile that forbids the waiting on multiple events at the same time. When an event comes, the sporadic thread is triggered and the port that caused the triggering is known by means of the `Port` field of the record. This mechanism works for both local and distributed cases. The listing 1.3 shows the provided interface of a thread component and the listing 1.4 shows the corresponding mapped EIB type.

4.3 Ports

We define an *exchanger* protected object as one that has an internal state along with `Get` and `Set` procedures to change that state. A *synchronizer* is a protected object with an internal state along with an `Await_Event` entry and a `Send_Event` procedure. For each incoming data port in a thread, we define an exchanger protected object and for each sporadic thread, we define a synchronizer.

In event `[data]` ports must have a subprogram designated to handle the reception of events. In general cases, it is the subprogram connected to the port. Otherwise, it is the subprogram specified by the `Compute_Entrypoint` standard property of the port.

4.4 Threads

AADL threads are transformed to Ada tasks. The thread characteristics are specified by means of AADL properties[3] :

- the standard property `Dispatch_Protocol` gives the thread kind, `Periodic` or `Sporadic`, the only two task kinds allowed by the Ravenscar Profile.
- the standard property `Source_Stack_Size` gives the stack size of a thread.
- the standard property `Period` gives the period of a periodic thread or the minimal inter arrival time for a sporadic thread.
- the custom property `Priority` gives the thread priority.

The mapped Ada tasks are instantiations of generic packages (one generic package for periodic threads and another for sporadic threads). In addition to the properties described above, these instantiation take a procedure without parameters called `<Thread_Name>_Dispatch` that is generated automatically. Generic instantiations are a popular pattern to design Ravenscar Profile compliant systems [BDV03]. We do not use them excessively to avoid the overhead in the executable size explained in 3.

For periodic threads the corresponding `<Thread_Name>_Dispatch` procedure calls the defined call sequence (if any) or calls the procedure given by the `Compute_Entry-point` property of the AADL thread. For sporadic tasks the `<Thread_Name>_Dispatch` procedure first blocks on the `Await_Event` entry of its synchronizer object (a sporadic thread has at least one `in event [data]` port), then calls the subprogram designated to handle the type of event that has dispatched it (received as an `out` parameter) upon return from the `Await_Event` entry.

---

[3] Other thread properties will be added in future revision of the mapping.

4.5 Local Communication

The communication infrastructure for co-located tasks consists of a set of exchangers and synchronizers that enable the tasks to communicate safely. For sporadic tasks with one or more in event [data] port(s), we generate a synchronizer protected object to discriminate the launching event. For each in data port, we create an exchanger object of the type specified in the port's declaration. We also define accessor stubs for each generated synchronizer/exchanger. These stubs facilitate the programming of the functional part of the task response code. A possible optimization of the generated code could consist on generating a simple Ada suspension object instead of a synchronizer when the thread contains only one in event port.

5 Extending the Code Generation for Distributed HI Applications

In this section, we first describe our middleware for HI systems: PolyORB-HI. Then we present the extra rules to generate Ravenscar Profile compliant code for distributed applications from their AADL models using Ocarina, our AADL toolsuite.

5.1 Distribution Model for HI Systems

HI distributed systems must be designed with respect to a set of requirements:

Language constructs: All language constructs used in PolyORB-HI are compliant with the Ravenscar Profile. Some additional language restrictions have been added in order to ensure compliance with HI systems (no goto statements, no slices...)

Memory model: In a HI system, dynamic memory allocation must be avoided. This protects the system from running out of memory during execution and from the non-deterministic behavior of memory allocators

Tasking and concurrency model: A large part of the Ravenscar Profile addresses tasking issues. The compliance to the Ravenscar Profile ensures static analyzability and the absence of deadlocks, priority inversion and non-deterministic scheduling

Transport layer: This part of the HI system is out of the scope of the Ravenscar Profile. However, the low-level transport layer should not affect the application properties obtained by respecting the Ravenscar Profile: in particular, it should bound priority inversion when accessing the communication channels, all communications channels must be created at initialization time and be non-terminating. PolyORB-HI will use the SpaceWire protocol which ensures all these properties

From these requirements, we derive the following distribution model: the application is made of pairs of caller/callee tuples, each located on a different node.

- The caller marshalls its data, retrieves the end-point to the callee, and then sends the data through the transport low-level layer.
- A protocol handler task is awaken on the callee side. It fetches the data, unmarshalls it and calls the corresponding processing code.

This model is notionally similar to typical RPCs, with the following limitations set to avoid blocking: (1) there is at most one communication channel per caller/callee couple, and one task handler per transport end-point; (2) requests are oneway; (3) data are of bounded size known at compile time.

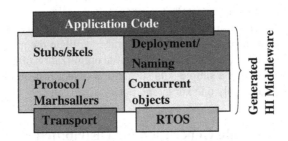

Fig. 3. Overview of PolyORB-HI

We have implemented this model in PolyORB-HI (figure 3) which is a core that contains the distribution features necessary for asynchronous distributed applications. As PolyORB, our *QoS-bases* middleware, PolyORB-HI is structured in several layers (transport, protocol, applicative aspect) but without any dynamic creation of components. This results in a small footprint size of the middleware ($\simeq 200KB$ including the real-time kernel and using GNAT for the ERC32 target).

Around the core, the remaining application code is generated automatically using Ocarina [VHPK05]. The next section describes the code generation rules for HI distributed applications.

5.2   Code Generation Rules for HI Distributed Applications

Most of the rules to generate code for monolithic distributed applications have been elaborated with the distributed case in mind. In other words the code generated for a single-node HI application is similar to the code of a distributed HI application. This section describes the rules that reflect the distribution aspects of a HI application.

5.2.1   Data Exchange

Data have to be converted into a data representation suitable for network transfer. The reader should note that the data transfer between nodes is request-oriented i.e.: all message sending in the AADL model are mapped to request invocations in the generated Ada code. This invocation is necessarily asynchronous to be compliant with the Ravenscar Profile.

For each distributed application, a discriminated record data type is generated. The discriminant of this record is the operation that is called by a node. For each operation that could be invoked remotely in the distributed application, a list of components corresponding to the operation parameters is added to the request type.

To convert a request into a data representation suitable to be transmitted through the network, we generate a package instantiation of the generic package Marshallers of

PolyORB-HI. The routines in this package provide deterministic ($O(data\ size)$) conversion functions suitable for communication systems of HI applications.

5.2.2 Communication Channels and Request Dispatching

To be compliant with the HI requirements, all the aspects of the distributed system have to be statically known (at compile time). Therefore, the entire task-set and all communication channels between different nodes have to be created at system initialization. To achieve this, a deployment package is generated for each node and contains the deployment information this node has on the other nodes of the distributed application. This information constitutes, in conjunction with the generated naming table (see below), the means for a node to send or receive invocations from another node. This mechanism, similar to the GLADE [PT00] way to deploy distributed applications, is completely static and does not use dynamic component creation (component factories in the CORBA Component Model [BMS03]). The deployment information is generated in a package called `Deployment` used by PolyORB-HI. It contains two Ada enumeration types:

- `Node_Type`: for each node we create an enumeration literal that lists all nodes reachable by the application. A literal is allocated for the local node (`My_Node`).
- `Port_Type`: for each `in` port, we declare an enumeration literal (see 4.2).

The naming information allows particular node to send (receive) requests to (from) another node in the distributed application. It contains, for each node, the information necessary to establish a connection with another node. This information is deduced statically from the AADL model's connection topology. The naming information is generated in a package called `Naming` used by the internal entities of PolyORB-HI.

5.2.3 Client Side Remote Activities

The communication between nodes can be assimilated to "method calls": the endpoint of a data port connection or an event data port connection is a subprogram call parameter. So, we can reflect the message sending by a call to a *stub* that builds a request from the parameters, marshalls this request and transmits it through the network to the receiver subprogram. For one interaction, the caller side is seen as a client; the called node a server. Besides, the compliance to the Ravenscar Profile reduces the invocation call protocol set to the single asynchronous way. Therefore, our code generator produces an asynchronous stub for each "method call". It also checks that the data flow between components is suitable for the asynchronous communication (remotely invoked subprograms must not have [in] out parameters).

Let us note the use of asynchronous communication is not sufficient to guarantee correctness of distributed applications sharing data across nodes. We are also designing a Ravenscar Profile compliant consensus algorithm between the different nodes.

5.2.4 Server Side Remote Activities

The receiver of a request is usually a sporadic AADL thread. Sporadic threads are mapped to sporadic Ada tasks. The work of a sporadic task consists of waiting for its dispatching event, then, when the dispatching event comes, doing the corresponding work. This work can be seen as the invocation of a request handler. As stated in [HZP06], an extra task plays the role of a protocol handler and dispatches the incoming requests to their respective handlers. The generated code for the request handler consists of an instantiation of a generic package since the work of all sporadic tasks is similar and a lot of code can be factorized. Generic instantiations does not cause significant overhead in our case because we use them only to create tasks and data marshallers/unmarshallers.

6   Conclusion and Future Work

Building HI distributed systems is a very tedious task since the application has to be verifiable and statically analyzable. The AADL fits these two requirements and allows the designer to describe different aspects of his distributed application (number of nodes, number of tasks in each node, connection between nodes...).

In this paper we presented rules for generating Ada code compliant with the Ravenscar Profile for HI applications from their AADL models. We also presented rules to generate code for HI distributed applications, with each node being compliant with the Ravenscar Profile. The generated code uses our middleware PolyORB-HI to guarantee the communication between application nodes.

This work is being done in the context of the IST-ASSERT project[4] that aims at developing new system engineering methods for DRE systems. We validated our code generator and middleware on case studies built by contributors of the ASSERT project. These examples have been successfully tested on native platforms; local examples have also been successfully tested using the tsim simulator for the LEON processor.

Future work will consider the enrichment of the coding rules to more complex cases; supporting field buses such as SpaceWire for LEON targets. Finally, a consensus algorithm will be provided to enable shared data between nodes (see 5.2.3).

Acknowledgements. The authors thank TULLIO VARDANEGA and JUAN ANTONIO DE LA PUENTE for their valuable feedback during the design of PolyORB-HI.

References

[BDV03]   Burns, A., Dobbing, B., Vardanega, T.: Guide for the use of the Ada Ravenscar Profile in high integrity systems. Technical report, University of York, UK (january 2003)

[BMS03]   Barros, M.C., Madeira, E.R., Sotoma, I.: An Experience on CORBA Component Deployment. In: Proceedings of the sixth International Symposium on Autonomous Decentralized Systems (ISADS'03) (April 2003)

[BV05]   Bordin, M., Vardanega, T.: Automated Model-Based Generation of Ravenscar-Compliant Source Code. In: ECRTS '05: Proceedings of the 17th Euromicro Conference on Real-Time Systems (ECRTS'05), pp. 59–67. IEEE Computer Society, Washington, DC (2005)

---

[4] ASSERT is part of the Sixth Framework Programme IST of the European Union, see http://www.assert-online.net

[HZP06]   Hugues, J., Zalila, B., Pautet, L.: Middleware and Tool suite for High Integrity Systems (December 2006)
[PT00]   Pautet, L., Tardieu, S.: GLADE: a Framework for Building Large Object-Oriented Real-Time Distributed Systems. In: Proceedings of the 3rd IEEE International Symposium on Object-Oriented Real-Time Distributed Computing (ISORC'00), Newport Beach, California, USA (June 2000)
[SAE04]   SAE. Architecture Analysis & Design Language (AS5506), (september 2004), available at http://www.sae.org
[SAE05]   SAE. Language Compliance and Application Program Interface. SAE 2005. The AADL Specification Document Annex D.
[SLNM05]   Singhoff, F., Legrand, J., Nana, L., Marcé, L.: Scheduling and memory requirement analysis with aadl. In: ACM Press (ed.) proceedings of the ACM SIGADA International Conference, vol. 25, pp. 1–10. ACM Press, New York (2005)
[Sof]   Ellidiss Software. STOOD. http://www.ellidiss.com/stood.shtml
[SRL90]   Sha, L., Rajkumar, R., Lehoczky, J.P.: Priority Inheritance Protocols: An Approach to Real-Time Synchronization. In: IEEE Transactions on Computers, pp. 1175–1185. IEEE Computer Society, Washington DC (1990)
[VHPK05]   Vergnaud, T., Hugues, J., Pautet, L., Kordon, F.: Rapid Development Methodology for Customized Middleware. In: Proceedings of the 16th IEEE International Workshop on Rapid System Prototyping (RSP'05), Montreal, Canada (June 2005)
[WG05]   Ada Working Group. Ada Reference Manual. ISO/IEC (2005), Available at http://www.adaic.com/standards/05rm/RM-Final.pdf.

Automatic Ada Code Generation Using a Model-Driven Engineering Approach*

Diego Alonso, Cristina Vicente-Chicote, Pedro Sánchez, Bárbara Álvarez,
and Fernando Losilla

División de Sistemas e Ingeniería Electrónica (DSIE)
Universidad Politécnica de Cartagena, Campus Muralla del Mar, E-30202, Spain
{diego.alonso,cristina.vicente,pedro.sanchez,balvarez}@upct.es

Abstract. Currently, Model-Driven Engineering (MDE) is considered one of the most promising approaches for software development. In this paper, a simple but complete example based on state-machines will be used to demonstrate the benefits of this approach. After defining a modelling language (meta-model) for state-machines, a graphical tool will be presented which is aimed at easing the description and validation of state-machine models. These models will then be used as inputs for another tool which will automatically generate the corresponding Ada code, including a simulation program to test the correctness and performance of the implemented application.

1 Introduction

In the last decades, programming languages and *Computer Aided Software Engineering* (CASE) tools promised an important improvement in the way software was developed. This improvement was due to the increase of the level of abstraction provided by the languages and tools used for software development. However, there have been several factors that have led to lower benefits than expected, such as: (1) the lack of accuracy of the used notations and, as a result, the loss of very relevant attributes (e.g. safety, reliability, etc); (2) the strong dependency of software on the execution infrastructure, i.e. the use of code-oriented designs; and (3) the impossibility of reusing most of the developed software artefacts in other projects (except when applying design patterns [9]). The main reason why all of these tools have failed to accomplish their promises can be summarized in the following sentence: all of them provide higher levels of abstraction in the *solution space* rather than in the *problem space*.

Model-Driven Engineering (MDE) is an emerging paradigm aimed at raising the level of abstraction during the software development process further than third-generation programming languages can. MDE technologies offer a promising approach to address the inability of third-generation languages to cope with increasing software complexity, allowing designers to describe domain concepts effectively [13]. This new paradigm uses models as first-class artefact's, making it possible to model those concepts needed to fully describe new systems, together with the relationships existing

---

* This work has been partially funded by the Spanish CICYT project MEDWSA (TIN2006-15175-C05-02) and the PMPDI-UPCT-2006 program (Universidad Politécnica de Cartagena).

N. Abdennahder, F. Kordon (Eds.): Ada-Europe 2007, LNCS 4498, pp. 168–179, 2007.

between them. Objects are replaced by models, and model transformations appear as a powerful mechanism for incremental and automatic software development [7].

The benefits of raising the level of abstraction from code blocks (either functions or classes) to models are clear. When generative techniques become more mature, MDE will exhibit all its potential for automating code generation, while keeping the final system compliant with the original requirements, following the correct-by-construction philosophy [5]. For this reason, MDE can be considered a very promising approach, especially in those domains where certain requirements must be guaranteed, a traditional field for Ada applications.

1.1 The Model-Driven Approach

MDE promotes a software development process centred on models which are systematically used everywhere. In this approach, models play a central role guiding not only the software development and documentation processes but also its management and evolution. In MDE [12] models are created starting from formal meta-models, which may describe complementary views of the same system, observed at different abstraction levels. The use of formal meta-models allow designers to build both models and transformations between them in a more natural way.

The *Model Driven Architecture* (MDA) proposal [1] is the particular view of the MDE process proposed by the *Object Management Group* (OMG). MDA defines a software development process aimed at separating the business logic from the technological platform. To achieve this, MDA proposes three modelling abstraction levels. Firstly, a *Computation Independent Model* (CIM) represents the system seen as a business process. Secondly, this CIM is refined into a *Platform Independent Model* (PIM) which describes different aspects of the CIM in more detail but which does not contain information about any specific execution platform. This PIM can evolve, through model transformations, to other more specific PIMs. Finally, when a PIM can not further evolve without specifying certain platform-dependent details, it evolves to one or more *Platform Specific Models* (PSMs), one for each platform being considered for system deployment. Each PSM can then evolve independently to other more specific PSMs until the final application code can be automatically generated.

The OMG has defined a series of standards to support MDA and to achieve interoperability among all the tools involved in the software development process defined by this approach. Among these standards, it is worth highlighting the *Meta-Object Facility* (MOF) [2] and the *XML Metadata Interchange* (XMI) standards. The MOF specification defines a meta-language and a set of standard interfaces aimed at defining and manipulating both models and meta-models. The XMI specification enables to store MOF artefact's into XML files, so they can be freely interchanged between tools that conform to these two standards. Although both MOF and XMI have been defined to support the MDA approach, they can also be used in the more general MDE approach, as it will be shown in this paper.

1.2 Goals of the Paper

The main goal of this paper is to highlight the advantages of the MDE approach by means of a complete example, i.e. from the meta-model definition, to the implementation of a graphical modelling tool and a model transformation to enable automatic Ada code generation. To achieve this goal, the following sub-goals will be addressed:

- The first step when using a MDE approach is to define the modelling language (meta-model) which should include those concepts relevant to the application domain being considered. We have chosen to define a simplified version of the UML 2.0 state-machine meta-model, since these artefacts are quite simple and well known in the real-time community. This sub-goal will be covered in section 2.
- A graphical modelling tool, based on the previously defined meta-model, has been implemented in order to help designers to build new state-machine models. This tool, together with a couple of example state-machines built with it, will be presented in subsection 3.1.
- Finally, the Ada code corresponding to one of the example state-machines will be automatically obtained using a model-to-text (M2T) transformation. This transformation will be described in subsection 3.2.

After covering these goals, the paper will present some related work together with some conclusions and future research lines.

2   A Motivation Example: Modelling State-Machines

This section presents an example based on the description of state-machines, which will be used through the rest of this paper to illustrate the benefits of the MDE approach. We have chosen state-machines since they are quite simple and widely used to describe high-integrity and safety critical systems, well-known application domains for the Ada community.

Applying a MDE approach to model state-machines (or any other general-purpose or specific application domain) requires selecting or defining the most appropriate modelling language (meta-model) for describing them. As stated in section 1, the OMG currently offers a set of standards related to MDA, which include MOF as the top level meta-meta-modelling language (language for describing meta-models, e.g. UML).

Nowadays, the most widely-used implementation of MOF is provided as an Eclipse[1] plug-in called *Eclipse Modelling Framework* (EMF) [6]. Although EMF currently supports only a subset of MOF, called *Essential MOF* (EMOF), it allows designers to create, manipulate and store (in XML format) both models and meta-models. Actually, many other MDE-related initiatives are currently being developed around EMF, such as *Graphical Modelling Framework* (GMF), *EMF Technology* (EMFT) or *Generative Modelling Technologies* (GMT).

All meta-models designed using EMF look very much like UML class diagrams where: (1) domain concepts are represented using boxes (*EClass* in EMOF), (2) inheritance arrows define concept specialisation (EMOF supports multiple inheritance),

---

[1] Eclipse is an open source, platform-independent software framework both for developing software (like a classical development environment) and for deploying final applications (what the project calls "rich-client applications"). It is available at http://www.eclipse.org

and (3) association arrows represent relationships between concepts (*EReference* in EMOF) with or without containment (composition). All these EMF elements will be shown in the state-machine meta-model which is presented in the following subsection.

In this paper a simplified version of the UML 2.0 state-machine meta-model has been chosen to illustrate the power and benefits of the MDE approach. Thus, some of the concepts currently included in the original UML 2.0 state-machines have been removed for the sake of simplicity, e.g. regions and certain kinds of pseudo-states (join, fork, choice, etc.).

As shown in Fig. 1, the simplified state-machine meta-model contains a set of `vertices` and `transitions`. Two different kinds of `vertices` can be defined: `states` and `pseudo-states`. The difference between them is quiet subtle: although a state-machine can only be in a certain observable `state` at a time and never in a `pseudo-state`, pseudo-states are needed to fully describe state-machine behaviour, e.g. defining the initial pseudo-state as the starting execution point of the state-machine. Conversely, a `finalstate` is observable and thus it should be considered a state, more specifically, the state where the state-machine execution ends.

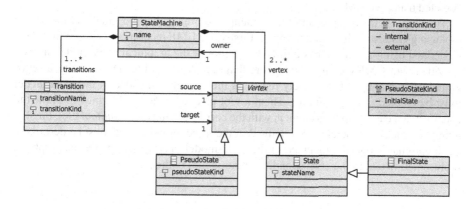

Fig. 1. The state-machine meta-model

Two different kinds of transitions have been included in the meta-model. On the one hand, external transitions exit the current state (calling its *onExit* activity) and, after executing their *fire* activity, they enter the same or another state (calling the corresponding *onEntry* and *do* activities). On the other hand, internal transitions do not change the current state. They only execute their *fire* activity and make the current state call its *do* activity (neither the *onEntry* nor the *onExit* activities are executed).

Transitions are not triggered by *events* and they have no *guards* (actually, these two concepts have not been included in the meta-model). Conversely, transitions are triggered by their names; this is why, in order to obtain a deterministic behaviour, all transitions leaving from the same state must have different names.

3   Tools for Modelling and Implementing State-Machines

This section presents the two tools implemented as part of this work, both of them based on the state-machine meta-model previously described. First, we describe a graphical modelling tool which allows designers to create and validate new state-machine models in a very intuitive way. The section ends showing a tool for automatically generating Ada code from any state-machine graphical model correctly built (and validated) with the previous tool.

3.1   A State-Machine Graphical Modelling Tool

A state-machine graphical modelling tool has been implemented using the facilities provided by the Graphical Modelling Framework (GMF) Eclipse plug-in. This tool is aimed at developing graphical model editors from any EMF meta-model. GMF integrates the facilities provided by other Eclipse plug-ins, namely: Graphical Editing Framework (GEF) and EMFT-OCL. The first of these plug-ins enables the definition of graphical elements that will represent the concepts included in the meta-model, while the second one enables the evaluation of OCL [4] queries and constraints in the models depicted using the GMF tool.

The steps of the process and the elements required to build a graphical modelling tool using GMF are illustrated in Fig. 2. Firstly, the EMF meta-model (*.ecore* file) must be defined using either the basic EMF tree-editor or the graphical meta-modelling tool provided with GMF (see the GMF ecore diagram shown in Fig. 1). Secondly, a set of graphical elements that intuitively represent the concepts included in the meta-model must be created (*.gmfgraph* file). Then, a tool palette has to be designed to allow the user to create each graphical element with the corresponding tool (*.gmftool* file). Finally, a mapping between the elements defined in the three previous files must be described, i.e. the domain concepts included in the meta-model must be mapped to its graphical representation and to the corresponding creation tool in the palette.

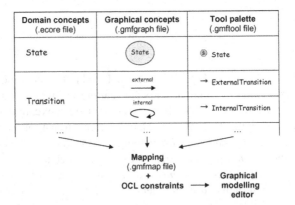

Fig. 2. Sketch of the process and the elements required for building a GMF tool

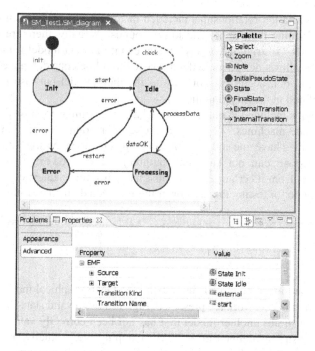

Fig. 3. A graphical state-machine model correctly validated

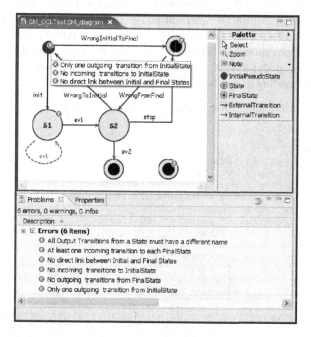

Fig. 4. Another graphical state-machine model. In this case, the validation process detects some incorrect elements (marked with small crosses).

Only the association relationships included in EMF meta-models can be somehow restricted by defining their upper and lower bounds. Actually, there are no means to include any further restrictions or any semantics into a meta-model using only EMF. However, GMF allows designers to define what should be considered a correct model and what should not, according not only to the meta-model but also to some OCL constraints defined in the mapping file.

The constraints included in our meta-model are very similar to those defined for the UML 2.0 state-machines. Some of these constraints are: (1) `Initial pseudo-states` have one and only one outgoing and no incoming `Transitions`; (2) `FinalStates` can not have any outgoing `Transition`; (3) All outgoing `Transitions` from a certain `State` must have different names; etc. As an example, the OCL code for testing the last constraint has been defined as follows:

```
self.owner.transitions -> forAll ( t1, t2 | (( t1.source = self )
    and ( t2.source = self ) and ( t1.target <> t2.target ))
    implies ( t1.transitionName <> t2.transitionName )
)
```

Next, two state-machine models built using the GMF graphical modelling tool implemented as part of this work are presented. Fig. 3 shows a valid state-machine model, while Fig. 4 illustrates another model that has not been correctly validated according to the OCL constraints defined in the GMF mapping file. Actually, as shown in the "Problems" tab under the diagram depicted in Fig. 4, six OCL constraints are violated, e.g. the following three errors appear associated to the initial state: (1) it can only have one outgoing transition (*init* or *WrongInitToFinal* has to be removed), (2) it can not have any incoming transition (*WrongToInitial* has to be removed), and (3) it can not be directly linked to a final states (*WrongInitToFinal* has to be removed).

The state-machine model shown in Fig. 3 will be used to obtain the corresponding Ada code with the model-to-text transformation described in subsection 3.2. Part of the XML file corresponding to this state-machine model is shown below.

Excerpt of the XML code corresponding to the state-machine model shown in Fig. 3:

```
<?xml version="1.0"
encoding="UTF-8" ?>
  <StateMachineTool:StateMachine xmi:version="2.0"
    xmlns:xmi="http://www.omg.org/XMI"
    xmlns:xsi="http://www.w3.org/2001/XMLSchema-instance"
    xmlns:StateMachineTool="StateMachineTool" name="SMExample">
  <transitions transitionName="init"
    source="//@vertex.0" target="//@vertex.1"
    transitionKind="external"/>
    ...
  <transitions transitionName="check"
    source="//@vertex.3" target="//@vertex.3"
    transitionKind="internal"/>
  <vertex xsi:type="StateMachineTool:PseudoState"/>
  <vertex xsi:type="StateMachineTool:State" stateName="Init"/>
  <vertex xsi:type="StateMachineTool:State" stateName="Error"/>
  <vertex xsi:type="StateMachineTool:State" stateName="Idle"/>
  <vertex xsi:type="StateMachineTool:State" stateName="Processing"/>
  </StateMachineTool:StateMachine>
```

3.2 Model Transformations: From Graphical State-machines to Ada Code

As already commented in section 1, model transformation is one of the key concepts of the MDE process, being one of the most powerful tools for designers. Actually, the OMG is about to finish the specification of the *MOF Query-View-Transformation* (QVT) [3], as the standard language for model transformations for their MDA approach.

Models can be transformed into other models or into any textual representation. *Model-to-Model* (M2M) transformations allow designers to refine abstract models (defined at the beginning of the design process) to obtain models that are closer to the final solution. These M2M transformations require defining a mapping between the corresponding meta-models, i.e. a transformation between the concepts represented in each meta-model. Once models are close enough to implementation, they can be transformed into a textual representation (e.g. code), using a *Model-to-Text* (M2T) transformation. Currently, it is possible to find some tools that make it possible to define both M2M and M2T transformations. Probably in the future, these tools will provide some interactive environment that will allow designers to guide the transformation process.

Among the M2T transformation tools currently available, we have chosen *MOF-Script*[2] to generate Ada code from the state-machine models previously built using the GMF tool presented in section 3.1. MOFScript enables the description of M2T transformations both in a declarative and in an imperative way. An excerpt of the MOFScript code implemented to obtain Ada code from any of the state-machine models previously defined, is shown below.

Excerpt of the MOFScript code implemented for transforming models into Ada code:

```
texttransformation SM_Model2Ada1 (in MetaModel:"StateMachineTool")
{
  MetaModel.StateMachine :: main ( ){
    ...
    // Writing StateMachine.adb
    file sm_adb (self.name + ".adb")
    var initialTransitions:List=self.transitions->select (
        t: MetaModel.Transition |
        t.source.oclIsTypeOf(MetaModel.PseudoState))
    var initial:MetaModel.Transition=initialTransitions.first()
    sm_adb.println("with Ada.Text_Io; use Ada.Text_Io;");
    sm_adb.print  ("with " + self.name+"_Code" + "; use ");
    sm_adb.println(self.name + "_Code" + ";");
    sm_adb.println("package body " + self.name + " is")
    sm_adb.print("\t Current_State : T_State := " )
    sm_adb.println (initial._getFeature("target").stateName+";")
    writeFunction("Get_Current_State","T_State","return Current_State;")
    transitionNames -> forEach ( tn:String ) { writeProcedure ( tn ) }
    sm_adb.println ("end " + self.name + ";")
    ...
  } // main
} // texttransformation
```

As stated in [9], state-machines can be implemented using (1) big `if..else` (or `case`) like blocks, that define state changes depending on the transition being fired;

---

[2] `http://www.eclipse.org/gmt/mofscript/`

(2) a look-up table that relates transitions and states; or (3) applying the State pattern. Each of these possible ways of coding the logic of a state-machine can be implemented by simply defining different M2T transformations. Due to limitations of space, only one of the possible transformations of type (1) will be presented. This transformation produces two Ada packages (both specification and body) and an animator for the generated state-machine. One package contains the logic of the transitions between the different states, while the other defines all the activities present in the model (*onEntry, do, onExit* and *fire*). In the first package, each Transition is associated to an Ada `procedure`, and each State is part of an enumerated type. An excerpt of the Ada code resulting from applying this M2T transformation to the model depicted in Fig. 3 is shown below. The package *SMExample* contains the logic of transition between states, while package *SMExample_Code* (not shown here) defines the activities. This schema follows a separation of concerns approach and avoids the unnoticed modification of the logic of the state-machine while the user was filling the code of the different activities.

Excerpt of the Ada code generated from the model shown in Fig. 3:

```
with Ada.Text_Io; use Ada.Text_Io;
with SMExample_Code;
package body SMExample is
    -- ------------------------------------
    Current_State : T_State := Init;
    -- ------------------------------------
    function Get_Current_State return T_State is
    begin
        return Current_State;
    end Get_Current_State;
    -- ------------------------------------
    procedure Start is
    begin
        case Current_State is
            when Init =>
                    SMExample_Code.Init_onExit;
                    SMExample_Code.Start_fire;
                    SMExample_Code.Idle_onEntry;
                    Current_State := Idle;
                    SMExample_Code.Idle_do;
            when others => null;
        end case;
    end Start;
    -- ------------------------------------
    ...
    -- ------------------------------------
    procedure Check is
    begin
        case Current_State is
            when Idle => SMExample_Code.Idle_do;
            when others => null;
        end case;
    end Check;
    -- ------------------------------------
end SMExample;
```

Lastly, the `null` statement in the `when others` line defines the reaction of the state-machine when the transition just triggered is not defined for the current state. This is just another way of handling semantic variation points, as stated in UML and [8].

Of course there can be different M2T transformations to support different policies for this semantic variation point, e.g. raise an exception. Another possible implementation for type (1) transformation could be to define both transitions and states as enumerated types, while using a unique and big `procedure` to specify the behaviour of the state-machine; again, it is also possible to define yet another M2T transformation to do this, which shows the potential benefits of developing software using a MDE approach.

4   Related Work

As already stated in the introduction, the purpose of this paper is to present a simple but complete example, based on state-machines, to demonstrate the benefits of applying a Model-Driven approach to software development. Although there are some tools that support the MDE approach (actually not many), we have chosen *Eclipse* as it is an open source project. Some of the alternative MDE environments we also considered were *MetaEdit+*[3] and *Microsoft Visual Studio with Domain-Specific Language Tools*[4], both of them available as commercial tools.

MetaEdit+ enables domain specific meta-model definition, graphical model specification and template-based model-to-code transformation. However, MetaEdit+ lacks two of the cornerstones of MDE, namely: (1) the underlying meta-meta-model is not available (Eclipse uses the MOF standard) and (2) it is not possible to define model-to-model transformations. Without a meta-meta-model it is not possible to clearly define and manipulate the meta-model elements, while without model-to-model transformations it becomes impossible to define different modelling abstraction levels.

On the other hand, the Visual Studio DSL Tools are the Microsoft answer to the OMG MDA initiative and they tightly integrated with other Microsoft and .NET tools. According to [10], "software factories use custom collections of DSLs to provide sets of abstractions customised to meet the needs of specific families of systems, instead of taking a generic, one-size-fits-all approach".

Although the state-machine graphical modelling tool and the model-to-Ada code transformation have only been developed as an example of the benefits of the MDE approach, it is worth to compare these tools with other well-known state-machine CASE tools. State-machines have been used in software system design since the early 1970s, being particularly useful in the embedded system domain. As a consequence, many different tools are currently available for describing and implementing state-machines in different programming languages. Among them, probably one of the most widely used is STATEMATE [11]. Later on, the UML adopted state-machines for describing the behaviour of the elements being modelled. Thus, new visual and UML-compliant tools appeared in the marketplace (e.g. Rational Rose, Raphsody or Poseidon, among many others), allowing designers to model and implement this artefacts. As the scope of these tools is wider than just generating code for state-machines, they commonly produce complex and cumbersome code making it difficult to extract the state-machine code. In this sense, the main advantage of the MDE approach is that developers can

---

[3] http://www.metacase.com

[4] http://msdn2.microsoft.com/en-us/vstudio/aa718368.apx

decide the abstraction level and the scope of their applications and the way models are transformed into code, giving them the full control of the development process.

5   Conclusions and Future Research Lines

Currently, Model-Driven Engineering (MDE) is considered one of the most promising approaches for software development. MDE merges new and matured technologies and is supported by an increasingly growing academic and commercial community.

In this paper we have presented a simple but complete example that demonstrates the great benefits of applying a MDE approach, both for modelling and implementing software systems. State-machines have been chosen as our example domain since these artefacts are quite simple and well known in the real-time community.

In order to allow designers to describe state-machines, we have defined a modelling language (meta-model) which is a simplified version of the one included in the UML 2.0. From this meta-model we have implemented a graphical modelling tool aimed at easing the specification and validation of state-machine models. These models can then be used to automatically generate Ada code using a model-to-text transformation also implemented as part of this work. All the specifications and applications presented in this paper have been implemented using some of the currently available MDE tools offered by Eclipse: such as EMF, GMF, EMFT-OCL and MOFScript, among others.

Although we have outlined different possible implementations of state-machines in Ada, only one of them has been addressed in this paper by means of a model-to-Ada code transformation. This transformation generates, among other Ada files, a simulation program that allows users to test the correctness and performance of the generated code.

Currently we are working on the definition of new model-to-text transformations in order to test the performance of other Ada state-machine implementations. We are also working in the definition of other model-to-code transformations to test different language implementations, in particular Java and VHDL. In the future we plan to extend the state-machine meta-model (and thus the graphical modelling tool) in order to include new domain concepts such as orthogonal regions and new pseudo-state kinds (i.e. join, fork, etc.).

Despite of the promising results shown by the MDE approach, it is still at a very early stage and there is a lot of research to be done before it can exhibit all its potential. Nevertheless, the increasingly growing interest of the software engineering community in the MDE approach envisages very good results in the coming years. Probably, one of the most promising features of this approach, in particular for the safety-critical real-time systems community, is in the field of automatic software V&V and certification. Some related research areas in this field include, among others: formal model transformations, automatic test generation, and robust and efficient code generation.

References

[1] Model Driven Architecture Guide Version v1.0.1, omg/2003-06- 01. Object Management Group (OMG) (2003), Available online:
http://www.omg.org/docs/omg/03-06-01.pdf

[2] Meta-Object Facility (MOF) Specification v2.0, ptc/04-10-15. Object Management Group (OMG) (2004), Available online:
http://www.omg.org/technology/documents/modeling_spec_catalog.htm#MOF

[3] Meta-Object Facility (MOF) v2.0 Query/View/Transformation Specification, ptc/05-11-01. Object Management Group (OMG) (2005), Available online: http://www.omg.org/technology/documents/modeling spec catalog.htm#QVT

[4] Object Constraint Language (OCL) Specification v2.0, formal/06-05- 01. Object Management Group (OMG) (2006), Available online:
http://www.omg.org/technology/documents/modeling-spec- catalog.htm#OCL

[5] Balasubramanian, K., Gokhale, A., Karsai, G., Sztipanovits, J., Neema, S.: Developing applications using model-driven design environments. IEEE Computer, vol. 39(2), IEEE Computer Society (2006)

[6] Budinsky, F., Steinberg, D., Merks, E., Ellersick, R., Grose, T.: Eclipse Modeling Framework. Eclipse series. Addison-Wesley Professional, Reading (2003) ISBN 0131425420

[7] Bézivin, J.: On the unification power of models. Software and Systems Modeling 4(2), 171–188 (2005)

[8] Chauvel, F., Jézéquel, J.M.: Code Generation from UML Models with Semantic Variation Points. In: Briand, L.C., Williams, C. (eds.) MoDELS 2005. LNCS, vol. 3713, pp. 54–68. Springer, Heidelberg (2005)

[9] Gamma, E., Helm, R., Johnson, R., Vlissides, J.: Design patterns: elements of reusable object-oriented software. Addison-Wesley Professional, Reading (1995)

[10] Greenfield, J., Short, K., Cook, S., Kent, S., Crupi, J.: Software Factories: Assembling Applications with Patterns, Models, Frameworks, and Tools, 1st edn. Wiley, Chichester (2004) ISBN 0471202843

[11] Harel, D., Naamad, A.: The STATEMATE semantics of statecharts. In: ACM Trans. Softw. Eng. Methodol., vol. 5(4), ACM Press, New York (1996)

[12] Kent, S.: Model Driven Engineering. In: Butler, M., Petre, L., Sere, K. (eds.) IFM 2002. LNCS, vol. 2335, pp. 286–298. Springer, Heidelberg (2002)

[13] Schmidt, D.C.: Model-Driven Engineering. In: IEEE Computer, vol. 39(2), IEEE Computer Society Press, Los Alamitos (2006)

Towards User-Level Extensibility of an Ada Library: An Experiment with Cheddar

Frank Singhoff and Alain Plantec

LISYC/EA 3883, University of Brest
20, av Le Gorgeu
CS 93837, 29238 Brest Cedex 3, France
{singhoff,plantec}@univ-brest.fr

Abstract. In this article, we experiment a way to extend an Ada library called Cheddar. Cheddar provides a domain specific language. Programs written with this domain specific language can be interpreted in order to perform real time scheduling analysis of real time systems. By the past, different projects showed that the Cheddar programming language is useful for the modeling of real time schedulers. But these experiments also showed that the interpreter is lacking of efficiency in case of large scheduling simulations. In this article, by designing a Cheddar meta-model, we investigate on how to compile such Cheddar programs in order to extend the Cheddar library. For such a purpose, we use *Platypus*, a meta CASE Tool based on *EXPRESS*. For a given Cheddar program and with a meta-model of Cheddar handled by *Platypus*, we can generate a set of Ada packages. Such Ada packages can be compiled and integrated as builtin schedulers into Cheddar. Then, the efficiency of scheduling simulations can be increased.

Keywords: Meta-modeling, Ada code generating, Cheddar, Platypus.

1 Introduction

This article deals with the Cheddar library [1]. Cheddar is a library designed for the performance analysis of real time applications. With Cheddar, a real time application is modeled as a set of tasks, processors, schedulers, buffers ... This library provides a set of real time schedulers and their analysis tools implemented in Ada. Schedulers currently implemented into Cheddar are mostly met in real time applications and the library can be used to perform performance analysis of many different types of real time applications. However, it exists a need to extend these Cheddar analysis tools to specific scheduler or task models. For such a purpose, it requires that the user understands the Cheddar design. Furthermore, designing a new scheduler or a new task model may be difficult without an environment which makes it possible to easily write and test the scheduler code. In order to ease the design of new schedulers, Cheddar provides a programming language. The model of a scheduler or of a task model described and tested with the Cheddar programming environment is interpreted: thus the designer can easily handle and experiment his scheduler models.

N. Abdennahder, F. Kordon (Eds.): Ada-Europe 2007, LNCS 4498, pp. 180–191, 2007.

Different projects showed that the Cheddar programming language is useful for the modeling of real time schedulers. But these experiments also showed that the interpreter is lacking of efficiency in case of large scheduling simulations.

This article presents a way to extend an Ada library. It presents a way to compile Cheddar programs by automatically producing Ada code corresponding to the modeled schedulers. For such a purpose, we use the *Platypus* meta CASE tool and a meta-model which specifies both the Ada 95 programming features and the Cheddar programming language features. Then, from the user-defined scheduler model, one can generate the new builtin scheduler fully integrated into the Cheddar library.

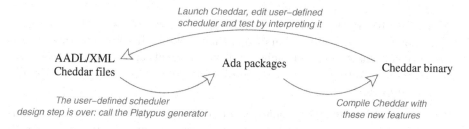

Fig. 1. The user-defined scheduler design process with Cheddar

The scheduler design and integration process proposed in this article is depicted by figure 1. This process is made of two main steps:

1. the first step is the new scheduler or the new task model design; a new scheduler and task model is specified with the Cheddar programming language; such a program can be interpreted by Cheddar allowing early testing and improvements;
2. the second step is the new scheduler or the new task model integration. It consists in the automatic generation of Ada packages from the user-defined scheduler; a Cheddar version integrating the new scheduler and task model is then recompiled.

This article is organized as follows. In section 2, we outline the Cheddar programming language and we give an example of its use. Then, we shortly describe the design of the Cheddar library in section 3. Section 4 is devoted to the process we use to generate Ada packages with the meta CASE Tool *Platypus*. In section 5, we propose a meta-model for the Cheddar programming language. The generated Ada code is briefly described in section 6. Finally, we conclude by describing the current status of the project in section 7.

2   The Cheddar Programming Language

In this section, we give an overview of the Cheddar programming language. A complete description of the language can be found in [2]. The use of the Cheddar programming language is illustrated by the example of the sporadic task model with an EDF scheduler [3].

2.1   Outline of the Cheddar Programming Language

The Cheddar programming language is composed of two parts:

1. a small Ada-like language which is used to express computations on simulation data. Simulation data are constants or variables used by the scheduling simulator engine of Cheddar in order to simulate task and scheduler behaviors. Examples of simulation data are task wake up times or task priorities. A program written with the Cheddar programming language is organized in sections. A section is a kind of Ada sub-program;
2. a set of timed automata such as those proposed by UPPAAL [4,5,6] which is a toolbox for the verification of real time systems. In Cheddar, these timed automata allow to model timing and synchronization behaviors of tasks and schedulers. Automata may run Ada-like sections in order to read or modify simulator data.

The Ada-like language provides usual statements such as loops, conditional statements, assignments. It also provides statements which are specific to the design and the debug of scheduling algorithms. Two kinds of such specific statements exist: high-level and low-level statements. High-level statements operate on vectors which store a simulation data for all tasks, messages, buffers, processors ... Low-level statements only operate on scalar simulation data.

The simplified BNF syntax of the language is given in figure 8. The *entry* rule specifies that a program is a set of sections. Most of the time, a program is composed of the following sections [1]: a *start_section* which contains variable declarations ; a *priority_section* which contains the code to compute simulation data on each unit of time during simulation; and an *election_section* which looks for the task to run on simulation time.

The *statement* rule gives the syntax of all available statements to the scheduler designer. The most important specific statements are the *return* statement and the *uniform/exponential* statements. The *return* statement gives the identifier of the task to run. *uniform/exponential* statements customize the way random values are generated during simulation time.

The language also provides operators and types. It provides usual Ada types such as scalar *integer*, *boolean*, *double*, *string* types or array and their attributes (*first*, *last*, *range*, ...). It also provides usual logical and arithmetic operators. As for the statements, scheduling specific types and operators are available. For instance, the *lcm* operator computes the last common multiplier of simulation data, the *max_to_index* operator looks for the ready task which has the highest value of an array variable and the *random* type provides random generator capabilities.

The second part of a scheduler or a task model is a specification of its timing and synchronization behavior with a set of automata. Automata used by Cheddar are timed automata as they are defined in the UPPAAL toolset [6].

A timed automaton is a finite state machine extended with clock variables. In UPPAAL, a system is modeled as a network of several timed automata. The model is extended with variables. A state of the system is defined by the locations of all automata, the clock constraints, and the values of the variables. Every automaton may fire a transition separately or synchronize with another automaton, which leads to a new state.

At least, each automaton has to be composed of some predefined locations and transitions. Transitions can run sections, read and write simulation data depending on the statements given by users on transitions (clock update, synchronization, guard, ...). The BNF syntax of a guard, a synchronization or a clock update can be read in [6].

2.2   Example of a User-Defined Task Model: The Sporadic Task Model

Figure 2 and figure 3 show an example of a user-defined task model: the sporadic task model. A sporadic task is a task which can be activated several times and which has a minimal delay between each of its successive activations [7].

Figure 2 shows a Cheddar program modeling a sporadic task. The *task_activation_section* specifies how inter-activation delays have to be computed. In this

```
: start_section
    dynamic_priority : array (tasks_range) of integer;
    gen1 : random;
    exponential(gen1, 100);
    cycle_duration : array (tasks_range) of integer;

sporadic_model : task_activation_section
    cycle_duration:=max(tasks.period, gen1);

: priority_section
    dynamic_priority := tasks.start_time
        + ((tasks.activation_number-1)*tasks.period)
        + tasks.deadline;

: election_section
    return min_to_index(dynamic_priority);

sporadic_model : automaton_section
    Initialize : initial state;
    Pended, Ready, Blocked, Run : state:

    Initialize —> [ ,tasks.activation_number:=0 ,start_section?] —> Pended
    Pended —> [ engine_clock>=tasks.activation_number+
      cycle_duration, cyclic_task_clock:=tasks.capacity, ] —> Ready
    Ready —> [ , cyclic_task_clock:=cyclic_task_clock+1,elect?] —> Run
    Blocked —> [ , , V!] —> Ready
    Run —> [ cyclic_task_clock>0, , preempt!] —> Ready
    Run —> [ ,cyclic_task_clock:=0, task_activation_section!] —> Pended
```

Fig. 2. Example of a user-defined task model : the sporadic task

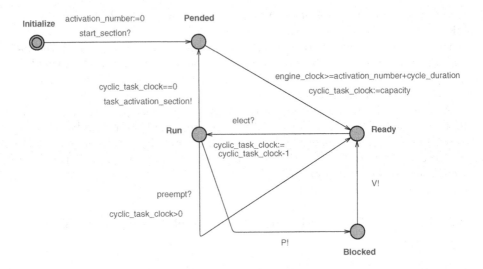

Fig. 3. Cyclic task modeling

case, the delay is the maximal value between the period of the task [1] and a value which is randomly generated according to an exponential density function.

The EDF scheduler run tasks according to task deadlines. These deadlines are computed in the *priority_section* and the task with the shortest deadline is chosen in the *election_section* sub-program.

Figure 3 models the synchronization and the timing part of the sporadic task model. In this example, the automaton describes the different task states: basically, a task can be *Pended* (it waits its next activation), *Blocked* (it waits for a shared resource access), *Ready* (it only waits for the processor), or *Run* (currently accessing the processor). The *task_activation_section* is called when the task goes from the *Run* location to the *Pended* location. During this call, the delay that the task has to wait upto its next activation time is computed and stored in the *cycle_duration* variable, as seen in figure 2.

3   Implementation of Cheddar

Before proposing a meta-model of Cheddar, let see how the library is implemented. The library implements the components showed in figure 4:

- Cheddar implements a data and a meta-data repository (eg. tasks, processors or schedulers are data; an automaton transition definition or a loop statement is a meta data);
- data and meta-data are read or written from or into the repository using the *Cheddar Data Acces Interface* (CDAI); the CDAI is used by every components of Cheddar library in order to read or write data and meta-data;

---

[1] The period is the minimal inter-activation delay.

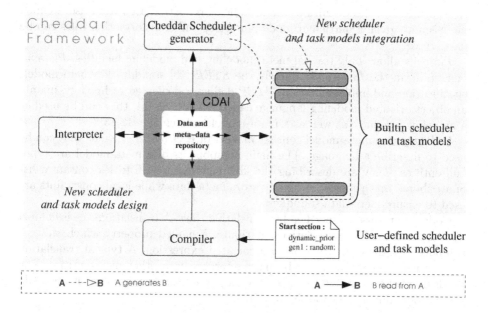

Fig. 4. The Cheddar library

- a new scheduler and task model is specified using the Cheddar programming language; the result is a Cheddar program; this program is read by a compiler that produces meta-data constituting an internal representation for it; meta-data are stored into the repository;
- the Cheddar interpreter is implemented in order to run user-defined schedulers; an interpreting process run statements and expressions stored as meta-data and interacts with Cheddar for data values reading and writing;
- the Cheddar scheduler generator is used to produce Ada packages from user-defined schedulers; for one user-defined scheduler, generated code consists in:
  - a package that implements the scheduler;
  - a package that extends CDAI for the new scheduler.

4   Modeling, Meta-modeling and Code Generating

Data and meta-data stored into the repository are described by a set of models and meta-models. All these models are handled by specific Ada code generators built with the meta CASE tool *Platypus* [8]. First, this section briefly describes the *Platypus* meta-CASE tool. Second, it describes *Platypus* using for code generating.

4.1   The Platypus Meta CASE Tool

Platypus [8] is a meta-environment fully integrated inside *Squeak* [9], a free *Smalltalk* system. *Platypus* allows meta-model specification, integrity and transformation rules definition. Meta-models are instantiated from user-defined models and, given a particular model, integrity and transformation rules can be interpreted.

Platypus allows only textual meta-modeling and modeling facilities. *Platypus* benefits from the *ISO 10303* namely the *STEP* [10] standard for meta-models specification and implementation. *STEP* defines a dedicated technology, mainly an object oriented modeling language called *EXPRESS* [11] that can be used as a modeling language as well as a meta-modeling language [12,13].

In *Platypus*, a meta-model consists in a set of *EXPRESS* schemas that can be used to describe a language. The main components of a meta-model are types and entities. They are describing the language features. Entities contain a list of attributes that provide buckets to store meta-data while local constraints are used to ensure meta-data soundness.

Code generators are specified by translation rules. A translation rule is defined within a meta-entity as a derived attribute: a named property which value is computed by the evaluation of an associated expression. A typical translation rule returns a string and can be parameterized with other meta-entities. The resulting string represents part of the target textual representation (eg. Ada source code, documentation, XML data).

4.2   Code Generating

As shown by figure 5, code generation is used at two levels of abstraction:

1. the first level is the Cheddar level. This level is related to a particular Cheddar version for which all handled object types (processors, tasks, buffers, ...) are fixed and described by the Cheddar model. The Cheddar model is an *EXPRESS* model, it is parsed by an Ada code generator that produces the CDAI set of packages. Translation rules applied by the generator are specified by an Ada for Cheddar meta-model. More explanations about this first level of design can be read in [14];
2. the second level is the Cheddar language level. It corresponds to Cheddar specializations driven by the specification of new schedulers and task models. These new parts are specified using the Cheddar programming language. The dedicated code generator is able to parse a Cheddar program and first, to produce a new scheduler implementation and second, to enrich the Cheddar object model. Then, the CDAI packages are regenerated and a new Cheddar version can be compiled.

5   Meta-modeling of the Cheddar Programming Model

The Cheddar programming language model is made of one meta model specified with *EXPRESS* that includes meta-data types (meta-entities), their relationships, constraints, and includes translation rules that are specified as meta-entities computed properties.

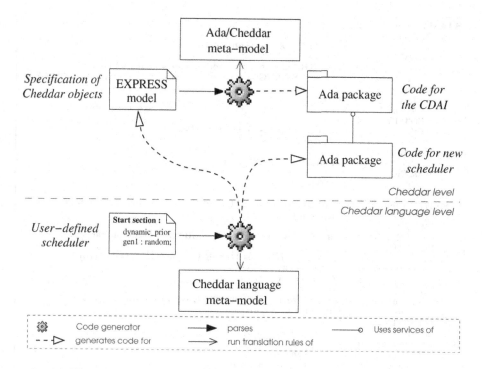

Fig. 5. Cheddar code generating from models and meta-models

The meta-model is made of several *EXPRESS* schemas. *cheddar_language* and *cheddar_automaton* schemas are the two main schemas. A part of their specification is shown in figure 6. *cheddar_language* includes the *cheddar_schema* entity that specifies what a Cheddar program is. A program is made of a set of sections. Two main kind of section can be specified, a *program_section* or an *automaton_section*. A *program_section* mainly contains a list of statements. An *automaton_section* is made of the specification of an automaton.

Cheddar compiler populates this meta-model. As an example, from one Cheddar program, one instance of *cheddar_schema* entity is created and stored into the repository.

Code generating consists in the reading of the two translation rules specified in *cheddar_schema* entity, namely the two derived attributes *cdai_entities* and *scheduler_package*:

– *cdai_entities* value is computed by the evaluation of the function *cheddar_schema_cdai_entities*; computing result consists in a new *EXPRESS* schema which extends the Cheddar model. From this new model we generate a new set of Ada packages which extends the CDAI.
– *scheduler_package* value is computed by the evaluation of the function *cheddar_schema_scheduler_package*; computing result consists in the new scheduler and task model Ada package.

```
SCHEMA cheddar_language;
  ENTITY cheddar_schema;
        sections : SET [1:?] OF section_definition;
      DERIVE
        cdai_entities : STRING:=cheddar_schema_cdai_entities(SELF);
        scheduler_package : STRING:=cheddar_schema_scheduler_package(SELF);
      WHERE
        have_one_and_only_one_election :
        sizeof(query(e <* sections | e.identifier = 'election_section'))=1;
  END_ENTITY;
  ENTITY section_definition ABSTRACT SUPERTYPE;
        identifier : STRING;
      INVERSE
        context : cheddar_schema FOR sections;
      UNIQUE
        context, identifier;
  END_ENTITY;
  ENTITY election_section_definition SUBTYPE OF (section_definition);
        task_id : return_stmt;
      DERIVE
        SELF\section_definition.identifier: STRING:='election_section';
  END_ENTITY;
  ENTITY program_section_definition SUBTYPE OF (section_definition);
        declarations : LIST OF variable;
        statements : LIST OF statement;
  END_ENTITY;
  ENTITY automaton_section_definition SUBTYPE OF (section_definition);
        automaton : automaton_definition;
  END_ENTITY;
    ...
SCHEMA cheddar_automaton;
  ENTITY automaton_definition;
        states : SET OF state_definition;
        transitions : SET OF transition_definition;
        initial_state : state_definition; ...
  END_ENTITY;
    ...
```

Fig. 6. A part of the meta-model for the Cheddar programming language

6   Cheddar Ada Packages Which Are Generated from a Cheddar Program

The Ada packages we generate for the Cheddar level is described in [14]. For the Cheddar language level, two different Ada packages are expected to be generated: packages implementing a new user-defined task model and packages implementing a new user-defined scheduler.

Cheddar tasks are implemented by a set of tagged records (see [14]): each task type is defined by a tagged record. The *Task_Activation* method of such a tagged record is able to compute the task wake up times. This sub-program is generated according to the statement the user gives in its Cheddar program (source code provided into the *task_activation_section*).

Cheddar schedulers are also implemented by a set of tagged records. A new scheduler is implemented by extending an abstract tagged record or any already existing schedulers which has a similar behavior. In order to be plugged with the Cheddar simulation engine, each scheduler tagged record has to implement a set of sub-programs such as:

```
10  procedure Build_Scheduling_Sequence(...) is
20  ...
30  begin
40    for I in Processor_Range loop
50       Check_Before_Scheduling(...);
60       Scheduler_Initialize(...);
70    end loop;
80
90    while(Current_Time < Total_Scheduling_Time) loop
100      for I in Processor_Range loop
110         Do_Election(...);
120         Next_Task(...);
130      end loop;
140      Current_Time:=Current_Time+1;
150   end loop
160 end Build_Scheduling_Sequence;
```

Fig. 7. Algorithm sketch of the Cheddar simulation engine

- *Scheduler_Initialize* which initializes variables used by the scheduler; this Ada sub-program contains the *start_section* code;
- some sub-programs to check scheduler assumptions (eg. the *Check_Before-Scheduling* sub-program);
- *Do_Election* which computes task priorities and chose the task to run; such a sub-program contains the *priority_section* and the *election_section* of the implemented scheduler;
- Finally, if a scheduler requires to store data for the tasks it provides scheduling facilities, it has to define a TCB[2] and a set of sub-programs to copy, initialize or display instances of such a TCB.

Figure 7 shows how these sub-programs work all together. The *Build_Scheduling_Sequence* is the main entry point of the Cheddar scheduling simulator. Since a system analyzed by Cheddar may model a multi-processors system, the *Build_Scheduling_Sequence* drives the simulation time unit per time unit. First, simulation data are initialized and some checks are performed to be sure that tasks meet scheduler assumptions (lines 30-70). Then, time unit per time unit, schedulers are called (line 110) and task wake up times are computed (line 120).

7 Conclusion

This article describes a way to extend an Ada library. The method is experimented with Cheddar, a library providing performance analysis tools. Cheddar provides a domain specific language which helps users to the design of real time schedulers. Programs written with this domain specific language can be interpreted in order to perform real time scheduling analysis of real time systems. By the past, different projects showed that the Cheddar programming language and its interpreter are useful for the modeling of real time schedulers. But these experiments also showed that the interpreter is lacking of efficiency in case of large scheduling simulations. In this article, we experiment a way to compile

---

[2] TCB stands for Task Control Block.

```
entry := sections
sections := section {sections}
section := program_section | automata_section
program_section := [identifier] ":"  section_type statements
automata_section := [identifier] ":"  "automaton_section" states transitions
section_type := "start_section" | "priority_section"
    | "election_section" | "task_activation_section" | ...

states := state {states}
transitions := transition {transitions}
state := identifier ["initial"] ":" "state" ";"
transition  := identifier "-->" "[" [guards] ,[clocks] ,
    [synchronizations] "]" "-->" identifier ";"
synchronizations : = synchronization {synchronizations}
synchronization := identifier '!' | identifier "?"
clocks := assignment {clocks}
guards := expression

statements := statement {statements}
statement := put | assignment | declare | while | for | if | return | random
put := "put" "(" identifier [, expression] [, expression]")" ";"
declare := identifier ":"  data_type [ ":=" expression ] ";"
assignment := identifier ":=" expression  ";"
if := "if" expression "then" statements [  "else" statements ] "end" "if" ";"
return := "return" expression  ";"
for := "for" identifier "in" ranges "loop" statements "end" "loop" ";"
while := "while" expression "loop" statements "end" "loop" ";"
random :=  "uniform" "(" identifier "," expression ","
        expression ")" ";"
    | "exponential" "(" identifier "," expression  ")" ";"

data_type := scalar_data_type
    | "array" "(" ranges ")" "of"  scalar_data_type
ranges := "tasks_range"
    | "buffers_range" |  "messages_range" ...
scalar_data_type := "boolean" |  "integer" |  "random" ...
operator := "and" | "or" | "mod" | "<" | ">" | "<=" | ">=" ...

expression := expression operator expression
    | "max_to_index" "(" expression ")"
    | "lcm" "(" expression "," expression ")" | ...
```

Fig. 8. BNF grammar of the Cheddar programming language

such a program. By designing a Cheddar meta-model, we show how to compile Cheddar programs in order to extend the Cheddar library. For such a purpose, we use *Platypus*, a Meta CASE Tool based on *EXPRESS*.

At the time we write this article, the CDAI is modeled and we are able to generate the corresponding Ada packages [14]. We are currently designing the meta-model of the Cheddar programming language and experimenting Cheddar scheduler and task generation.

References

1. Singhoff, F., Legrand, J., Nana, L., Marcé, L.: Cheddar: a Flexible Real Time Scheduling Framework. ACM Ada Letters journal. Also published in the proceedings of the International ACM SIGAda Conference, Atlanta, USA, vol. 24(4), pp. 1–8 (2004)

2. Singhoff, F.: Cheddar Release 2.x User's Guide. Technical report, number singhoff-01-2007 (2007), Available at http://beru.univ-brest.fr/šinghoff/cheddar
3. Liu, C.L., Layland, J.W.: Scheduling Algorithms for Multiprogramming in a Hard Real-Time Environment. Journal of the Association for Computing Machinery 20(1), 46–61 (1973)
4. Hopcroft, J.E., Ullman, J.D.: Introduction of Automata Theory, Languages and Computation (2001)
5. Alur, R., Dill, D.L.: Automata for modeling real time systems. In: Paterson, M.S. (ed.) Automata, Languages and Programming. LNCS, vol. 443, pp. 322–335. Springer, Heidelberg (1990)
6. Behrmann, G., David, A., Larsen, K.G.: A Tutorial on Uppaal. Technical Report Updated the 17th November 2004 (Department of Computer Science, Aalbord University, Denmark) (2004)
7. Sprunt, B., Sha, L., Lehoczky, J.: Aperiodic Task Scheduling for Hard-real-time Systems. The. Journal of Real. Time. Systems 1, 27–60 (1989)
8. Plantec, A.: Platypus Technical Summary and download. (http://cassoulet.univ-brest.fr/mme)
9. Team, T.S.: Squeak web site. (http://www.squeak.org)
10. ISO 10303-1: Part 1: Overview and fundamental principles. (1994)
11. ISO 10303-11: Part 11: EXPRESS Language Reference Manual (1994)
12. Plantec, A., Ribaud, V.: Experiences using an Application Generator Builder. In: Proceedings of the 11th International Conference on software engineering and knowledge engineering, Kaiserslautern, Germany (June 16-19, 1999)
13. Mimoune, M.E.H., Pierra, G., Ait-Ameur, Y.: An ontology-based approach for exchanging data between heterogeneous database systems. In: ICEIS 2003: Proceedings of the 5th International Conference On Enterprise Information Systems, Angers - France, École Supérieure d' Électronique de l' Ouest (2003)
14. Plantec, A., Singhoff, F.: Refactoring of an Ada 95 Library with a Meta CASE Tool. ACM Ada Letters journal. Also published In: the proceedings of the International ACM SIGAda Conference, Albuquerque, USA, vol. 26(3), pp. 61–70 (2006)

Modelling Remote Concurrency with Ada
Case Study of Symmetric Non-deterministic Rendezvous

Claude Kaiser, Christophe Pajault, and Jean-François Pradat-Peyre

CEDRIC - CNAM Paris
292, rue St Martin, F-75003 Paris
{kaiser,christophe.pajault,peyre}@cnam.fr
http://quasar.cnam.fr/

Abstract. When developing concurrent software, a proper engineering practice is to choose a good level of abstraction for expressing concurrency control. Ideally, this level should provide platform-independent abstractions but, as the platform concurrency behaviour cannot be ignored, this abstraction level must also be able to cope with it and exhibit the influence of different possible behaviours. We state that the Ada language provides such a convenient abstraction level for concurrency description and evaluation, including distributed concurrency. For demonstrating it, we present two new cooperative algorithms based on remote procedure calls which, although simply stated, contain actual concurrency complexity and difficulties. They allow a distributed symmetric non-deterministic rendezvous. One relies on a common server and the second is fully distributed. Both realize a symmetric rendezvous using an asymmetric RPC modelled by Ada rendezvous. These case studies show that Ada concurrency features provide the adequate abstraction level both for describing and evaluating concurrency and for carrying out design decisions.

1   Introduction

1.1   The Need of High-Level Concurrency Description

Concurrency is a prolific source of complexity and is a serious cause of errors when developing software. Thus it is a challenge for developers of long-lived, high-quality software that needs reliable software technologies.

Current approaches to software development use patterns or models as a set of guidelines for structuring application specification, design and implementation. Providing significant examples is of prime importance for mastering the additional temporal dimensions of correctness introduced by concurrency, i.e., safety and liveness. Even if you never employ them directly, reading about different special-purpose design patterns can give you ideas about how to attack real problems.

Moreover when developing concurrent software, a proper engineering practice is to choose a good level of abstraction for expressing concurrency control. Ideally, this level should provide platform-independent abstractions [1]. However the

N. Abdennahder, F. Kordon (Eds.): Ada-Europe 2007, LNCS 4498, pp. 192–207, 2007.

concurrency semantics of platforms associated with POSIX standards or with languages like Ada, Java or C# are different and this diversity may influence the correctness of some models or patterns. In [7], we have shown examples where the weak liveness semantics of Java and C# run time causes deadlock in some programs, which nevertheless have been proven safe with the Ada strong liveness semantics. As the platform concurrency behaviour cannot be ignored, the abstraction level should be able to cope with it and to analyse the influence of the different possible behaviours.

1.2   Ada as a Concurrency Description and Modelling Language

We state that the Ada language provides such a convenient abstraction level and thus may be used for concurrency description and evaluation, including distributed concurrency. Our statement is based on four assumptions.

First Ada proposes today the most powerful set of high level concurrency features available in an imperative language and its concurrency semantics is well and precisely defined. For expressing cooperation through a shared memory, protected objects can be used together with the requeue statement and with the entry family facility. For analysing communication without a shared memory, the rendezvous together with the use of the requeue statement allows to simulate simply the semantics of a remote procedure call.

Second the behavioural semantics of shared memory platforms used for other languages such as POSIX, C# or Java can be emulated with Ada [7]. Similarly, the remote procedure call, which is used in message passing protocols, can be simulated by Ada task rendezvous.

Third, as Ada concurrency semantics is precisely defined, model programs expressed in Ada can be analysed automatically for detecting correctness deficiencies such as deadlock or starvation. Our tool QUASAR [6], based on slicing, followed by Petri net generation and by model checking of the generated net, is devoted to concurrent Ada programs analysis. It allows evaluating and validating a concurrency model description at the design and specification stage.

Fourth, Ada provides an executable description language. This allows running simulations and testing the concurrency behaviour of programs.

Indeed, our approach that we teach also to our students aims at mixing design and evaluation. We are convinced that this encourages choosing simpler concurrency architectures in order to render them more readable, understandable, and finally easier to validate, maintain, reuse and modify.

This is the most necessary, as our students are not lucid enough about concurrent programming; as many designers they underestimate its difficulties and the need of a language for coping with clear concurrency ideas and structures. Todays programming approaches, whatever the pedantic name they use, are often close to cut-and-paste techniques and lack concurrency analysis.

We have already shown how data sharing paradigms which use the monitor concept [13] can be expressed in Ada and validated while running on platforms with different fairness semantics. We will now deal with remote procedure call.

Cooperative algorithms based on message passing tend to grow complicated especially when they include some form of consensus among participants. It is our statement that Ada is really suitable for expressing them when they rely on remote procedure calls. Thus our presentation focuses on such distributed concurrency. Although simply stated, our case study contains actual concurrency complexity and difficulties. We show that Ada can be used for analyzing them and carrying out design decisions.

2 Representing Remote Procedure Call Protocols by Ada Tasking

In the following case study, we focus on the use of the remote procedure call concept for expressing, analysing and validating a protocol resolving the symmetrical rendezvous required by processes scattered in a distributed system. It may be useful for installing a peer-to-peer communication and it is an instance of the more general problem of group making in asynchronous distributed systems. The partners do not share a common memory; they communicate only by messages and use remote procedure call.

The case study is modelled in Ada as concurrent tasks that communicate only by rendezvous, without shared variables.

Recall that a concurrency protocol or a distributed application that is modelled in Ada is compiled and analysed as a single program. The first purpose of the model is to express and analyse its concurrency properties. It does not necessarily need to be a distributed program itself. If it were necessary however (for example, for running some simulation programs), the analysed model could be distributed and run on several platforms. Since Ada 95, distributed applications may be programmed with Ada partitions, according to postpartitioning and to the distributed annex choices. Active partitions have no global clock and communicate by asynchronous transfer of messages. Thus tasks are not visible across partitions: Ada has no remote rendezvous between tasks of different partitions, no distributed delay or time management and no distributed task management. This must be coped with and is well mastered by the partition model and the post-partitioning process (also called post-compilation partitioning)[17,11]. This is an additional advantage of choosing Ada, an executable description language.

2.1 The Basic Binary Rendezvous

The binary rendezvous has been suggested first for CSP [13] and Ada 83 [14]. In a binary rendezvous a communication involves the synchronization of exactly two processes. CSP provides a symmetric, nondeterministic and synchronous communication construct. Synchronous communication requires that both processes involved in a communication be ready to communicate before the communication can proceed. Nondeterministic selection allows a process to participate in one of many possible communication and symmetric communication allows both send and receive commands in a nondeterministic selection construct. Surveys of centralized and distributed CSP binary rendezvous implementations can be found in [3,19].

2.2   Ada Former Implementations of a Symmetric Rendezvous

The Ada rendezvous between tasks is said to be asymmetric since the nondeterministic selection is possible only for receive commands. Moreover during the rendezvous, data may pass in both directions. This leads to an extended rendezvous or a remote invocation construct abstracting a remote procedure call from another task.

A programming challenge is how to implement a symmetric rendezvous using the Ada asymmetric rendezvous. A synchronous communication where a controller task performs an anonymous rendezvous between one producing and one consuming tasks has been given in [20]; this was also named three ways synchronization in the early book on concurrent programming in Ada [4]. This gave us insights for our server solution. We have not yet found any published implementation using the asymmetric Ada rendezvous for non deterministic pairwise choice in distributed systems (not even in the early review of Ada tasking [5]), possibly because it was cumbersome to do it in Ada 83 without the possibility of fixing a caller state when the requeue statement did not exist, and because Ada 83 did not aim at programming distributed applications. However symmetric intertask communication has been proposed as an additional feature of Ada 83 and was not held [10]. We shall show how it can be programmed with Ada 95.

2.3   Specification of a Non-deterministic Symmetric Binary Interaction

In distributed applications the binary remote rendezvous is often named binary interaction. For example, peer to peer collaboration starts by a binary interaction which can be performed in a purely decentralized manner directly between network hosts or in an indirect scheme using supernodes as rendezvous servers [2].

Let us now specify the case study that we consider in this paper. The distributed system is made of a set of at least two asynchronous processes that are labelled by distinct Ids. Sometimes a process that considers performing some peer-to-peer communication becomes a candidate partner, and seeks to constitute a pair with another candidate partner. Candidate partners behave all similarly, i.e. their rendezvous is symmetrical (they candidate in the same way, and all have the same capabilities for sending or receiving partners requests), the pair is the result of the non-deterministic interaction between two (or more) candidate partners and its Id values are returned to both successfully chosen candidate partners. We suppose that the partnership ends after a while allowing both processes of the pair to return to the state of possible candidate partners. The absence of candidate partners will not last forever.

To start with, we suppose that processes do not fail. Afterwards, we examine briefly the consequences of some process or communication failures, assuming nevertheless that procedure calls are atomic operations. Recall that distributed applications have to face site crash or message failures as well as absence of correspondants and that solving agreement problems in purely asynchronous distributed systems prone to process failures has been shown to be impossible deterministically [8,9]. Thus we shall only examine how to increase the probability of non-faulty behaviour.

3   A Server for Anonymous Non-deterministic Pairing

We describe now a first solution relying on a centralized server. According to the use of Ada as a description and evaluation language, we first complete the protocol specification using remote procedure call (the RPC acronym will be used now on); then we model it in Ada which allows validating its safety by Quasar and evaluating its performances by simulation runs. We end the protocol analysis by some fault tolerance insights.

3.1   Specification

Each candidate partner calls the server by RPC, communicating its Id and waiting until the pair is notified. The pair notification contains the caller Id. An additional result is returned to paired partners, which is the choice of a leader arbitrary chosen by the server in the pair. The server specification follows:

1. The server is callable by any candidate at any moment, whatever the server state may be.
2. All the calls are registered and a caller is not acknowledged before it is paired.
3. The server waits until it has received two requests, before giving notifications.
4. Notifications of the pair values are sent as soon as possible, i.e. as soon as the server has two not yet acknowledged waiting calls.
5. Both notifications are done before starting preparing another pair.

Multithreading the service could help when notification transmission delays are long. However if the arriving calls are dispatched among the threads, several candidates may wait although they should be paired according to 4. This harmful situation is avoided if solely a unique thread does the pairing service. In case of lengthy transmission delays, the server may require auxiliary tasks controlled by a producer-consumers schema to perform concurrently these notifications. Similarly, other auxiliary tasks may intervene in a producers-consumer schema if registering the calls is lengthy.

Both RPC calls and the server sequence are indivisible actions (when failures will be considered, they should then be atomic).

3.2   Description and Modelisation in Ada

A concurrent solution using shared data controlled by a monitor has been modelled with Ada protected objects and implemented also in Java and POSIX [15] and we have shown how to care of weak fairness semantics of Java and POSIX. We present here a solution where the symmetric rendezvous is controlled by an Ada task modelling a remote server called by RPC.

The RPC is modelled by a call to the server task, which exports a unique visible entry. According to Ada, this call blocks the caller until the results have been delivered.

The server has to hold on a first accepted entry call and to wait for a second one and, as soon as its second one is accepted, it has to return out parameters values to both accepted callers. Embedding two accept statements of the same entry is forbidden in Ada. However it is feasible when two embedded accept statements concern an entry and a private entry to which a former call has been requeued. The indivisibility of the server sequence is a property of the accept blocks.

The pairing action is realised as follows. The first accepted calling partner is requeued to a private entry (i.e., an entry not callable by another task). This removes its call from the visible queue and allows accepting another call on this entry. The server then accepts another call to the unique visible entry and the first statement of this accept block is to accept the call that was previously requeued to the private entry. Accept statements are nested and this nesting performs the symmetrical rendezvous as an indivisible action. Once this nesting done, the server exchanges candidate partner parameters and both calls are returned, allowing hereafter a new couple of calling partners to use the server.

```
Nb_Process : constant := N; type Id is range 1.. Nb_Process;

task Server is
  entry Cooperate(X: in Id; X_Other: out Id; Group_Leader: out Id);
private
  entry Waiting(X1: in Id; X_Other1: out Id; Group_Leader1: out Id);
end Server;

task body Server is
begin
 loop -- cyclic server
   accept Cooperate(X: in Id; X_Other: out Id; Group_Leader: out Id) do
     Group_Leader := X; -- server chooses arbitrarily the first member as leader
     requeue Waiting;    -- done for being able to nest two calls of the same entry
   end Cooperate;
   accept Cooperate(X: in Id; X_Other: out Id; Group_Leader: out Id) do
     accept Waiting(X1: in Id; X_Other1: out Id; Group_Leader1: out Id)
     do
       X_Other := X1; X_Other1 := X; Group_Leader := X1;
     end Waiting;
   end Cooperate;
 end loop;
end Server;
```

When implemented in other languages, their RPC semantics and the indivisibilities required has to be compared to Ada solutions in order to behave similarly when concurrency is involved. This concerns especially preventing perturbations caused by other calling candidates and respecting the notification completion as soon as possible and before starting up another pair. For example calling partners should not emit concurrent RPC calls, RPC servers should not process concurrently several rendezvous calls.

This Ada implementation has been validated as deadlock-free by our tool Quasar [6] and running simulation programs is straightforward.

We have not yet found a previously published version of this simple Ada solution. This solution can be extended to group formation, which for example might be useful before starting some grid-computing algorithm.

3.3   Failure Considerations

We give some hints just to show that in presence of faults the concurrency problems discussion may go ahead still using Ada as a concurrency design, description and analysis language. Failure considerations lead using atomic procedure calls [16]and atomic actions, which have been devised for Ada [18,21]. As ending the pairing action requires sending a notification to a pair of processes, this has also to cope with consensus on commit [12].

However according to the impossibility results recalled in section 2.3., there is a nonzero probability that the partners of an announced pair are not exactly two. Suppose that processes A and B have called the server, that A received correctly the notification and that B did not and exits from the RPC (the commit failed). B does not know A and will not answer to it. A is orphan especially if it was chosen as Group_Leader. But as B has not found a partner, it may start a new seek ending with C. B is now paired with both A and C. If the pairing data arrive to C and not to B (suppose B is in a jammy part of the network), B may try again with another partner, say D.

4   A Cooperative Non-deterministic Symmetric Rendezvous

We describe now a fully distributed solution relying on process cooperation. Here also we use Ada as a description and evaluation language. First we refine slightly the partner behaviour specification and examine some simplifying choices; they lead to two policies and two versions in each policy; then we model the more reliable solution in Ada and this allows validating its safety by Quasar and testing its performances by simulation runs. We end the protocol analysis by some fault tolerance insights.

4.1   Specification Refinement

In this approach, each candidate partner tries to find directly another candidate partner willing also to constitute a pair. In the absence of failure, once a pair is formed, both partners of the pair share the same cooperation knowledge. Each one has registered the decision, i.e. the paired partners names. But each partner is also confident that its partner shares this information. If the pair is (A, B), partner A knows that its partner is B and that B knows that its partner is A. Symmetrically B knows that its partner is A and that A knows that its partner is B. We shall return to this when we examine the effects of failures.

We suppose that a partner can reach two states only in which it can seek a rendezvous. Either it sends a call to another partner which it supposes willing to answer to it (i.e. expected to be in the listening state or on the way to it), or it is listening, awaiting a remote call from any calling partner. The success supposes that while seeking for a pair the candidate partners finally achieve being in different states, one sending, the other one listening. If all partners wait forever in the same state (all listening or all calling), a communication deadlock occurs.

Let us recall that we assume that there is no failure (reliable communication and reliable processes). We shall consider successively two kinds of behaviour for processes that are not candidate partners. At first they do respond to any request and answer whether they are candidate or not. In a second version, they may be non-responding and remain silent, ignoring the request of a candidate partner.

4.2   Local Concurrency Level

First let us examine whether simultaneous communications or multithreading may help.

Simultaneous communications imply a global decision. Suppose that a candidate partner is allowed to manage concurrently its two communicating states or to seek several partners in parallel when it is calling (for example, broadcasting its request). Thus if it receives successively multiple proposals, it may concurrently start a rendezvous with several other candidate partners which themselves may already have started other rendezvous. Due to these possible transitivity and symmetry, the decision must be global and supposes some complex global serialization.

Local decision concerning two candidates at most. As the final choice concerns only two candidate partners, a global decision can be avoided. Introducing a local serialization of actions and a fixed dissymmetry between partners, the choice can rely on a local decision taken by one partner only. This leads to a simpler solution which is presented now. First a candidate partner manages each of its communicating states exclusively and then it is either calling or listening. Thus it examines only one other candidate at a time. Second suppose that a listening partner (candidate or not) is able to execute as an indivisible operation the acceptance of one and only one pairing request followed by the processing of its answer. This listening partner is then able to commit the final decision for both partners: it can accept or refuse to constitute a pair with the candidate calling partner since it knows whether it is itself also willing to pair or not. This is possible if the successive pairing request calls are acknowledged serially and if the calling partner is blocked until the end of the RPC. By chance, this is the semantics of the synchronous remote procedure call and of the Ada rendezvous accept statement. This dissymmetry gives precedence to the listening partner over the calling partner for decision taking.

4.3   Required Indivisible Actions

For each process X, we introduce the following local variables:

```
Candidate      : Boolean ;  -- X is requiring a partner
Paired         : Boolean ;  -- X has got a partner
Partner        : Id ;       -- X has got a partner which Id is the value
Next_Neighbor  : Id ;       -- Function delivering a process Id, different at each call
Site(X)        : T_Site ;   -- Network address of X
```

Let us summarize the concurrency assumptions for candidate processes:

1. Each candidate is either requesting or listening.
2. A requesting candidate sends only one request at a time (there is no calling concurrency).
3. A listening candidate picks and serves its received requests one at a time.
4. The pairing implies that both partners are candidates and that one is requesting and the other is listening.
5. The pairing decision is taken by the listening partner.

Each process X may be remotely called by RPC. This is modelled in Ada by the following entry which is visible by other processes:

```
entry Cooperate (Calling_Partner: in Id; Listening_Partner: out Id;
                 Accepted        : out Boolean);
```

According to the previous assumptions, a cooperating process may run either of the following action sequences, CS1 during the requesting state, or CS2 during the listening state. This can be specified in Ada as follows.

```
(|CS1|) {Candidate , not Paired }
|Requesting a possible candidate partner|
   Z := Next_Neighbour ;            -- trying Z as candidate partner; Next_Neighbour
                                    -- delivers a different Id at each call
   Site(Z).Cooperate(X, Z, OK) ;  -- calling Z with possibly a time limit
   -- if OK is returned within time limit and is True, then rendezvous(Z, X) has been decided
   -- by Z while X was waiting for the end of this call, therefore X is no longer candidate
   Candidate := not OK;             -- following statements are executed only when the
                                    -- call is accepted within the time limit
   Paired := OK;
   if OK then Partner := Z; end if ;
   {Requesting success = not Candidate }
```

```
(|CS2|) {True}
|Listening and accepting a remote call|
   accept Cooperate(Calling_Partner : in Id; Listening_Partner : out Id;
                    Accepted          : out Boolean) do
   -- request from remote candidate Calling_Partner, accepted with possibly a time limit
   -- returns name X and Accepted to caller Calling_Partner,
   -- if Candidate, the rendezvous(Y, X) is decided by X while Y is waiting for this decision
   -- X no longer Candidate once the rendezvous is decided
   Accepted:= Candidate;
   -- if X is Candidate, it decides to form the pair and returns Accepted = True
   Paired := Accepted;
   if Paired then Partner:= Calling_Partner; Listening_Partner := X;
   end if ;
   Candidate := False ; -- either X is no longer candidate or was already not candidate
   end Cooperate ;
```

4.4   Navigation Policies When Seeking Another Candidate

We consider now two policies that may be used by a process for managing both calling and listening states and for navigating in the system when seeking another candidate: polling alternatively these two states or reacting when any one of these two states is triggered.

For simplicity, we suppose that each process is granted an assistant task that is in charge of the seeking policy.

Polling Policy. When polling, a process assistant loops alternatively listening for a call from any candidate partner and calling a process while changing the called process Id at each cycle. In the first version, the assistant task is supposed to acknowledge remote calls even if its process is not candidate for partnership and in that case to return a negative answer to the request. If all candidates happen to be in the same state, this leads to deadlock; this deadlock probability can be lessened, but not annulled, by using a probabilistic succession of states. Another version for avoiding deadlock is to wait in each state only during a given delay (large enough to allow message transmission - in a distributed system where transmission delays have a known upper limit, this delay can be chosen as twice this limit). As this allows also caring about processes non-responding since they are not candidate, the assistant task needs not necessarily to acknowledge every call when its process is not candidate. However this latter version may lead to livelock, even if livelock probability may be lessened similarly as above.

The kernel of the assistant task body is then the following.

```
-- function Hazard return Boolean; generates a value with some probability distribution
loop                      --polling loop of the assistant task
 case Hazard is
  when True  => CS1; -- possibly requesting during an exponential delay
  when False => CS2; -- possibly listening during an exponential delay
 end case;
 -- possible exit when not Candidate
 if not Candidate then return partner Id to the process; end if;
end loop
```

Reacting Policy. In this solution, when both states are simultaneously triggered, one state only has to be chosen. This supposes a nondeterministic symmetric selection of send or receive commands, as it is possible with CSP. We have devised such a scheme in Ada. Each process assistant task loops using a select statement, which nondeterministically accepts either a remote call from other candidates (the assistant is then listening) or a local call which aim is to emit a call to another process (the local process requires its assistant to perform such a call). The local call is performed repeatedly by the candidate partner to its assistant until a partner is found by the assistant, either by calling or by listening, and the assistant task must address each time a different process in order to hit a candidating one.

In the first version, the assistant task is supposed to accept remote calls even when the process is not candidate for partnership and in this latter case to return a negative answer to the request. In this version, it may happen that all candidate assistant tasks have been triggered by local calls for calling a remote partner and that this leads to circular situations such as candidate A requesting candidate B, candidate B requesting candidate C, candidate C requesting candidate A. This can be avoided by ordering processes and forbidding a candidate to call a process having a lower rank (a smaller Id for example). Thus an assistant task calls only processes (in fact it calls the other processes assistant tasks) with higher ranks that its own process. The highest rank process assistant does not emit a request and requeues the local call to a private entry Waiting, which allows it to wait until a successful remote call has to be returned to the process (see below).

In the second version, the assistant task needs no longer be present when its process is not candidate. Thus the assistant task of a candidate partner waits in each state only during a given delay using Ada selective accept with a delay alternative or Ada timed entry call.

In both versions, the assistant task must acknowledge the call of its local process and indicate whether seeking failed or succeeded and in the latter case returning the partner Id. Thus the first operation to do when examining a local call is to examine whether a distant call was successfully accepted since the last local call. Such a success must also forbid new distant call acceptance before its acknowledgement (the corresponding entry guard is set to False) and withdraws calling a new candidate partner.

4.5   The Ada Symmetric and Non-deterministic Cooperative Rendezvous Protocol

We introduce some additional local entities:

```
Peer_To_Register : Boolean ;      -- assistant task has acknowledged a distant call
function Next_Neighbour(X) : Id ;-- delivers the Id of a Process with a rank greater
                                  -- than X; each call still delivers a different value.
function Top(X) return Boolean;   -- indicates whether process X has the highest rank
entry Waiting;                    -- for requeueing the highest rank process
```

The kernel of the assistant task body is then the following, giving priority to distant call when both local and distant call are triggered.

```
loop forever -- assistant task cyclic behaviour
  select
   accept Local_Call do
    if Peer_To_Register then
      Candidate := False; Peer_To_Register := False;
      -- acknowledges beforehand the local caller when a remote call was
      -- successfully accepted since last local call
    else
      Candidate := True; -- local call is considered as a candidature for pairing
      if not Top(X) then
        CS1; -- for requesting Neighbour(X) when candidate and not Last(X)
      else
        requeue Waiting; -- just wait for acknowledging a remote call
      end if;
    end if;
   end Local_Call;
  or

  when Peer_To_Register =>
```

```
    accept Waiting do
      Candidate := False; Peer_To_Register := False;
      -- acknowledges local caller when a remote call was accepted since last local call
    end Waiting;
  or
    when not Peer_To_Register =>
      accept Distant_Call do -- accepting a remote call
        CS2;
        Peer_To_Register := Accepted;
        -- a partner has been committed; local process has to be informed
      end Distant_Call;
  end select;
end loop;
```

This description holds for Ada concurrency semantics of the task rendezvous. When the protocol is implemented using other languages or platforms, their RPC semantics and the required indivisibilities must be confronted with Ada choices.

The complexity of this cooperative protocol, the possible concurrency simplifications and the resulting algorithm are easy to express and to analyse using ADA. This shows the expressive power of Ada for concurrency problems.

Two policies, polling and reactive, and two versions in each policy have been devised. The full Ada solution of the first version of the reactive policy is given in Annex and its implementation has been analysed as deadlock-free by our tool Quasar [6].

The second version with delayed call or accept is suitable for an asynchronous network with bounded transmission delays, but it is prone to communication uncertainty in a purely asynchronous distributed system (in this latter, when a called process does not answer, the caller doesnt know whether the called process is non responding since it is not a candidate or the candidate called process has sent an answer which is very late to arrive, so any delay may be erroneous since there is no bounded transmission delay).

The polling versions are never absolutely safe (they are prone to deadlock or to livelock) and have some probability of failure.

4.6   Failure Considerations

Again we give just some hints to show that the concurrency errors due to the presence of faults may still be considered using Ada as a description and analysis language. Faulty processes or variable network delays may be simulated with abort and timed rendezvous and delayed entry.

Anew, failure considerations lead using atomic procedure calls and atomic actions in order to reduce the faults outcome. As all communications are point to point, the consensus on commit is not necessary this time. However when some messages are not received either by failure or when the waiting delays are too short for network propagation or for processor overload, a candidate partner may still be associated with any number of other candidates in a dissymmetrical association. This again may be simulated in Ada when requesting candidates use timed entry calls and when listening candidates use delayed accepts. Recall that this may also lead to livelocks.

5   Conclusion

In the introduction, we have stated that Ada can be used for concurrency description and evaluation. We pointed out that its concurrency features are powerful and have been settled at a convenient abstraction level, and that this allows expressing most of the useful concurrent algorithms as well as emulating other language constructs or semantics.

In a former paper we have shown how the use of Ada protected objects allowed to describe and validate a monitor based implementation and to derive it for Java and POSIX safe implementations.

In this paper we have designed step by step and analysed RPC based concurrent and distributed protocols. The first one, a server protocol, is so simple that it is directly apprehensible in Ada. The second, a cooperative protocol, was described by parts and all, including the global architecture which is the most delicate part, were able to be expressed in Ada. With these protocols, we have also fulfilled twice the programming challenge of implementing a symmetric rendezvous using the Ada asymmetric rendezvous. These case studies emphasise the suitability of Ada as a domain-specific language for distributed concurrency description and evaluation.

These protocols, either based on protected objects or tasking rendezvous, are programmed by our students as a starting step of the chameneos game [15] which they have to implement, validate and simulate.

Our final claim is that Ada concurrency programming richness is largely underestimated and its capabilities not yet fully understood, especially by designers of new languages. With this presentation we would also like to contribute pointing out its power and its elegance.

References

1. AADL workshop (2005), www.axlog.fr/R_d/aadl/workshop2005_fr.html
2. Androutsellis-Theotokis, S., Spinellis, D.: A survey of peer-to-peer content distribution technologies. ACM Comput. Surv. 36(4), 335–371 (2004)
3. Bagrodia, R.: Process synchronization: Design and performance evaluation of distributed algorithms. IEEE Trans. Softw. Eng. 15(9), 1053–1065 (1989)
4. Burns, A.: Concurrent programming in Ada, New York. Cambridge University Press, Cambridge (1985)
5. Burns, A., Lister, A.M., Wellings, A.J.: A review of Ada tasking. Springer, Berlin Heidelberg New York (1987)
6. Evangelista, S., Kaiser, C., Pradat-Peyre, J-F., Rousseau, P.: Quasar: a new tool for analyzing concurrent programs. In: Rosen, J.-P., Strohmeier, A. (eds.) Ada-Europe 2003. LNCS, vol. 2655, pp. 166–181. Springer, Heidelberg (2003)
7. Evangelista, S., Kaiser, C., Pradat-Peyre, J-F., Rousseau, P.: Comparing Java, C# and Ada monitors queuing policies: a case study and its Ada refinement. Ada Lett. XXVI(2), 23–37 (2006)
8. Fich, F., Ruppert, E.: Hundreds of impossibility results for distributed computing. Distrib. Comput. 16(2-3), 121–163 (2003)
9. Fischer, M.J., Lynch, N.A., Paterson, M.S.: Impossibility of distributed consensus with one faulty process. J. ACM 32(2), 374–382 (1985)

10. Francez, N., Yemini, S.A.: Symmetric intertask communication. ACM Trans. Program. Lang. Syst. 7(4), 622–636 (1985)
11. Gasperoni, F.: Programming distributed systems (2003)
12. Gray, J., Lamport, L.: Consensus on transaction commit. ACM Trans. Database Syst. 31(1), 133–160 (2006)
13. Hoare, C.A.R.: Communicating sequential processes. Commun. ACM 21(8), 666–677 (1978)
14. Ichbiah, J.D.: Preliminary Ada reference manual. SIGPLAN Not. 14(6a), 1–145 (1979)
15. Kaiser, C., Pradat-Peyre, J.F.: Chameneos, a concurrency game for Java, Ada and others. In: ACS/IEEE Int. Conf. AICCSA'03, IEEE Computer Society Press, Los Alamitos (2003)
16. Lin, K-J., Gannon, J.D.: Atomic remote procedure call. IEEE Trans. Softw. Eng. 11(10), 1126–1135 (1985)
17. Pautet, L., Tardieu, S.: GLADE User Guide (2000)
18. Romanovsky, A.B., Mitchell, S.E., Wellings, A.J.: On programming atomic actions in Ada 95. In: Hardy, K., Briggs, J. (eds.) Ada-Europe 1997. LNCS, vol. 1251, pp. 254–265. Springer, Heidelberg (1997)
19. Schneider, F.B.: Synchronization in distributed programs. ACM Trans. Program. Lang. Syst. 4(2), 125–148 (1982)
20. Le Verrand, D.: Le langage Ada. Manuel d'évaluation. Dunod (1982)
21. Wellings, A., Burns, A.: Implementing atomic actions in Ada 95. IEEE Trans. Softw. Eng. 23(2), 107–123 (1997)

Annex: The Cooperative Non-deterministic Symmetric Rendezvous Program

This runnable Ada program contains the cooperative protocol in the first version of the reactive policy together with a simulation where Nb_Process processes require each a non-deterministic rendezvous Nb_Trial times. This simulation may not terminate when all processes but one have ended after their successful Nb_Trial rendezvous. The remaining lonely process cannot find a pairing partner. This runnable program can be downloaded at: http://quasar.cnam.fr/files/concurrency_papers.html.

```ada
with Text_IO; use Text_IO;

Procedure Cooperative is
  Nb_Process : constant := 9; type Id is range 1..Nb_Process;
  Nb_Trial   : constant := 6; -- number of rendezvous requested by each process
     ---- set of Assistants ----
  task type T_Assistant is
  entry Get_Id        (Y: in Id);
  entry Local_Call    (X: in Id; X_Other: out Id; Group_Leader: out Id;
                       Accepted : out Boolean); -- local call
  entry Distant_Call  (X: in Id; X_Other: out Id; Group_Leader: out Id;
                       Accepted : out Boolean); -- remote call
  private
  entry Waiting       (X: in Id; X_Other: out Id; Group_Leader: out Id;
                       Accepted : out Boolean); -- for Id'last Process
  end T_Assistant;
  Assistant: array(Id) of T_Assistant;
     ---- Assistant task body ----
```

```
task body T_Assistant is
  Ego                  : Id ;                  -- Caller_Id
  Partner              : Id ;                  -- the result of search
  Peer_To_Register : Boolean := False ;        -- partner found by CS2 through an
                                               -- accepted Distant_call
  Candidate            : Boolean := False ;    -- searching a partner
  --- Process neighbourhood management --
  Current : Id := Id'Last ; -- used for managing Next_Neighbour
    -- Next_Neighbour provides a neighbour name which is always larger than
    -- the caller's name (this avoids deadlock due to circular calls)
  function Next_Neighbour return Id is
  begin
    if Current = Id'Last then Current := Ego + 1;
    else Current := Current + 1; end if ;
    return Current ;
  end Next_Neighbour ;
  function Top(X : in Id) return Boolean is -- X has the highest rank
  begin return X = Id'Last ; end Top;
  Y : Id ;   -- records a value returned by Next_Neighbour
    --- end of neighbourhood management --

begin
  -- attaching each Assistant to a different Process
  accept Get_Id(Y: in Id) do Ego := Y; end Get_Id ;

  -- cyclic Assistant Ego waiting for a request from a remote process or from a local call
  loop
    select
      -- CS1 : FIRST MUTUALLY EXCLUSIVE ACTION : local call to propagate to Next_Neigbour
      accept Local_Call(X: in Id; X_Other: out Id; Group_Leader:
                        out Id; Accepted : out Boolean) do
        -- a new partner may have been already found and has to be registered
        if Peer_To_Register then
          X_Other := Partner ; Group_Leader := Ego;
          Accepted:= True; -- a partner has been found and registered;
                           -- reset Assistant state
          Peer_To_Register := False ;
        else
          Candidate := True; -- a local request is made for searching a partner
            -- calls a neighbour process, hoping it might be a partner assume: every
            -- assistant that is called will answer positively or negatively to remote call
          if not Top(Ego) then
            -- calls a neighbour holding a name strictly bigger than Ego
            Y := Next_Neighbour; -- each time a different neighbour process
            Assistant(Y).Distant_Call(X, X_Other, Group_Leader, Accepted);
            if Accepted then
              Candidate := False; -- a partner is found, reset Assistant state
            end if ;
          else
            requeue Waiting; -- X holds the biggest name, it never calls a neighbour
          end if ;
        end if ;
      end Local_Call ;

    or

      -- used only by Assistant(Id'Last) for returning the partner name
      when Peer_To_Register =>
      accept Waiting(X: in Id; X_Other: out Id; Group_Leader: out Id;
        Accepted : out Boolean) do
        -- a new partner has called, was accepted and then has to be registered
        X_Other := Partner ; Group_Leader := Ego;
        Accepted:= True; -- a partner has been registered; reset Assistant state
        Peer_To_Register := False ;
      end Waiting ;

    or
```

```
      -- CS2 : SECOND MUTUALLY EXCLUSIVE ACTION : waiting for a distant call
      -- barrier forbids accepting a new distant call before acknowledging the previous one
      when not Peer_To_Register =>
        accept Distant_Call (X: in Id; X_Other: out Id; Group_Leader: out
          Id; Accepted : out Boolean) do
          Partner := X; X_Other := Ego; Group_Leader := Ego;
          Accepted := Candidate; -- the pair is accepted only if process Ego is seeking
          Peer_To_Register := Candidate; -- for triggering its local registration
          Candidate := False; -- whatever the answer, process Ego is no longer seeking
        end Distant_Call;
      or
        terminate;
      end select;
    end loop;        -- end of cyclic Assistant code
  end T_Assistant;    -- end of Assistant body


      --- set of processes ---
  task type T_Process is
    entry Get_Id (Y : in Id);
    entry Start_Peering (Pilot : in Id; Copilot : in Id; Leader : in Id);
    entry Finish_Peering (Copilot: in Id; Pilot : in Id; Leader : in Id);
  end T_Process;
  Process: array(Id) of T_Process;


      --- Process task body ---
  task body T_Process is
    Ego, Partner, Leader: Id;
    Done                : Boolean := False;
begin
  -- giving each Process a different name
  accept Get_Id (Y: in Id) do Ego := Y; end Get_Id;

  -- each process loops seeking a partner just for recording its name and the rendezvous
  -- peer-to-peer asymmetric communication is simulated only
  for I in 1.. Nb_Trial  loop
    -- get a partner
    loop
      Assistant(Ego).Local_Call(Ego, Partner, Leader, Done);
      -- repeats request until a partner is found
      delay (0.001);
      exit when Done;
    end loop;
    Put_line ("Process" & Id'Image(Ego) & " is  paired  with  " &
          Id'Image(Partner) & ". Leader is " & Id'Image(Leader));
    if Ego = Leader then
    -- sends initializing RPC
      Process(Partner).Start_Peering(Ego, Partner, Leader);
      accept Finish_Peering (Copilot : in Id; Pilot : in Id;
                             Leader : in Id); -- waits until peering ends
    else
      accept Start_Peering (Pilot : in Id; Copilot : in Id;
                           Leader : in Id); -- waits partner call
      delay (1.0); -- simulates peer interchange and processes corresponding activity
      Put_line ("PROCESS" & Id'Image(Ego) & " acts as COPILOT while " &
            "PEERING with" & Id'Image(Partner) & " as PILOT");
      -- peer exchange ends; sends releasing RPC
      Process(Partner).Finish_Peering(Ego, Partner, Leader);
    end if;
  end loop;
end T_Process;

      --- allocating names to tasks ---
begin
  for I in Id loop Assistant(I).Get_Id(I) ; end loop;
  for I in Id loop Process(I).Get_Id(I) ; end loop;
end Cooperative;
```

Design and Performance of a Generic Consensus Component for Critical Distributed Applications

Khaled Barbaria, Jerome Hugues, and Laurent Pautet

GET-Télécom Paris – LTCI-UMR 5141 CNRS
46, rue Barrault, 75634 Paris CEDEX 13, France
{Khaled.Barbaria,Jerome.Hugues,Laurent.Pautet}@enst.fr

Abstract. This paper addresses the design and implementation of a generic middleware component for solving the consensus problem. This component can transparently provide critical applications with the consensus algorithm that best fits their requirements. The interactions between the consensus component and the underlying middleware layer are defined in terms of functional services among which tasking and transport are the most important. A complete design and configuration of the middleware is proposed. Performance measurements and source code analysis prove the efficiency and the ability to evolve of our design.

1 Introduction

Critical applications have dramatically evolved during the last few decades. The migration of the functionalities of these applications from specialized hardware to software, and the increase in their complexity have created new challenges. On one hand, the complexity of these applications gives rise to new needs to produce software with guaranteed quality and the ability to be deployed on various, sometimes heterogeneous, hardware architectures. On the other hand, there is a need for reducing development costs and accelerating product delivery. New critical applications have increasingly stringent requirements in terms of customization capabilities, and of the ability to dynamically react to costs and time-to-market pressures.

In this context, the notion of *middleware* [1] is of great help. Middleware consists of a set of abstractions provided to the applications regardless of the underlying operating systems communication protocols. Middleware increases productivity, quality, and reliability, while reducing production costs and implementation delays. [10] argues for the use of middleware technology for developing critical applications. The middleware, as a reusable software, has to come with the necessary abstractions and with guarantees to allow rapid and inexpensive development of critical applications.

Informally, the consensus problem can be defined over a set of processes; each process initially proposes a value and all correct (e.g.: non crashed) processes agree on a common value. A more formal definition can be found in [2].

Critical distributed applications have strong requirements for various kinds of agreements, especially when they are implemented on top of unreliable asynchronous

N. Abdennahder, F. Kordon (Eds.): Ada-Europe 2007, LNCS 4498, pp. 208–220, 2007.

systems. The consensus is a general abstraction to which the majority of agreement problems can be reduced [16]. This is the case with atomic broadcast, group membership, leader election, etc. Reducing these problems to consensus has been the subject of many research efforts. For instance, [9] introduces the notion of consensus filters which solve many agreement problems by adapting a consensus algorithm.

The design and implementation of a consensus component has two essential motivations. First, the genericity of this problem makes it possible to provide many critical applications with the appropriate abstractions they need to solve their agreement problems. Second, the development of a reusable Component-Off-The-Shelf (COTS) for consensus allows for rapid and cheap development of distributed critical applications.

Generally, the *genericity* of a component allows it to anticipate many usage circumstances. This capability of adaptation may have a strong impact on the implementation, which would suffer from many inefficiencies. For instance, this can cause a need to write too much code to handle all the possible use cases. We believe that a careful design can help minimizing the risk of inefficient implementations and of huge development and financial costs when new usage circumstances appear. In our case, we analyze the requirements and define the functional relations between the consensus component and the other middleware services. This allows us to minimize the risk of re-writing an application if it requires the use of a new consensus algorithm (e.g.: if new requirements appear) or re-writing some middleware components if there are needs to support new consensus algorithms.

Middleware has to support the consensus algorithm's requirements not only by guaranteeing that the assumptions about failure modes and system model hold, but also by providing means to allow resource management, performance and maintainability guarantees. This paper addresses the design and implementation of a generic middleware component providing application-level entities with an abstraction of the consensus. Because many algorithms require the presence of a failure detector, we have also designed and implemented a component providing an abstraction of a failure detector.

The paper is organized as follows: section 2 presents a summary of the requirements of a generic consensus building block. In section 3, we analyze these requirements and present our design proposal. Section 4 focuses on some implementation details based on intensive reuse of some components from an existing middleware. Section 5 proposes an evaluation of our architecture. Section 6 concludes the paper.

2   Requirements

The consensus component provides application-level entities with an interface to run consensus instances. This component interacts with other middleware components to correctly provide its service. The assumptions made by the consensus algorithms being run by the consensus component are to be fulfilled by other middleware components. A generic consensus component is designed to provide application level entities with an Application Programming Interface (API) to run consensus. In this section, we define the key requirements of the generic consensus component, we also deal with the support that should be provided by the middleware for the consensus and failure detection components.

2.1   Target Applications

Target applications are critical applications that need to solve some agreement problems by running instances of consensus. Typical applications are those that need distributed agreement to consistently achieve functions such as active redundancy, system reconfiguration (e.g.: after the failure of a processor), consistent global decision (e.g.: sensor reading) or distributed transaction management. More generally, every application that requires an agreement despite the possible occurrence of failures can use the consensus abstraction [8]. Under certain environments, the assumptions of the consensus or the failure detector algorithm cannot be fulfilled (e.g.: reliable channels or synchronized clocks). Therefore, the consensus component has to transparently support the execution of many consensus algorithms and to provide an easy way to select the consensus algorithm that best fits the requirements of the application. This increases the portability of applications and the usability of the middleware that provides the consensus abstraction.

2.2   Non-functional Requirements

Using a middleware stipulates that it provides the applications with enough guarantees in terms of safety and liveness. The consensus component as well as the low-level middleware services it uses must not violate application requirements and assumptions. Since the middleware components will be part of the final distributed application, its source code should fulfill the same constraints as the application code. Below, the most important non-functional requirements of a middleware component responsible for providing a consensus abstraction are given.

- Performance : typical applications need to run many instances of consensus per second. Even if the convergence time of consensus rounds depend on the used algorithm, there is a need to take care of the possible overhead introduced by the middleware functionalities.
- Compliance to certification guidelines: if applications of extreme criticality are in the set of the target applications, middleware code (and thus the code implementing the consensus component) has to provide strong guarantees and artifacts to pass the rigor of certification standards such as DO-178B [14].
- Partitioning: some critical applications are built upon an operating system that supports partitioning. In such operating systems, partitions are seen as separate entities that can be run and fail independently from each other. The consensus component should support this notion, at least, by giving the possibility to concurrently run many instances of consensus for many processes on the same computing platform.
- Tasking model: the consensus component can require using multitasking, according to the requirements of the consensus algorithms it can support. Depending on the criticality of the target application and on its need for static schedulabity analysis, the use (or not) of the Ravenscar tasking profile [3] may be needed. The implementation of the consensus component should not bypass the middleware : all the tasking functionalities it uses may be provided by the middleware.

3   Design of Components for Consensus and Failure Detection

In this section, we provide short descriptions of the components in charge of providing consensus and failure detection abstractions. Then, we define the underlying mechanisms used to support the execution of these components independently of the actual consensus and failure detection algorithms utilized.

3.1   Middleware Support for Consensus and Failure Detection

Consensus and failure detection components should be part of the middleware, so that they can be reused. From a functional point of view, it is possible to divide a middleware providing the consensus abstraction into two layers: the first one, referred to as "consensus layer" contains the components needed to provide consensus and failure detection abstractions. The second one can be seen as a low level layer providing general purpose services such as support for data exchange, tasking, etc. This vision is depicted in figure 1. The "core services" layer is responsible for supporting the execution of these algorithms and for ensuring that the assumptions of the components running on top of it hold. In the next paragraphs, we characterize the role of these two layers and define the interactions between them.

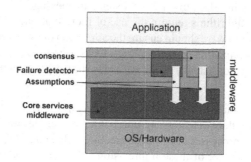

Fig. 1. middleware components

3.2   Consensus Layer

This layer is composed of two components that cooperate to provide applications with consensus. The failure detection configuration depends on the consensus algorithm. In some cases, the presence of a failure detector may be useless (e.g.: if the core services middleware exports a synchronous behavior).

Consensus. The consensus component is designed to be independent of the actual consensus algorithm. We used the strategy design pattern [7] to decouple the consensus object from the algorithms. The algorithms can access basic middleware functionalities such as simple primitives to exchange messages. They are also allowed to access the information provided by compatible failure detectors. Compatibility means that the failure detector satisfies the requirements specified by the consensus algorithm in terms of accuracy and completeness, more details will be provided in the next paragraph.

In order for this component to have the larger set of possible target applications, a trade-off should be solved. On one hand, some impossibility results, (e.g.: [6]) require the computational model to guarantee certain properties and as a consequence the core services middleware to implement certain functionalities (e.g.: quasi-reliable or reliable channels, bounded message delays, etc.). On the other hand, the weaker the assumptions on the computational model are, the larger is the set of applications that can use this component. This trade off is very hard, if not impossible to solve in the general case, but the middleware tailoring and customization properties can solve this challenge once the application requirements and deployment platform are known.

The consensus module provides a simple interface with a unique procedure that takes a "value" as an *in out* parameter and updates it with the agreed value. The call of this procedure is blocking, the application is blocked until the end of the consensus run. The chief interactions with other middleware components are :

- Failure detector : the consensus component has an access to the list of the processes suspected by the failure detector.
- Transport : the consensus component comes with a set of messages that have to be exchanged among the processes that need an agreement. The consensus component uses the transport interface to send and receive its messages.
- Tasking : many algorithms require the use of more that one task. In this case, the core services middleware should ensure the allocation of these tasks and provide the necessary synchronization primitives (e.g.: locks, semaphores, condition variables, etc.) to ensure the consistency of the variables shared between the tasks.

Failure Detection. A failure detector maintains and exports a list of the processes that it suspects. Generally, failure detectors are unreliable, they are allowed to make mistakes by suspecting correct processes or by not suspecting failed ones. [2] proposes two basic properties that limit the set of these imprecisions : accuracy, and completeness. Failure detectors can be classified according to these properties. This classification allows a wide range of consensus algorithms to exactly specify the properties of the failure detectors they need. For instance, before accessing the information about the suspected processes, the consensus component should check the class of the failure detector which must be *stronger* than a certain class assumed by the algorithm.

Generally, failure detection algorithms build their lists of suspects by sending heartbeat messages and running timeouts. Just like consensus algorithms, failure detection algorithms require the use of a transport service. They also may require advanced tasking primitives and an abstraction of a monotonic local clock.

3.3   Core Services Middleware

The implementation of consensus algorithms requires two important features provided by the middleware. First, the middleware has to ensure that the assumptions the consensus and failure detection algorithms make hold during the whole system life-cycle. Second, the middleware provides an interoperable functional support to these algorithms by acting as a distribution middleware and as a host to infrastructure middleware [15]. Host to infrastructure middleware isolates application level and high level middleware entities from the underlying operating system and hardware. Distribution middleware isolates the same entities form the communication subsystem.

Ensuring the Assumptions of Consensus Algorithms. Consensus algorithms state a set of assumptions about the failures that can occur and about the system computational model. These assumptions have to be enforced by the low level set of software and hardware upon which the consensus algorithm runs. Since the middleware hides the details of the operating system and hardware, it has to ensure that these assumptions hold on their behalf. Thus, the failure modes and the system computational model are those made visible by the middleware. The assumptions of consensus algorithms are seen as functional requirements for the middleware. For instance, if a consensus algorithm assumes a totally synchronous system model, the middleware is required to provide an upper bound on message transmission delay [4]. A straightforward consequence of the impossibility result of Fischer, Lynch and Paterson [6] is that if the "core services" middleware layer exports a totally asynchronous model then the use of a failure detector is required. The middleware can ensure an assumption by loading the adequate version of a given service. This allows to use some technologies like "wrapping" to let weak components exhibit failure modes simpler than the ones that they would have exhibited otherwise [13].

Host Infrastructure Middleware. Host infrastructure middleware provides a platform-independent way of executing operations independently on the operating systems and hardware architectures.

Many algorithms for consensus and failure detection require the use of multithreading. This is the case with the majority of timeout-based failure detection algorithms. Implementations of these algorithms require the middleware to provide the adequate tasking service and to offer thread pools and synchronization primitives. The middleware as "an interface to the operating system" or host infrastructure middleware in [15] should support these functionalities.

Distribution Middleware. Distribution middleware ensures transparent communication between entities despite possible heterogeneity with regard to hardware configuration, programming language and even the distribution model itself [17].

The middleware transport component requires an API to be implemented by low level transport protocols. It consists of a set of primitives to send, receive and to block until the reception of a message. This property allows the components to use the transport protocol that best fits the application requirements. This allows the application to use domain specific transport protocols such as SCPS-TP [5].

3.4 Middleware Configuration

Generally, a critical application comes with a set of requirements to be satisfied by the middleware. If these requirements include agreement then a consensus algorithm should be selected and customized. A (semi-) automatic configuration of the middleware functionalities as a function of the application requirements, including the consensus, allows application designers to save time and money.

The definition of a configuration process raises some problems to be solved. Such a process should reconcile the requirements caused by the selection of the consensus algorithm and the other requirements of the application. It also should handle multiple configuration dimensions (e.g.: the parameters of the consensus algorithms, the deployment information, the tasking model, etc).

The design we propose isolates the essential functional services, each in a specialized component. We believe that its clarity and principles will be a determining factor while defining this configuration process.

4   Implementation

Our implementation reused some components of PolyORB [1]. Thanks to its architecture [17] it has been possible to reuse neutral components: i.e.: components that are independent of the distribution model.

For the transport component we adapted the UDP-based transport service to our interface. The consensus component provides two algorithms. The first one is the well known rotating coordinator proposed by Chandra [2]. The second was proposed by Mostefaoui in [12]. The failure detector implements two algorithms of classes $\diamond S$ and $\diamond P$ respectively published in [2] and [11].

Generally, each consensus or failure detection algorithm comes with its own message types. While implementing an algorithm, primitives to marshal and unmarshal the messages should be provided. In our implementation, the group configuration and the parameters of the algorithms (e.g.: timeouts) can be loaded from a configuration file. The association of network addresses to process identifiers is also part of the group configuration.

Despite its advantages, the use of object oriented programming can be inappropriate for some safety critical applications. Avoiding some constructs and features like dynamic dispatching enhances the efficiency and predictability of the executions. Instead objects (i.e.: tagged types) we used parametrized Ada types. Our components are implemented as Ada packages. The provided functionalities are visible in the package specifications, the required functionalities are initialized through package dependencies. The remainder of this section describes the most important elements of our implementation.

4.1   Consensus

Listing 1.1 shows an excerpt of the interface of the consensus component. The main functionalities are to create and run consensus instances. The definition of a consensus entity contains a reference on the partition on which the consensus instance will run. This allows it to interact with the other participants by sending and receiving messages.

The application defines the set of consensus algorithms that it requires by declaring a dependency upon the packages that implement each of them. Each consensus

---
[1] http://polyorb.objectweb.org

algorithm is defined as a child package of *Consensus*. Ada provides some mechanisms for executing code at elaboration time, i.e.: before the main program starts executing. During its elaboration phase, each package registers the algorithm it provides and an access type that defines the procedure to call when an application entity wants to run the algorithm. Once all the child packages of *Consensus* are elaborated, the application can choose the consensus algorithm by creating a consensus entity with a call to *Create_Consensus_Instance*. The application can now run instances of consensus.

```ada
1  with Values;
   with Failure_Detector;
3  with Process_Identifiers;
   package Consensus is
5     type CS_Type is private;
      type CS_Access is access all CS_Type;
7     type Run_Consensus_Type
      is access procedure
9        (Pid : Process_Id;
         Value : in out Values.Value);
11
      type CS_Algo is
13       (Rotating_Coordinator, ..., etc);
      procedure Run_Consensus
15       (CS     :        CS_Access;
         Value : in out Values.Value);
17    procedure Create_Consensus_Instance
         (Algo     :        CS_Algo;
19        P        :        Process_Id;
          With_FD :        Boolean;
21        FD       :        Failure_Detector.FD_Access;
          Success : out Boolean;
23        Result  : out CS_Access);
      [...]
25 private
      type CS_Type is record
27       Partition : Process_Id;
         Run          : Run_Consensus_Type;
29       [...]
      end record;
31    procedure Register
         (Algo : CS_Algo;
33        Run  : Run_Consensus_Type);
   end Consensus;
```

Listing 1.1. Consensus

4.2 Failure Detection

Listing 1.2 shows an excerpt of the interface of the failure detector component. We use the same process to let the application create entities that represent failure detectors. If the only interaction between the consensus package and its child packages is to define the procedure that should be called to run the consensus, the relation between the package *Failure_Detector* and its child packages is more subtle. This is due to the need to export the list of suspects independently of the actual failure detection algorithm. The failure detector implementing a given algorithm calls the *Notify_Suspects_List* procedure each time it updates its internal lists of suspects. This list of suspects is made

```
 1  with Process_Identifiers;
 2  package Failure_Detector is
 3     type FD_Algo is (A_Chandra, A_Larrea, ...);
 4     type Run_FD_Access
 5     is access
 6        procedure (FD : FD_Access);
 7     procedure Run_Failure_Detector
 8        (FD : FD_Access);
 9     procedure Stop_Failure_Detector
10        (FD : FD_Access);
11     function Get_Suspects
12        (FD : FD_Access) return Process_List;
13     procedure Create_Failure_Detector
14        (Algo    : FD_Algo;
15         P       : Process_Id;
16         Success : out Boolean;
17         Result  : out FD_Access);
18     function Get_Failure_Detector
19        (Pid : Process_Id) return FD_Access;
20  [...]
21  private
22  [...]
23     procedure Notify_Suspects_List
24        (FD     : access FD_Type;
25         P_List : Process_List_Access);
26
27     procedure Register
28        (Algo : FD_Algo;
29         Run : Run_FD_Access);
30  end Failure_Detector;
```

Listing 1.2. Failure_Detector

visible via calls to *Get_Suspects*. Note that there is a possibility to stop a failure detector instance, this allows us to simulate a crash failure on a partition.

4.3   Transport Interface

Listing 1.3 shows an excerpt of the interface of the high level transport API. the package responsible for providing these abstractions is called *partition_protocols*. It is responsible for message exchanges across logical or physical partitions. The private part of this package illustrates the use of the tasking component of PolyORB. The type *Runnable* is an abstraction of a unit of execution (e.g.: an Ada task). In each partition, there is a runnable responsible for receiving entering messages, targeting them to the interested entities or storing them in a message queue. The functionalities for receiving messages allow consensus and failure detection components to poll on the message queue or to block until the arrival of messages.

5   Assessment

To assess our design and implementation we achieved two complementary evaluations. First, we carried out performance measures to evaluate the efficiency of our design and

```
1  with PolyORB.Tasking.Threads;
2  with [...]
3  package Partition_Protocols is
4    function Create_Partition_Transport
5      (Nid  : Process_Id) return Partition_Transport_Access;
6    function Is_There_A_Message
7      (Self : access Partition_Transport)
8      return Boolean;
9    function Is_There_A_Message_Of_Type
10     (Self    : access Partition_Transport;
11      M_Type : Message_Type)
12     return   Boolean;
13   function Receive_Message
14     (Self       : access Partition_Transport;
15      M_Type    : Message_Type;
16      From      : Process_Id;
17      Blocking  : Boolean := False)
18     return      C_Message;
19     -- Receive a specific message (identified by its sender and its type)
20   function Receive_Any_Message
21     (Self       : access Partition_Transport;
22      Blocking  : Boolean := False)
23     return      C_Message;
24   procedure Send_Message
25     (Self : access Partition_Transport;
26      M    : C_Message;
27      To   : Process_Id);
28   procedure Shutdown (Self : access Partition_Transport);
29  private
30   type T_Runnable is new PolyORB.Tasking.Threads.Runnable with record
31     T_Partition : Partition_Transport_Access;
32   end record;
33   procedure Run (R : access T_Runnable);
34  end Partition_Protocols;
```

Listing 1.3. Transport interface

implementation. Second, we analyzed the distribution of code between the architectural elements of our design to assess the validity and ability to evolve of our design.

5.1 Performance Evaluation

Performance evaluations of consensus and failure detection algorithms are often done theoretically by assessing their complexities. Communication cost is traditionally given by an approximation of the total number of messages, while computations costs are approximated by the number of rounds necessary to reach consensus. Even if these parameters are indicative, they are not enough for a critical application that has stringent timing constraints. Generally, testing a consensus algorithm on top of real distributed systems is a hard task due to the efforts needed to implement the communications and tasking primitives as well as the message marshalling and unmarshalling primitives. In our case, the implementation task was facilitated by the reuse of some services from PolyORB. We have chosen the rotating coordinator algorithm proposed by Chandra and Toueg in [2]. This algorithm requires an *eventually strong* failure detector (i.e.: a failure detector that belongs to the class $\diamond S$). The test application consists of a variable number of processes running a consensus and a compatible failure detection algorithm. After an initialization phase in which the partitions are set up and the

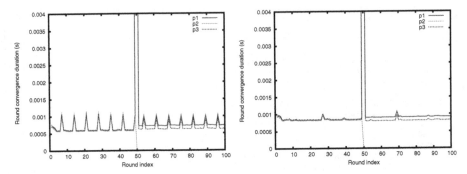

Fig. 2. Rotating coordinator with Chandra $\diamond S$ detection algorithm

Fig. 3. Rotating coordinator with Larrea $\diamond P$ failure detection algorithm

consensus and failure detection algorithms are loaded, the three processes run 100 instances of consensus by proposing an integer value. The experiments were performed using a P4 machine with 1 GB of RAM and running Linux (kernel 2.6.15-27-386). For simplicity reasons, the deployment is done in one Ada program. This has two advantages. First, there are no clock synchronization problems. Second, we can test the isolation between the partitions (i.e.: the fact that instances of consensus and failure detector that run in one partition do not misbehave by "stealing" messages or computing resources that belong to other partitions). We use the UDP protocol for message exchanges.

Figure 2 presents the results of a first experiment using Chandra's rotating coordinator with a $\diamond S$ failure detector. There are three participants at the beginning, a crash is simulated on the coordinator partition by shutting down the transport and the failure detectors. We notice that the decision duration is around $1 ms$ and that generally the measures are very close to the mean value. The second remark is about a peak in the round 50, this peak is due to the fact that the processes cannot decide about the failure of the coordinator before they receive the information from the failure detector which runs timeouts of $100\ ms$. The measured peak was around $208\ ms$. After the round 50 we notice a slight increase of the convergence times. This is due to two mutually compensating phenomena: the time spent before defining a coordinator and the availability of additional resources after the crash of the coordinator.

Figure 3 presents the results of a second experiment similar to the first one but using another failure detector of class $\diamond P$. The conclusions are similar, but we notice that the mean value for consensus instances is slightly higher despite the fact that the timeouts are the same as in the first experiment. This is due to the additional treatments done in the second failure detection algorithm and to the size of the exchanged messages. Note that the timeouts can be reduced but this can be at the expense of system resources availability and failure detection properties. In conclusion, these performance measures are expected and demonstrate the validity of our design and the efficiency of our implementation.

5.2 Source Code Analysis

Source code analysis provides not only information on the important elements of a design, but also indications on the coding effort needed to implement new algorithms. In our design, the reusable part is obviously the PolyORB neutral layer but also the transport and the interfaces of the consensus and failure detection components. We computed Source Lines Of Code (SLOCs) of these components. Using SLOCCount[2], table 1 presents the SLOCs of these parts. We note that the majority ($\approx 89\%$) of the involved code is reused from PolyORB or developed as reusable utilities (such as message representation, message transport, etc.). The consensus and failure detection components on their own have not required too many lines of code. The generic reusable consensus and failure detection components are presented in boldface in the table, the other numbers represent the size of the implemented algorithms. This analysis shows clearly that the majority of the involved code is generic and thus reusable. This clearly reduces the need to write large portions of code when implementing new algorithms, the written code will be simple, easily traceable and relatively inexpensively certifiable.

Table 1. Source code distribution

PolyORB neutral layer	Consensus			Failure detection			Transport	Other utilities
SLOCs	Algo	ref	SLOCs	Algo	ref	SLOCs	SLOCs	SLOCs
$\approx 5000^3$	generic	N/A	144	generic	N/A	333	833	2200
	Chandra	[2]	273	Chandra $\diamond S$	[2]	170		
	Mostefaoui	[12]	273	Larrea $\diamond P$	[11]	279		

6 Conclusion and Future Work

In this paper, we presented the advantages of implementing a middleware - level consensus service for critical distributed applications. After analyzing the typical requirements of such a service, we proposed a design for a middleware layer providing a consensus abstraction, as well as some indications to customize the middleware to the requirements of its target applications. The performance measures and the source code analysis we have done prove the efficiency or our design and the extensibility of our implementation.

The perspectives opened by this work include technical work such as extending the set of the values on which consensus algorithms can be run or extending the set of supported consensus and failure detection algorithms. The configuration of the middleware, including the consensus component, as a function of the application requirements, is a natural extension to this research work. We plan to take advantage of our clear design to automate the middleware configuration using an architecture description language. Finally, this work can be the base of other research contributions such as comparative performance analysis of various consensus algorithms or enhancing the architecture to support other agreement protocols.

---

[2] http://www.dwheeler.com/sloccount/

[3] The neutral layer of PolyORB is about 40000 SLOCs, the amout of code effectively used is about 5000.

References

1. Bernstein, P.A.: Middleware: a model for distributed system services. Commun. ACM 39(2), 86–98 (1996)
2. Chandra, T.D., Toueg, S.: Unreliable failure detectors for reliable distributed systems. Journal of the ACM 43(2), 225–267 (1996)
3. Dobbing, B., Burns, A.: The Ravenscar tasking profile for high integrity real-time programs. In: Proceedings of SigAda'98, Washington, DC, USA (November 1998)
4. Dolev, D., Dwork, C., Stockmeyer, L.: On the minimal synchronism needed for distributed consensus. J. ACM 34(1), 77–97 (1987)
5. Durst, R.C., Miller, G.J., Travis, E.J.: Tcp extensions for space communications. Wirel. Netw. 3(5), 389–403 (1997)
6. Fischer, M.J., Lynch, N.A., Paterson, M.: Impossibility of distributed consensus with one faulty process. J. ACM 32(2), 374–382 (1985)
7. Gamma, E., Helm, R., Johnson, R., Vlissides, J.: Design Patterns: Elements of Reusable Object-Oriented Software. Addison Wesley, Reading, Massachusetts (1994)
8. Guerraoui, R., Schiper, A.: Software-based replication for fault tolerance. Computer 30(4), 68–74 (1997)
9. Guerraoui, R., Schiper, A.: The generic consensus service. IEEE Transactions on Software Engineering 27(1), 29–41 (2001)
10. Haverkamp, D.A., Richards, R.J.: Towards safety critical middleware for avionics applications. In: LCN '02: Proceedings of the 27th Annual IEEE Conference on Local Computer Networks, Washington, DC, USA, p. 716. IEEE Computer Society Press, Los Alamitos (2002)
11. Larrea, M., Fernndez, A., Arvalo, S.: the impossibility of implementing perpetual failure detectors in partially synchronous systems (2001)
12. Mostefaoui, A., Raynal, M.: Consensus based on failure detectors with a perpetual accuracy property. In: IPDPS '00: Proceedings of the 14th International Symposium on Parallel and Distributed Processing, Washington, DC, USA, p. 514. IEEE Computer Society Press, Los Alamitos (2000)
13. Rodriguez, M., Fabre, J.-C., Arlat, J.: Wrapping real-time systems from temporal logic specifications. In: Bondavalli, A., Thévenod-Fosse, P. (eds.) Dependable Computing EDCC-4. LNCS, vol. 2485, pp. 253–270. Springer, Heidelberg (2002)
14. RTCA. Software considerations in airborne systems and equipment certification. do-178b / ed-12b (1992)
15. Schmidt, D.C., Buschmann, F.: Patterns, frameworks, and middleware: their synergistic relationships. In: ICSE '03: Proceedings of the 25th International Conference on Software Engineering, Washington, DC, USA, pp. 694–704. IEEE Computer Society Press, Los Alamitos (2003)
16. Schneider, F.B., Lamport, L.: Paradigms for distributed programs. In: Distributed Systems: Methods and Tools for Specification, An Advanced Course, London, UK, April 3-12, 1984 and April 16-25, pp. 431–480. Springer-Verlag, Berlin Heidelberg (1985)
17. Vergnaud, T., Hugues, J., Pautet, L., Kordon, F.: PolyORB: a schizophrenic middleware to build versatile reliable distributed applications. In: Llamosí, A., Strohmeier, A. (eds.) Ada-Europe 2004. LNCS, vol. 3063, pp. 106–119. Springer, Heidelberg (2004)

SANCTA: An Ada 2005 General-Purpose Architecture for Mobile Robotics Research

Alejandro R. Mosteo and Luis Montano

Departamento de Informática e Ingeniería de Sistemas. Universidad de Zaragoza
Instituto de Investigación en Ingeniería de Aragón, I3A
c/ María de Luna 1, 50018 Zaragoza, Spain
{amosteo,montano}@unizar.es

Abstract. We present SANCTA, a flexible control architecture for multi-robot teams. It is fully written in Ada 2005, except for the reuse of some C libraries. In this paper we highlight the architectural elements of our implementation and also present our experiences using the cutting-edge 2005 implementation from GNAT, through its GPL 2005 and 2006 iterations. We expect to exemplify the kind of advantages and challenges that developers can find in using the new Ada 2005 features. Since this architecture makes use of a wide range of Ada capabilities, from low level hardware interaction to graphical user interfaces, we believe it is a good example of a successful mid-size project using Ada 2005 in academy.

Keywords: multi-robot, control architecture, Ada 2005, GNAT GPL.

1 Introduction

Mobile robot teams is a flourishing research topic motivated by problems like planetary exploration, autonomous mapping, search and rescue applications in urban settings, automated transportation and so on. The use of multiple robots has benefits like higher throughput, higher reliability due to redundancy, and the possibility of tackling problems that a single robot could not.

These multi-robot teams present new challenges: coordination needs among robots, long-term mission planning, communication with human operators in manageable ways that are not overwhelming in feedback nor too demanding on inputs, for example.

Such broad necessities, ranging from embedded software to distributed computation and interaction, make Ada a natural language choice due to its ingrained principles in software safety, reusability, portability and maintainability. Hence we want to disseminate our experience with Ada development in this field.

We firstly introduce our research domain in Sect. 2. Next, we show the architectural elements of our implementation in Sect. 3. Ada implementation insights on relevant parts of it are then presented in Sect. 4. Section 5 is devoted to bindings to foreign language libraries. Finally, we comment in Sect. 6 our experience using the new features of Ada 2005.

N. Abdennahder, F. Kordon (Eds.): Ada-Europe 2007, LNCS 4498, pp. 221–234, 2007.
© Springer-Verlag Berlin Heidelberg 2007

2   Mobile Robot Teams and Task Allocation

The SANCTA architecture receives its name from *Simulated Annealing Constrained Task Allocation*, since these are the first novel features that it implemented [1] in the field of multi-robot task allocation. Simulated annealing [2,3] is a probabilistic tool useful for optimization problems with large solution spaces, able to escape local minima and, with enough running time, find good solutions or even the optimal one. It imitates the metallurgical process of annealing, where controlled heating and cooling is used to reach configurations with desired properties. By analogy, the simulated annealing uses a temperature variable to balance greedy and randomized behavior in the optimization process.

Semiautonomous robot teams introduce the critical need of deciding how to assign tasks to robots in order to optimize performance. Ideally, this would be a completely automatic operation without the need of human intervention beyond high-level description of missions. Our research focuses in this kind of problem, aiming for optimality and autonomy of decision in mobile robot teams intended to be deployed in hostile environments.

A typical sequence of events would be: robots are deployed awaiting orders; a human operator relays a high-level description of mission to the robot team; the mission is refined into low-level tasks executable by robots; robots negotiate the ownership of tasks and needs of cooperation; execution of tasks starts; on-line replanning and task allocation is performed when new environment data requires it. All these operations should be preferably done in a distributed manner with good scalability properties. Examples of missions are: build a map of an unknown environment; locate a vehicle in a parking lot; patrol an area in such a way that an intruder could not remain undetected; visit a series of spots of interest to take ground samples.

Several requirements arise in this context: communication among robots themselves and human supervisors; sharing and synchronization of data; ability to cope with faulty networking and lost robots; algorithms for task allocation, path planning, obstacle avoidance; graphical visualization of status; etc.

3   Architecture

SANCTA was born initially as just the testing implementation of our research. Soon it was evident that, better than have stand-alone programs for each element of research, a reusable solution was more desirable. We could have integrated our code in one of the many existing robot control libraries. However, most are oriented to single robot control, so we preferred to create a new Ada layer on top of one of these, namely Player [4]. This way we retain more control over what we could do, while minimizing dependencies on other software. We chose Ada because we believe in its advantageous properties over other popular languages.

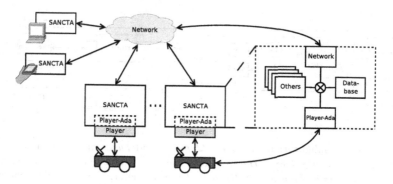

Fig. 1. Key elements in the SANCTA architecture. Components are interconnected as determined by the configuration file. Some important components are explicitly shown. Grayed blocks are C code corresponding to the Player library, accessed through the Player-Ada binding.

Also, we had previous exposure to it, since it is actively used for teaching in our university.

There are two principles that are paramount in the design of our system:

– *Simplicity*: Albeit always desirable, a tool that may be potentially used by several researchers must be kept as simple as possible. In SANCTA this is achieved reducing the elements to its simplest expression. The approach taken is modularity, and the building blocks are *components*. Each component operates as a black box, except for its defined inputs and outputs. Several components can thus interact without having to know any internals of each other. Table 1 shows a selection of some relevant components available for our architecture.
– *Flexibility*: We wanted to impose minimum constraints on component programmers, so they must conform to a very simple interface. Additionally, some basic execution scheduling is offered. Namely, programmers can choose between periodic, asynchronous and event-driven execution (or a combination of these). Direct component interaction is achieved connecting matching inputs and outputs, allowing the construction of powerful flows of data. Fig. 2 exemplifies this chaining construction, that corresponds to a *pipes and filters* flow pattern [5]. Indirect interaction is also available through a *shared repository* approach.

Notable components of our architecture are shown in Fig. 1. Nodes can be robots, laptops showing a GUI[1] or in general any connected computing device. A node configuration is defined and constructed with just a collection of component instances and their interconnections. To simplify configuration, some components are predefined and always created automatically, though this could be easily changed if necessary due to hardware constraints.

---

[1] Graphical User Interface.

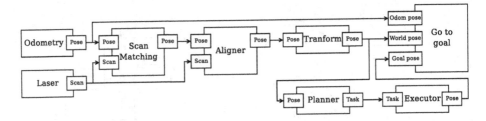

Fig. 2. A node configuration example. *Odometry* and *Laser* are sensor readers. *Scan matching, Aligner* and *Transform* are processing algorithms. *Planner* is a task allocation component (*i.e. Annealer* or *Bidder*). *Executor* determines the robot commands necessary to perform a task, while *Go to goal* directly commands the robot hardware.

3.1 Configuration Definitions

A node configuration is maintained in a simple XML file. This configuration is read (using XmlAda [6]) at start-up by the SANCTA executable launched in each robot or device. Fig. 2 shows a visualization for a superset of the configuration snippet shown in listing 1.1.

Listing 1.1. Snippet of configuration file

```
<config_example>
    <agent id="Ari" kind="robot">
        <component name="odometry" enabled="true">
            <provides data="pose"
                      as="odometric_pose"
                      type="types.pose" />
        </component>
        <component name="scan_matching" enabled="true">
            <requires data="pose"
                      as="odometric_pose"
                      type="types.pose" />
            <provides data="pose"
                      as="corrected_pose"
                      type="types.pose" />
        </component>
    </agent>
<config_example>
```

Several relevant characteristics are apparent:

– The top-level element names the configuration.
– Each node (robot or not) is defined in an "agent" element. Assuming that every node has synchronized copies of the configuration files, this allows to configure the whole team in one file. Each node can have a different configuration according to its capabilities.
– Each component instance is defined in a "component" element. Attributes are used to configure specific component behavior.
– Component inputs/outputs are respectively defined in "requires"/"provides" elements.

- "data" attributes are predefined and detailed in the component documentation. "as" attributes are an arbitrary identifier (Fig. 3). "data" names need not to be unique among components, but external names can only appear once as output in each node (unlimited as inputs). Matching external names create an output → input connection. "type" attributes are informative and optional, but data types of connected outputs/inputs should match.
- Unused outputs can be omitted to avoid clutter.

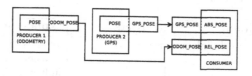

Fig. 3. *data/as* attributes in configuration files correspond to internal/external names of a same value

Following a *factory method* pattern [10], what the configuration does is to instance a collection of components, each one providing and requiring a series of data that the user must connect appropriately. Components can be data filters, hardware drivers, network modules or any necessary algorithm. Some predefined components naturally act as *singletons* and are automatically created:

- *Network*: Provides messaging among nodes. A straightforward implementation uses UDP packets. A predefined abstract interface exists for network components, so it can be seamlessly replaced with another network/messaging layer.
- *Local database*: Used for communications among the rest of components.
- *Player-Ada*: Interfaces with our robot hardware (Pioneer3 platforms). Again, an abstract interface exists so a change of platform should have an isolated impact.

3.2 Execution Modes

We have advanced that components have two ways of receiving execution time that are supported by the architecture, plus a third that is self-management. More precisely, the modes are:

- *Periodic*: When created, the component receives an initial call. Each component can specify, at that moment and at each subsequent run slice, the next time to be invoked. There is a single Ada task managing these calls, so this is the mode indicated for soft real-time execution of brief-lasting calls.
- *Event-driven (or synchronous)*: A component can subscribe to database records of interest, using an *observer* pattern [5,11], and will be notified each time the monitored ones change. Event chains can be constructed this way. It is the responsibility of the user to avoid infinite recursive calls, although some cases can be detected.

– *Asynchronous*: Computationally intensive components should create its own Ada task. This could also be done when hard real-time scheduling is desired (although, in our case, this has not been necessary for our research until date). The predefined components are tasking safe, so they can be used in a typical client-server approach for *rate monotonic analysis* (RMA) or similar techniques.

Table 1. Some available components, ordered in decreasing abstraction level

Component	Inputs	Outputs	Explanation
Global database	Network link	Database	Globally accesible database for data sharing among nodes with built-in replication
Local database	None	Database	Local data storage and sharing among components
Annealer	Pose, Database	Task allocation	Computes a best effort task allocation for a multi-robot team using simulated annealing techniques [1]
Bidder	Pose, Network link	Task allocation	Bids on auctioned tasks using market-based techniques [7]
Map	Pose, Laser scan	Map	Builds an environment grid map
Network	None	Network link	Provides messaging between nodes
Transformer	Pose	Pose	Transforms a pose in robot coordinates to world coordinates
Scan matching	Pose, Laser scan	Pose	Uses MBICP [8] to improve odometry using laser readings
Aligner	Pose, Laser scan	Pose	Corrects the pose angle when the robot is in an environment with known principal orientations (i.e. orthogonal walls)
GPS	Pose	Pose	Combines an odometry pose with GPS readings to produce global localization
Executor	Task list	Robot commands	Determines the robot actions needed to perform a task
Go to goal	Pose, Goal	None	Issues Player [4] movement calls
GUI relay	Robot state, Network link	None	Relays information to remote GUIs
Logger	Any	None	Logs some input to disk
Watchdog	Any	None	Aborts execution if input remains unchanged for some time
Player_Ada	Robot commands	Robot sensors	Proxy to robot hardware [9]

4 Implementation Details

We will now explore some details of Ada code, highlighting fragments related to the explained aspects of the architecture.

4.1 Component Specification

Listing 1.2 shows that components, as advanced, are really simple. They are just a code container, with an added facility for periodic soft real-time calls, that are managed by a priority queue sorted by time.

Listing 1.2. Root component type

```ada
type Object is abstract tagged limited null record;
--  Root type.

type Object_Access is access all Object'Class;
type Object_Creator is access
   function (Config : in Xml.Node)
            return       Object_Access;
--  For a factory approach.

procedure Run (This : in out Object;
               Next :     out Ada.Calendar.Time)
is abstract;
--  Invoked on component creation.
--  Next should be filled with the next call time.
```

A creation function must be registered (for example on component body elaboration) following a typical factory pattern. This function receives the XML element corresponding to the component configuration. The factory will then be used to create the components as specified in the configuration file.

4.2 Local Database Specification

The database component exports a type that is actually a protected wrapper over a standard Ada.Containers.Indefinite_Sorted_Maps.Map. Keys are strings, and stored values are descendants of a root type, so the database can store any variety of non-limited objects. Thus, asynchronous data sharing is simply a matter of using the functions in listing 1.3:

Listing 1.3. Some database accessing functions

```ada
function Get (This : in Database;
              Key  : in Object_Key)
             return      Object_Data'Class;

procedure Put (This  : in out Database;
               Key   : in     Object_Key;
               Value : in     Object_Data'Class);
```

A simple view renaming allows for comfortable use of typed data.

Now we present the facilities for event registration, following an *observer* pattern. Components can obtain automatically from the configuration file the equivalence between its internal keys (the "data" attribute) and the particular name bound to it (the "as" attribute), in fact allowing for the connection of inputs/outputs:

The user must define a descendant type of *Key_Listener*, and register an instance in the database with the *Listen* subprogram (listing 1.4). Every time the key receives an update, the *On_Key_Stored* dispatching procedure will be invoked for each listener. Using a tagged type instead of a function pointer has the advantage that the listener can store any necessary contextual data right within it.

Listing 1.4. Database data observing

```
type Key_Listener is
   abstract tagged limited null record;
type Key_Listener_Access is
   access all Key_Listener 'Class;

procedure On_Key_Stored
   (This  : in out Key_Listener;
    Key   : in      Object_Key;
    Value : in      Object_Data 'Class )
is abstract;

procedure Listen
   (This     : in out  Database;
    Key      : in       Object_Key;
    Listener : not null Key_Listener_Access );
```

We provide also a default empty component with a listener member and convenient functions for registration (listing 1.5). This could have been done with the new language interfaces, but we encountered compiler problems.

A typical event-driven component will register itself on creation to the inputs he needs. This is particularly useful for filtering components. In Fig. 2 is depicted a typical chain of components used to correct the robot pose.

Listing 1.5. Component with embedded listener

```
type Listener (Parent : access Base_Component) is
   limited new Key_Listener with null record;
-- Base_Component has been declared in public part.

type Base_Component is limited new Component.Object with record
   Listener : aliased Listener (Base_Component 'Access );
end record;

not overriding
procedure Subscribe (This : in out Base_Component;
                     Key  :          String );
```

4.3   Advantageous Ada Features

Our simulated annealing algorithm does not require high precision, but takes advantage of exact repeatability of results when operating on task costs. This repeatability is a key factor to make our algorithm $O(n \log n)$ instead of $O(n^2)$. This can be naturally handled in Ada by means of fixed types instead of floating point ones or integer workarounds.

5   New Bindings

We believe in code reuse, and sometimes a little effort spent in creating a binding to foreign libraries pays over reimplementing the wheel in every favorite language. As part of our work we have implemented some bindings of interest for the Ada community.

5.1   Player-Ada Binding

Our choice for low level robot interaction is the Player library [4]. Its advantages are many: portability across robot platforms, open source nature, dedicated volunteers and developers, acknowledgment within the robotic community, and availability of a quite realistic multi-robot simulator to say a few. Many client libraries existed for it but unfortunately not one written in Ada. Our binding is called Player-Ada [9]. The C library uses object oriented (OO) techniques and so our Ada 95 binding uses the support for OO programming in the form of tagged and controlled types.

Listing 1.6. C auxiliary file in Player-Ada

```
#include "libplayerc/playerc.h"

size_t get_device_t_size ()
{
  return sizeof (playerc_device_t);
}
```

Listing 1.7. Player-Ada specification detail

```
function Get_Device_T_Size return Interfaces.C.size_t;
pragma Import (C, Get_Device_T_Size);

type Pad_Array is array (Positive range <>) of
  System.Storage_Elements.Storage_Element;
pragma Pack (Pad_Array);

type Position2d is record -- A new Device_T
  Reserved : Pad_Array (1 .. Natural (Get_Device_T_Size));
  -- Note the function call to Get_Device_T_Size.
  -- Other fields here.
end record; pragma Convention (C, Position2d);
```

Our binding uses some auxiliary C functions to improve the portability of the Ada part in the event of changes in the underlying C library. For example, some constant sized structures that are opaque to the user may likely change in size between versions.

The construct shown in listings 1.6 and 1.7 abstracts the size of the C structure from the Ada binding, thanks to the Ada type elaboration capabilities. A single recompilation will take care of this aspect in the event of changing the Player version. The same technique has been used for other relevant constants. We believe this is valuable over a pure Ada binding that is specially useful when the C library is still evolving. We have been able to successfully use our binding with three different Player versions over the time doing only minor modifications, and indeed this technique has proven useful in at least one version change.

5.2 Concorde Binding

Concorde [12] is an advanced TSP[2] solver, free for research purposes. Only suited for the single-traveler with symmetric costs problem, with graph transformations it can be used for asymmetric and multi-robot cases. We have implemented a thick binding for it and also the appropriate transformation functions. With our binding, asymmetric, open and MTSP[3] problems of moderate size[4] can be solved.

6   Ada 2005 Experiences

Our attempts at using new Ada 2005 features is a mix of success and failure. Some features are ready for use, whereas other are either partially or totally unimplemented. We must note that the reported failures herein may have been caused in part or in full by a lack of complete understanding in our part, despite our best effort to keep up to date [13,14]. See Table 2 for a quick overview of our subjective perceptions.

- **Standard containers:**
  This is a very fruitful addition in our experience: Most of our data structures that require collections use the new standard containers. Before its availability we used a mixture of open source libraries but we have completely replaced them in favor of the standard containers. We have not found any critical bug in the last two compiler releases.

  The safety requirements of the containers, materialized in checks in subprograms with *access-to-subprogram* parameters (Query_Element and Update_Element, among others), will prevent the improper use of cursors and

---

[2] Traveling Salesman Problem.

[3] Multiple Traveling Salesmen Problem.

[4] This is due to the use of large numbers in the transformations involved and the use of integers in the C library. We have solved problems involving several hundred cities.

Table 2. Our perception of some Ada 2005 features

Feature	Frequency of use	Usefulness
Containers	All the time	Very useful
Limited with	Not used	–
Private with	Frequently	Useful
Anonymous access types	Regular	Useful
Box initializer	Rarely	Somewhat useful
Task termination	All the time	Useful
Overriding marks	All the time	Very useful
Interfaces	Abandoned	Useful
Dot notation	All the time	Very useful

modification of elements (*tampering with cursors* and *tampering with elements* are the RM expressions). These checks have aided us in preventing some errors, in circumstances that would have been difficult to debug. Once again, the safety emphasis of Ada mandates these checks where other languages would prefer to omit them for a marginal gain in efficiency. In our case, these checks have been proved a valuable feature.

Another related 2005 addition that nicely blends here is the new access scope rules. Declaring trivial subprograms in place for simple processing of container elements has worked flawlessly and contributes to maintain code locality without added burden. See listing 1.8 for an example.

Listing 1.8. Containers and access subprograms

```
declare
    procedure Do_Something (Key :         Key_Type;
                            Val :  in out Element_Type) is
    begin
        --   Operate in-place with the Val element
    end Do_Something;
begin
    Some_Map.Update_Element (Some_Map.Find (Some_Key));
end;
```

– **Limited with:**
We were keen to use this new feature but unfortunately the GNAT GPL 2005 version was not behaving as we expected, so we ended not using it. Superficial tests in the most recent 2006 version show that either the problems with this feature have been solved or our understanding of the operations we could do with the incomplete view of a type is more thorough.

We regret not having more up to date information and use cases to report on this major addition to the language.

– **Private with:**
This feature works flawlessly in our experience and helps in adding clarity to specifications.

– **Anonymous access types:**
This is another interesting feature that has contributed to remove some now unnecessary access type declarations. However, functions returning anonymous access types was not completely implemented to the best of our knowledge so we did not use it. The latest patches we have seen submitted to gcc improving support for this feature are [15].

– **Box notation for default initializations:**
This seemingly minor feature is a nice addition to the language, aiding in the simplification of some code: Although intended to allow for some impossible initializations in Ada 95 related to limited types, we have found it useful for defaults in subprogram specifications. We have identified however a dangerous possibility: it is now easy to indulge in it for the initialization of record components, so neglecting the utility of specifying every record member to get a compilation error if some new components are added.

We reported a bug when used it for controlled types initialization in the 2005 version, which was already corrected for the 2006 version. Due to this bug, some calls to Initialize in controlled members of a type would be omitted. We use it now regularly without problems.

– **Ada.Task_Termination:**
This new package is a nice addition allowing a standard way of tracking unusual task terminations. We have incorporated it into our architecture and it has proved to be useful for extra debugging awareness.

– **Overriding notation:**
Another feature not likely to have a great impact, but which we use and find very useful in aiding to document specifications. It also has helped in preventing a few bugs, identifying some unintended overridings. Being an optional feature, it is in the hand of the programmer to remember to use it. A specific warning devoted to its omission could be a fine addition for the object-oriented practitioners.

– **Interfaces:**
Curiously, we had more success with them in the 2005 version than in the current one. In the former, we were able to use synchronized interfaces to specify network layers, and actually implemented a UDP based component. Other, simpler interfaces (not synchronized), were also used. However, we were unable to get them working in the 2006 version due to compiler crashes, so we had to revert to abstract tagged types (listing 1.9). This was fortunately very little work, since we had made few use of multiple inheritance, and we could simply go back to abstract types in most cases, or move to a vertical hereditary design in the remaining ones.

Listing 1.9. Problems with interfaces

```
type Object is abstract tagged limited null record;
--  Root type as currently defined with GPL 2006.

type Object is limited interface;
--  The version we used with the GPL 2005 compiler.
```

In any case, we think this is one of the most interesting language additions, providing a manageable form of multiple inheritance and also contributing to more informative specifications.

- **Dot notation:**

We close this section with the much anticipated dot notation. The 2005 implementation was certainly buggy, although one could use it if really determined, specially if compilation units were small. Typically, it could be used without noticeable problems until some specific construct would cause the compiler to crash in any dot notation instance in the compilation unit (which previously compiled fine). We submitted two bugs that were accepted and corrected.

In contrast, the 2006 implementation has been solid in this respect, allowing us to use it without any contempt now.

7   Conclusions

We have presented an Ada architecture currently used for research on heterogeneous multi-robot mobile teams. It makes use of modularity in the form of black box components to allow manageable complexity and enable easy cooperation among developers. During its ongoing development we are testing several Ada 2005 features, following its addition to the GNAT GPL compiler, with mixed but promising results.

Our architecture gives access to a wide range of capabilities through several implemented components and the reuse of available libraries: configuration is parsed with XmlAda; graphical displays are implemented with GtkAda [16]; robot control is achieved via Player-Ada, a binding authored by ourselves. Several ready for use components related with our research are presented.

We valuate greatly the GNAT effort in bringing a fully usable GPL compiler to the Ada community. Also, the evident improvements between the 2005 and 2006 versions evidence the compromise of AdaCore in having a complete 2005 implementation as soon as possible.

Acknowledgments

This work is partially funded by the Spanish MCYT-FEDER projects DPI2003-07986 and DPI2006-07928.

References

1. Mosteo, A.R., Montano, L.: Simulated annealing for multi-robot hierarchical task allocation with flexible constraints and objective functions. In: IROS'06 workshop on Network Robot Systems: Toward intelligent robotic systems integrated with environments (2006)

2. Kirkpatrick, S., Gelatt, C.D., Vecchi, M.P.: Optimization by simulated annealing. Science 4598(220), 671–680 (1983)
3. Cerny, V.: Thermodynamical approach to the traveling salesman problem: An efficient simulation algorithm. Journal of Optimization Theory and Applications 45(1), 41–51 (1985)
4. Gerkey, B.P., Vaughan, R.T., Howard, A.: The player/stage project: Tools for multi-robot and distributed sensor systems. In: International Conference on Advanced Robotics, pp. 317–323 (2003)
5. Avgeriou, P., Zdun, U.: Architectural patterns revisited - a pattern language. In: 10th European Conference on Pattern Languages of Programs (EuroPlop'05), July 2005, pp. 1–39 (2005)
6. Briot, E., Baillon, C., Krischik, M.: XmlAda. [Online]. Available: `https://libre2.adacore.com/xmlada/`
7. Dias, M.B., Zlot, R.M., Kalra, N., Stentz, A.T.: Market-based multirobot coordination: a survey and analysis, Robotics Institute, Carnegie Mellon University, Tech. Rep. CMU-RI-TR-05-13 (April 2005)
8. Minguez, J., Lamiraux, F., Montesano, L.: Metric-based scan matching algorithms for mobile robot displacement estimation. IEEE Int. Conf. on Robotics and Automation, Barcelona, Spain (2005)
9. Mosteo, A.R.: Player-Ada. [Online]. Available: https://ada-player.sf.net
10. Gamma, E., Helm, R., Johnson, R., Vlissides, J.: Design Patterns: Elements od Reusable Object-Oriented Software. Addison-Wesley Professional Computing Series. Addison-Wesley Publishing Company, New York (1995)
11. Riehle, D.: A role-based design pattern catalog of atomic and composite patterns structured by pattern purpose, Union Bank of Switzerland, Switzerland, Tech. Rep. 97-1-1 (1997)
12. Applegate, D., Bixby, R., Chvatal, V., Cook, W.: Concorde TSP solver. [Online]. Available: `http://www.tsp.gatech.edu/concorde.html`
13. Miranda, J., Schonberg, E.: GNAT and Ada 2005, AdaCore, Tech. Rep. (January 2005)
14. Barnes, J.: Rationale for ada 2006. Ada. User. Journal, vol. 26,27 (2006)
15. Charlet, A.: Add support for function returning anon access type (October 2006) [Online]. Available: http://gcc.gnu.org/ml/gcc-patches/2006-10/msg01690.html
16. Briot, E., Brobecker, J., Charlet, A., Setton, N.: GtkAda. [Online]. Available: `https://libre2.adacore.com/GtkAda/main.html`

Incorporating Precise Garbage Collection in an Ada Compiler

Francisco García-Rodríguez[1], Javier Miranda[2,*], and José Fortes Gálvez[1]

[1] Departamento de Informática y Sistemas
Universidad de Las Palmas de Gran Canaria
Canary Islands, Spain
francisco.garcia.100@gmail.com
jfortes@dis.ulpgc.es
[2] Instituto Universitario de Microelectrónica Aplicada
Universidad de Las Palmas de Gran Canaria
Canary Islands, Spain
jmiranda@iuma.ulpgc.es

Abstract. In recent years an increasing effort to develop garbage collectors for real-time applications has been undertaken by the Java community. Currently it seems appropriate to evaluate the effort required to integrate such a facility into Ada.

This paper presents an ongoing project to accomplish this goal by modifying the GNAT compiler to incorporate support for precise garbage collection. The approach taken can be immediately applied to current Ada 95 code, and allows coexistence of explicit and implicit deallocation. The text describes the extra code generated by a modified version of the front end and the corresponding run-time support for a mark-and-sweep collector.

1 Introduction

Garbage collectors have proved to be valuable for the construction of safer programs. Complex designs with intensive memory usage can benefit from implicit memory deallocation [13]. In the context of real-time applications, garbage collectors have been traditionally avoided because of efficiency and schedulability considerations. However, during the past decade the industry has invested substantial resources to develop garbage collectors appropriate for real-time systems, e.g., Real-Time Java implementations [10,16], embedded systems [2] and hardware assisted methods [15]. While Ada implementations have traditionally provided memory management facilities beyond unchecked deallocation and controlled types, support for garbage collection has been ignored by most.

In this paper we summarize the current state of an ongoing academic project consisting in the modification of the GNU Ada compiler (GNAT) to incorporate

---

* This work was done during a six-month visit to the NYU Courant Institute funded by the Spanish Minister of Education and Science under proyect PR2006-0356.

N. Abdennahder, F. Kordon (Eds.): Ada-Europe 2007, LNCS 4498, pp. 235–245, 2007.

precise recovery of implicitly deallocated data. The approach taken relies on a new implementation-defined pragma used to mark data types for implicit deallocation. Legacy sources using explicit deallocation can be easily adapted for garbage collection, or for simultaneous use of both deallocation paradigms, thus allowing to evaluate the impact of the garbage collector on existing applications.

The rest of this paper is structured as follows. Section 2 briefly introduces the garbage collector scenery. Section 3 presents the current design of the integrated support for our garbage collector. Section 4 describes the overall workings by means of a short example. Section 5 presents the results of some performance tests. We close with some conclusions and the bibliography.

2   Garbage Collectors

Garbage collectors have evolved and become widely used since the early 1960s. Initially, they were confined to specialized areas and programming languages, specially symbolic languages as Lisp, for which one of the first garbage collectors was built by McCarthy [14].

Limited resources in earlier computers gained garbage collection a reputation for slowing down program execution to unacceptable levels. Recently, the use of garbage collection in the Java Virtual Machine has shown that the reliability of implicit deallocation of dynamic variables and the automatic recovery of its memory space can be combined with sufficient efficiency on current machines [20].

Despite having matured, adapted to new requirements, and taken advantage of new computing features, most garbage collectors continue to work around the same original algorithms. These fall under two basic categories, namely *tracing* and *reference counting* [19,13].

Algorithms. Tracing collectors locate and free those heap-allocated data blocks that are currently unreachable, directly and through any path, from any pointer in the rest of storage areas (typically stack and static areas). Knowledge of such pointers is essential for the proper functioning of precise garbage collectors and are commonly referred as *roots*, hence their collective name of *root set*. The tracing approach has been used to develop most garbage collector variations, including support for cache optimization, concurrency, data compaction, generational sets, etc. [19,13]

In reference counting [9], a counter is associated with each individually heap-allocated data block to count the number of references to it. Accordingly, counters must be updated at every pointer assignment. When a counter reaches zero, its corresponding data block can be deallocated. Unreachable cyclic data structures prevent their node counters from reaching zero, and thus, in the basic algorithm, they cannot be freed when they become garbage. However, this can be solved with modern techniques [3].

Finally, some recent research focus on alternative, region-based methods [18].

Integration. Garbage collection has been included in some programming languages since their inception, e.g., Lisp and Java. In these cases, semantic restrictions are generally present in the language specification to facilitate its implementation, e.g., restricting or avoiding pointer arithmetic. This allows compiler writers to build a proper framework for the garbage collector and let it work with an exact knowledge of the memory layout, eventually resulting in detailed and complete recovery of unreachable data, what is known as *precise* garbage collection.

The situation is quite different when trying to introduce a garbage collector after the language has been defined and implemented. Most problems relate to memory identification, and heuristics must be devised to identify pointers. False references might lead to unreachable data blocks not being collected. However, Zorn has argued that they will not lead to significant memory leaks [20].

A widely used solution to this problem is the fully *conservative* collection [7,6], particularly the family of collectors implemented by Boehm et al. [5], which are used in C and C++ implementations among others. Zorn [20] has suggested that this solution can be as time-effective as explicit memory deallocation, at the cost of considerable memory usage overhead. Some collectors mix both conservative and precise styles, as in the compacting garbage collector by Bartlett [4].

Finally, integration of garbage collection with real-time restrictions poses particular problems. For instance, Real-Time Java [8] offers a mixture of programmer-controlled and implicit deallocations, which some consider inappropriate and for which they propose less intrusive and more homogeneous approaches [16,2].

3   Adding Garbage Collection to GNAT

Ellis and Detlefs [11] analyze the steps and conditions to incorporate a garbage collector into a compiler for a language with no specific provisions for it. Inspired by their work, we established the following guidelines to design a widely acceptable implementation through evolutionary improvements.

- *Precise memory identification.* We consider that the more predictable behavior and lower execution support overhead of precise collectors are valuable, specially when extending our project for concurrent and real-time programming. Moreover, in these cases, the programmer may possibly want to identify some data structures for explicit deallocation.
- *Minimize changes to the compiler.* Collector support must be as unintrusive as possible, and must avoid slowing down code sections which do not use implicit deallocation. Following the GNAT architecture, we restrict our changes to the front end and run-time support.
- *Minimize the impact on the programmer.* It is important to facilitate the use of the garbage collector with legacy applications and libraries that use explicit deallocation.
- *Flexibility.* It is desirable to allow the programmer to choose the collector. The implementation should be as independent of the collector algorithm as possible.

Garbage Collection Algorithm. According to these requirements, we have chosen a basic *mark-and-sweep* [14] algorithm for our initially nonconcurrent implementation of a garbage collector. We found it to be the least intrusive in the compiler and in its generated code. It only requires the ability to locate the root pointers needed to start the mark phase, and to register during allocation calls the data block addresses required for the sweep phase.

A reference count algorithm, although not requiring the building and maintenance of a root set, requires the insertion of code at pointer assignments. In addition, single deallocations become recursive.

Nonetheless, most of the infrastructure has been designed to provide support for future implementation of other garbage collection algorithms.

Pragma *Garbage_Collected.* In order to use implicit deallocation, the programmer simply has to apply a new implementation-defined pragma *Garbage_Collected* on those data types whose dynamic variables will be implicitly deallocated by the garbage collector. These types will be called *collected* types. At compile time the pragma leads to extra semantic checks and code expansion to provide the support discussed in the following sections.

The approach we have taken has almost immediate application, or easy adaptation, to previous sources that use explicit deallocation. Moreover, both explicit and implicit deallocation paradigms can be simultaneously used in the same program, thus allowing the gradual incorporation of implicit deallocation in legacy software. Nevertheless, we do not exclude the possibility of providing eventually, as an option, general garbage collection compatible with real-time.

Currently, the pragma can only be applied to tagged types. If a collected type is derived, the pragma must be applied at least to its ultimate ancestor. The compiler propagates the collected-type property to all its derivations. However, for documentation purposes, if the pragma is not applied to a type derived from a collected type, the front end generates a warning message suggesting to the programmer the addition of the pragma to such sources.

The mentioned restrictions result from the following considerations.

- *Object type identification.* We rely on the ability of some run-time support to identify the type of a given object. In Ada this support is only available by default for tagged types through the tag of the object (see the standard package Ada.Tags [12, Section 3.9]). In future versions we will investigate how to remove this restriction.
- *Ultimate ancestor and all its derivations.* Allowing the use of the pragma on a type with a noncollected ancestor leads to complex schemes that need further analysis. For example, if the programmer applies the pragma to a type T2 derived from tagged type T1, which is defined in some legacy library (and is therefore noncollected), the garbage collector may erroneously deallocate objects of type T2 that may remain referenced by access-to-T1'Class objects in the legacy library.

A direct consequence of the latter restriction is that controlled types cannot be implicitly deallocated, because their ultimate ancestor is defined in a standard Ada package [12, Section 7.6]. The main benefits of this corollary restriction is that it helps us to keep our conceptual model simple. We plan to investigate the combination of controlled and collected types in future versions.

Finally, pragma `Controlled` is used in Ada to prevent any automatic reclamation of storage (garbage collection) for the objects created by allocators of a given access type [12, Section 13.11.3]. Therefore, it is an error to apply this pragma to a collected type.

Data Structures. Our prototype implementation has the following three main data structures. The following sections describe how they are updated and used by the run-time system.

- *Descriptor Table*, containing one descriptor for each collected type. Each descriptor entry is generated by the compiler and used to know at run-time the type size and alignment, and the address of some functions generated by the frontend to know the object layout and deallocate objects of such type. The tag of the collected type is used as the hash key to register the descriptor in the run-time system during program initialization.
- *Collectable-Block Table*, containing an entry for each allocated block of each collected type. Each entry contains the block's address and meta-data (as needed by the garbage collection algorithm, e.g., mark bit). This physical separation from the respective block's data avoids intrusive components that could lead to problems with legacy applications containing Ada representation clauses [12, Section 13.5.1]. The table is implemented as a hash table, and addresses are used as hash keys.[1] The entries are inserted at each allocation, and are removed when their corresponding blocks are deallocated.
- *Root-Set Stack*, containing the address of each access-to-collected-type object in the program stack or static area.

3.1 Root-Set Maintenance

Siebert [17] reviews the best known strategies for real-time root scanning. Just like collectors, they can be precise, conservative or mix both styles. As mentioned before, we prefer the well defined behavior of precise algorithms.

Our implementation keeps the root-set stack continuously updated. Whenever the declaration of a variable holding one or more pointers to collected types is placed in the stack, the address of each such pointer is saved in the root-set stack. When the execution of the program leaves the scope containing such variable declarations, all these addresses are removed from the root-set stack.

The following example shows the definition of a collected type *Cell*. Part of the code that is automatically generated by our modified front end is shown as comments.

---

[1] This approach has the added benefit of allowing us to check whether an address points to a collectable block.

```
type Cell;
pragma Garbage_Collected (Cell);

type Cell_Ptr is access all Cell;
--   for Cell_Ptr'Storage_Pool use GC.Pool;

type Cell is tagged record
    Prev  : Cell_Ptr;
    Key   : Positive;
    Next  : Cell_Ptr;
end record;
```

The *collected pool* (GC.Pool) is used to allocate objects created by allocators of collectable objects. The programmer is free to use the standard storage pool, as well as other pools, to manage explicitly deallocated data.

For each declaration of an access type to collectable type (like Cell_Ptr in the example), extra code is generated in place by the front end to associate such an access type with the collected pool.

Given these declarations, the following example presents as comments the actions performed by the run-time system to manage the root-set stack.

```
procedure Foo is
    --   GC.MarkTop;
    P : Cell_Ptr;    --   GC.Push (P'Address);
    N : Cell;        --   GC.Push (N.Prev'Address,
                     --                N.Next'Address);
begin
    ...
    --   GC.PopUntilMark;
end Foo;
```

The top of the root-set stack is saved when the procedure is entered, and is restored before the procedure returns. During the elaboration of each declaration of a pointer (like *P*) or composite object containing pointers (as the *Prev* and *Next* components of *N*) to collected type, the addresses of such pointers are pushed onto the root-set stack.

3.2   Layout Functions

For each collected type, our modified front end generates a layout function. These functions are necessary for the tracing process to follow the pointers stored in collectable blocks. They return an array of offsets that is used by the garbage collector to locate such pointers. In order to support both fixed and variant records, the code generated by the front end makes use of the standard Ada attribute Position [12, Section 13.5.2]. Here is the function generated for type Cell of our example.

```
function Cell_Offsets
  (Obj_Addr : Address) return GC.Offset_Array
is
    type Cell_Acc is access Cell;
    function To_Cell_Acc is
       new Unchecked_Conversion (Address, Cell_Acc);

    Offsets : Offset_Array (1 .. 2) :=
       (1 => To_Cell_Acc (Obj_Addr).Prev'Position ,
        2 => To_Cell_Acc (Obj_Addr).Next'Position );
begin
    return Offsets ;
end Cell_Offsets ;
```

3.3 Coexistence with Noncollected Types

References between both kind of types, collected and noncollected, present some difficulty. Figure 1 shows the storage areas considered by our conceptual model and the pointers allowed by our implementation. Pointers like a and b have a known lifespan and are managed as already explained. Pointers like c can be overlooked because handling them is programmer's duty. Pointers from noncollected pools are obviously not managed by the collector: the collector cannot know how long they live, nor any data blocks that they may point into the collected heap. Accordingly, their presence would imply that the automatic deallocation of any data block in the collected heap is no longer safe.

Our compiler rejects pointers from noncollected types to collected ones. A more complex solution could accept these references, at the cost of some execution time overhead on noncollected types.

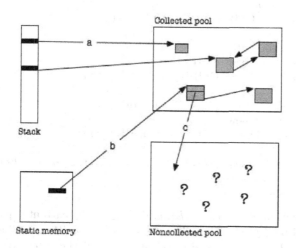

Fig. 1. Storage areas and allowed pointers

242   F. García-Rodríguez, J. Miranda, and J. Fortes Gálvez

4   The Collector at Work

Let us complete our previous example with an overview of the steps taken during
the execution of code with automatic deallocation generated by our compiler.

The following example code first builds two double linked nodes, with values
8 and 13, and then creates and links a new node with value 31 replacing node
with value 13, which becomes garbage. See Fig. 2.

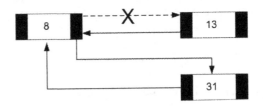

Fig. 2. Double-linked list example

Similarly to our previous example, here we have the code of this program and
the extra actions it performs when executed.

```
procedure Example is
   —  GC.MarkTop;
   P1 : Cell_Ptr;      —  GC.Push (P'Address);
   P2 : Cell;          —  GC.Push (P2.Prev'Address,
                        —          P2.Next'Address);
begin
   P1 := new Cell;

   —  Element A
   P1.all := Cell'(null, null, 8);

   —  Element B
   P1.Next := new Cell;
   P1.Next.all := Cell'(P1, null, 13);

   —  Element C makes B garbage!
   P1.Next := new Cell;
   P1.Next.all := Cell'(P1, null, 31);

   P2.Next := new Cell;      —  GC triggered here!
   —  GC.PopUntilMark;
end Example;
```

When execution of procedure *Example* begins, the current top of the root-set
stack is saved by *GC.MarkTop*. Then, the address of *P1*, as well as addresses of
P2.Last and *P2.Next*, are saved in the stack. Next, the successive allocations of
Cell objects are captured by the collected pool `GC.Pool`, and each newly allocated
data block's address, along with its mark-bit set to unmarked, is stored in the

table of collectable blocks. So far, only normal program code along with the extra support code has been executed.

Now let us suppose that the final allocation for *P2* triggers a mark-and-sweep garbage collection. The execution of the mutator program is then temporarily paused and the tracing process starts from each address stored in the root-set stack. For instance, the address in *P1* is examined in the collectable-block table to check whether it points to some block in GC.Pool. If it does, its mark bit is set to *marked* and, by reading the block's tag, its related descriptor is read from the descriptor table. From *Cell*'s descriptor, its associated layout function is invoked to obtain the offsets of pointer components to collected-type objects. This information is used by the algorithm to trace collectable blocks and thus to recursively mark all the accessible ones.

Next the sweep phase proceeds. By exploring every allocated address contained in the table of collectable blocks, each one is visited, and its mark bit set to unmarked for the next mark phase of algorithm. In our example, only *Cell* block with value 13 has its mark-bit initially unmarked when visited, since it could not be reached during the mark phase. Therefore, the *Cell*-specific unchecked deallocator is called for this block after finding its type descriptor from the block's tag.

5 Testing

We have applied some performance tests to have a preliminary evaluation of the overhead of our current implementation. All these tests use linked lists of heap-allocated nodes and perform the following actions: build the list, remove half of the list elements at different positions while preserving the list integrity, and finally manually launch the garbage collector. The Ada compiler is our modified version of the GAP 2005 distribution [1]. We used a 2.4 GHz Pentium 4 PC with 512 MB RAM under the Ubuntu 5.10 Linux distribution to run the tests.

In each test we evaluate the cost of our implementation support (including the additional code expansion and the run-time cost of the garbage collector) versus the cost of the same algorithm using explicit deallocation only. The following table summarizes our test results.

Test variant	Expanded code length	Execution time dep. on list length		
		5,000	10,000	20,000
Without any support	663	261.4ms	1.670s	11.59s
With support code plus collector	953	267.8ms	1.684s	11.74s
No. of push instructions		49,986	99,986	199,986

The column titled *Expanded code length* has the number of lines of the expanded code. This information was obtained using a GNAT switch that produces a listing of the expanded code in Ada source form.

The source test program is 63-lines long. According to the table results, after expansion, $953 - 663 = 290$ lines correspond to the additional code generated by our modified frontend to maintain the root-set stack and the collectable-block table, as well as the collected-type related functions for table management, descriptor construction, layout, and deallocation.

The next column presents the execution time of the program using a list with 5000, 10000, and 20000 nodes. The execution times shown in the the table have been averaged over 8 runs of the test program (these values were obtained from the *user* time information provided by the Unix `time` command). The execution time growth rate is justified by the quadratic complexity of the list algorithm used in the test program.

These figures must be regarded with caution, as they represent only preliminary estimations that will be reduced as the implementation improves, in particular with the integration of more efficient collection algorithms.

6   Conclusions

Garbage collector capabilities are being added to GNAT in an ongoing academic project. The design is focused on changes to the GNAT front end to ease its portability. Precise garbage collection allowing the coexistence of explicitly and implicitly deallocated types is provided. Our current implementation has several limitations that we plan to relax in future enhancements, particularly the collection of untagged and controlled types, and precise collection in a multitasking environment. The latest version of this work is available at `http://www.iuma.ulpgc.es/~jmiranda/gc`.

Acknowledgments

We would like to thank Ed Schonberg and Ben Brosgol for their insightful comments on drafts of this paper.

References

1. AdaCore. GNAT Academic Program (2007), http://www.adacore.com/home/academia
2. Bacon, D.F., Cheng, P., Rajan, V.T.: The Metronome: A simpler approach to garbage collection in real-time systems. In: Meersman, R., Tari, Z. (eds.) On The Move to Meaningful Internet Systems 2003: OTM 2003 Workshops. LNCS, vol. 2889, pp. 466–478. Springer, Heidelberg (2003)
3. Bacon, D.F., Rajan, V.T.: Concurrent cycle collection in reference counted systems. In: Knudsen, J.L. (ed.) ECOOP 2001. LNCS, vol. 2072, pp. 207–235. Springer, Heidelberg (2001)
4. Bartlett, J.F.: Compacting garbage collection with ambiguous roots. Research Report 88/2, Western Research Laboratory, Digital Equipment Corporation (1988)
5. Boehm, H.-J., Demers, A.J., Shenker, S.: Mostly parallel garbage collection. In: PLDI '91: Proceedings of the ACM SIGPLAN 1991 conference on Programming language design and implementation, pp. 157–164. ACM, New York (1991)

6. Boehm, H.-J.: Space efficient conservative garbage collection (with retrospective). In: McKinley, K.S. (ed.) Best of PLDI, pp. 490–501. ACM, New York (1993)
7. Boehm, H.-J., Weiser, M.: Garbage collection in an uncooperative environment. Software: Practice and Experiencie 18(9), 807–820 (1988)
8. Bollella, G., Brosgol, B., Furr, S., Hardin, D., Dibble, P., Gosling, J., Turnbull, M.: The Real-Time Specification for Java. Addison-Wesley, London (2000)
9. Collins, G.E.: A method for overlapping and erasure of lists. Communications of the ACM 3(12), 655–657 (1960)
10. TimeSys Corp. RTSJ reference implementation. http://www.timesys.com/java/
11. Ellis, J.R., Detlefs, D.: Safe, efficient garbage collection for C++. In: John, R. (ed.) Proceedings of the 1994 USENIX C++ Conference, Cambridge, Massachusetts, pp. 143–178 (1994)
12. Intermetrics Inc. and the MITRE Corporation. Annotated Ada Reference Manual with Technical Corrigendum 1. Language Standard and Libraries. ISO/IEC 8652:1995(E). (2000) http://www.adaic.org/standards/95aarm/AARM.PDF
13. Jones, R., Lins, R.: Garbage Collection: Algorithms for Automated Dynamic Memory Management. Wiley and Sons, New York (1996)
14. McCarthy, J.L.: Recursive functions of symbolic expressions and their computation by machine, part I. Communications of the ACM 3(4), 184–195 (1960)
15. Schmidt, W.J., Nilsen, K.D.: Performance of a hardware-assisted real-time garbage collector. In: William, J. (ed.) Proceedings of the Sixth International Conference on Architectural Support for Programming Languages and Operating Systems. ACM SIGPLAN Notices, vol. 29, pp. 76–85 (1994)
16. Siebert, F.: Hard real-time garbage-collection in the Jamaica virtual machine. In: Proceedings of the 6th International Workshop on Real-Time Computing and Applications Symposium (RTCSA'99), pp. 96–102. IEEE Computer Society, Los Alamitos (1999)
17. Siebert, F.: Constant-time root scanning for deterministic garbage collection. In: Wilhelm, R. (ed.) Compiler Construction, CC 2001, as part of ETAPS 2001. LNCS, vol. 2027, pp. 304–318. Springer, Heidelberg (2001)
18. Tofte, M., Talpin, J.-P.: Region-based memory management. Information and Computation 132(2), 109–176 (1997)
19. Wilson, P.R.: Uniprocessor garbage collection techniques. In: Bekkers, Y., Cohen, J. (eds.) Memory Management, International Workshop (IWMM 92). LNCS, vol. 637, pp. 1–42. Springer, Heidelberg (1992)
20. Zorn, B.G.: The measured cost of conservative garbage collection. Software: Practice and Experience 23(7), 733–756 (1993)

Author Index

Lecture Notes in Computer Science

For information about Vols. 1–4471

please contact your bookseller or Springer

Vol. 4515: M. Naor (Ed.), Advances in Cryptology - EU-ROCRYPT 2007. XIII, 591 pages. 2007.

Vol. 4514: S.N. Artemov, A. Nerode (Eds.), Logical Foundations of Computer Science. XI, 513 pages. 2007.

Vol. 4513: M. Fischetti, D.P. Williamson (Eds.), Integer Programming and Combinatorial Optimization. IX, 500 pages. 2007.

Vol. 4511: C. Conati, K. McCoy, G. Paliouras (Eds.), User Modeling 2007. XVI, 487 pages. 2007. (Sublibrary LNAI).

Vol. 4510: P. Van Hentenryck, L. Wolsey (Eds.), Integration of AI and OR Techniques in Constraint Programming for Combinatorial Optimization Problems. X, 391 pages. 2007.

Vol. 4509: Z. Kobti, D. Wu (Eds.), Advances in Artificial Intelligence. XII, 552 pages. 2007. (Sublibrary LNAI).

Vol. 4508: M.-Y. Kao, X.-Y. Li (Eds.), Algorithmic Aspects in Information and Management. VIII, 428 pages. 2007.

Vol. 4507: F. Sandoval, A. Prieto, J. Cabestany, M. Graña (Eds.), Computational and Ambient Intelligence. XXVI, 1167 pages. 2007.

Vol. 4506: D. Zeng, I. Gotham, K. Komatsu, C. Lynch, M. Thurmond, D. Madigan, B. Lober, J. Kvach, H. Chen (Eds.), Intelligence and Security Informatics: Biosurveillance. XI, 234 pages. 2007.

Vol. 4505: G. Dong, X. Lin, W. Wang, Y. Yang, J.X. Yu (Eds.), Advances in Data and Web Management. XXII, 896 pages. 2007.

Vol. 4504: J. Huang, R. Kowalczyk, Z. Maamar, D. Martin, I. Müller, S. Stoutenburg, K.P. Sycara (Eds.), Service-Oriented Computing: Agents, Semantics, and Engineering. X, 175 pages. 2007.

Vol. 4501: J. Marques-Silva, K.A. Sakallah (Eds.), Theory and Applications of Satisfiability Testing – SAT 2007. XI, 384 pages. 2007.

Vol. 4500: N. Streitz, A. Kameas, I. Mavrommati (Eds.), The Disappearing Computer. XVIII, 304 pages. 2007.

Vol. 4499: Y.Q. Shi (Ed.), Transactions on Data Hiding and Multimedia Security II. IX, 117 pages. 2007.

Vol. 4498: N. Abdennadher, F. Kordon (Eds.), Reliable Software Technologies – Ada Europe 2007. XIV, 247 pages. 2007.

Vol. 4497: S.B. Cooper, B. Löwe, A. Sorbi (Eds.), Computation and Logic in the Real World. XVIII, 826 pages. 2007.

Vol. 4496: N.T. Nguyen, A. Grzech, R.J. Howlett, L.C. Jain (Eds.), Agent and Multi-Agent Systems: Technologies and Applications. XXI, 1046 pages. 2007. (Sublibrary LNAI).

Vol. 4495: J. Krogstie, A. Opdahl, G. Sindre (Eds.), Advanced Information Systems Engineering. XVI, 606 pages. 2007.

Vol. 4494: H. Jin, O.F. Rana, Y. Pan, V.K. Prasanna (Eds.), Algorithms and Architectures for Parallel Processing. XIV, 508 pages. 2007.

Vol. 4493: D. Liu, S. Fei, Z. Hou, H. Zhang, C. Sun (Eds.), Advances in Neural Networks – ISNN 2007, Part III. XXVI, 1215 pages. 2007.

Vol. 4492: D. Liu, S. Fei, Z. Hou, H. Zhang, C. Sun (Eds.), Advances in Neural Networks – ISNN 2007, Part II. XXVII, 1321 pages. 2007.

Vol. 4491: D. Liu, S. Fei, Z.-G. Hou, H. Zhang, C. Sun (Eds.), Advances in Neural Networks – ISNN 2007, Part I. LIV, 1365 pages. 2007.

Vol. 4490: Y. Shi, G.D. van Albada, J. Dongarra, P.M.A. Sloot (Eds.), Computational Science – ICCS 2007, Part IV. XXXVII, 1211 pages. 2007.

Vol. 4489: Y. Shi, G.D. van Albada, J. Dongarra, P.M.A. Sloot (Eds.), Computational Science – ICCS 2007, Part III. XXXVII, 1257 pages. 2007.

Vol. 4488: Y. Shi, G.D. van Albada, J. Dongarra, P.M.A. Sloot (Eds.), Computational Science – ICCS 2007, Part II. XXXV, 1251 pages. 2007.

Vol. 4487: Y. Shi, G.D. van Albada, J. Dongarra, P.M.A. Sloot (Eds.), Computational Science – ICCS 2007, Part I. LXXXI, 1275 pages. 2007.

Vol. 4486: M. Bernardo, J. Hillston (Eds.), Formal Methods for Performance Evaluation. VII, 469 pages. 2007.

Vol. 4485: F. Sgallari, A. Murli, N. Paragios (Eds.), Scale Space and Variational Methods in Computer Vision. XV, 931 pages. 2007.

Vol. 4484: J.-Y. Cai, S.B. Cooper, H. Zhu (Eds.), Theory and Applications of Models of Computation. XIII, 772 pages. 2007.

Vol. 4483: C. Baral, G. Brewka, J. Schlipf (Eds.), Logic Programming and Nonmonotonic Reasoning. IX, 327 pages. 2007. (Sublibrary LNAI).

Vol. 4482: A. An, J. Stefanowski, S. Ramanna, C.J. Butz, W. Pedrycz, G. Wang (Eds.), Rough Sets, Fuzzy Sets, Data Mining and Granular Computing. XIV, 585 pages. 2007. (Sublibrary LNAI).

Vol. 4481: J. Yao, P. Lingras, W.-Z. Wu, M. Szczuka, N.J. Cercone, D. Ślęzak (Eds.), Rough Sets and Knowledge Technology. XIV, 576 pages. 2007. (Sublibrary LNAI).

Vol. 4480: A. LaMarca, M. Langheinrich, K.N. Truong (Eds.), Pervasive Computing. XIII, 369 pages. 2007.

Vol. 4479: I.F. Akyildiz, R. Sivakumar, E. Ekici, J.C.d. Oliveira, J. McNair (Eds.), NETWORKING 2007. Ad Hoc and Sensor Networks, Wireless Networks, Next Generation Internet. XXVII, 1252 pages. 2007.

Vol. 4478: J. Martí, J.M. Benedí, A.M. Mendonça, J. Serrat (Eds.), Pattern Recognition and Image Analysis, Part II. XXVII, 657 pages. 2007.

Vol. 4477: J. Martí, J.M. Benedí, A.M. Mendonça, J. Serrat (Eds.), Pattern Recognition and Image Analysis, Part I. XXVII, 625 pages. 2007.

Vol. 4476: V. Gorodetsky, C. Zhang, V.A. Skormin, L. Cao (Eds.), Autonomous Intelligent Systems: Multi-Agents and Data Mining. XIII, 323 pages. 2007. (Sublibrary LNAI).

Vol. 4475: P. Crescenzi, G. Prencipe, G. Pucci (Eds.), Fun with Algorithms. X, 273 pages. 2007.

Vol. 4474: G. Prencipe, S. Zaks (Eds.), Structural Information and Communication Complexity. XI, 342 pages. 2007.

Vol. 4472: M. Haindl, J. Kittler, F. Roli (Eds.), Multiple Classifier Systems. XI, 524 pages. 2007.